Library of Congress Control Number: 2006940670
ISBN 978-0-9662736-2-5

Marker Press
Box 390
Brimfield, MA 01010
marker_press@comcast.net

TRYING TO DO MY DUTY

The Civil War Letters of Capt. Francis D. Lincoln and Rebecca Cox Lincoln

Edited and Annotated by Larry and Koren C. Lowenthal

I am not only deprived of your society, of which Heaven knows I ought to think as much as you can of mine, but the children are far away too. And we have for the most part a dull routine of duty to occupy ourselves with. A few friends, the letters from home, with the consciousness of trying to do my duty sustain me in my efforts.

—Captain Francis D. Lincoln to Rebecca Lincoln, 1863.

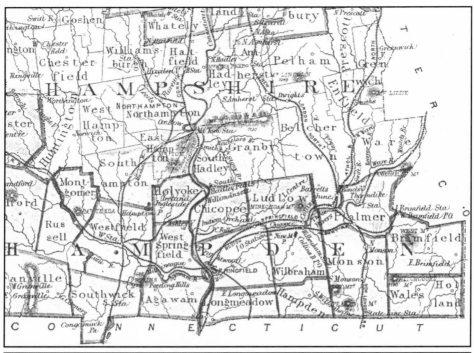

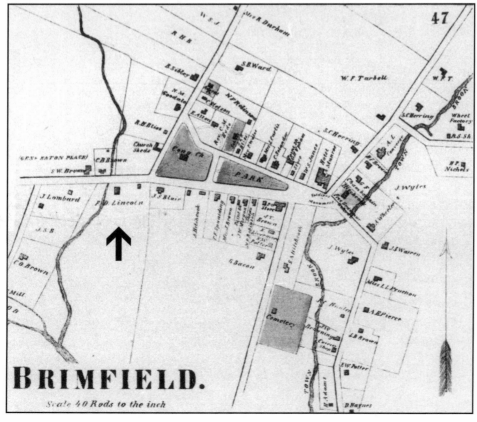

BRIMFIELD.

Scale 40 Rods to the inch

PREFACE

As soon as I saw these letters, I knew that they were voices that deserved to be heard. The people who wrote them, Captain Francis D. Lincoln and his wife Rebecca, of Brimfield, Massachusetts, would be appealing in any case; but the greater importance of these letters derives from being written during the Civil War.

Everyone who participated in the Civil War understood that they were engaged in mighty events, upheavals that would leave the world forever altered. This feeling of being involved in affairs of overwhelming importance is the common element that unites all participants, regardless of which side they were on or the particular nature of their activity.

The nearly century and a half that has passed has only confirmed the original assessment: the Civil War remains the great dividing line, the decisive period, in American history. Anything written during that tumultuous period absorbs something of its grandeur and commands our attention in a way that ordinary correspondence 20 years earlier or later would not. The sheer human drama, the scale of the tragedy and the response of people swept up in it, becomes compelling.

If all Civil War writings are innately interesting, these letters, mostly written while Capt. Lincoln was on duty with the 46th Regiment of Massachusetts volunteers in eastern North Carolina and Rebecca was at home in Brimfield, are especially so. First, it is relatively unusual to have both sides of a wartime correspondence preserved to this extent. Both writers are intelligent and observant, though not favored by a great deal of formal education. They are provincial insofar as they spent their lives in small Massachusetts towns, but they made sure to keep informed about larger issues.

Frank and Rebecca seemed to have a very "modern" relationship—or at least the kind of relationship that most modern couples believe they are striving for. What has been termed the Victorian "cult of domesticity" was firmly established by the Civil War. Middle-class women were supposed to be household goddesses, confined to a limited sphere of activity and dependent on their husbands. The legal system, controlled by men and endorsed by religious authority, supported this arrangement. Probably the gender separation was less rigid in rural areas, where women had a larger share in managing farm operations, but the equality of Frank and Rebecca's relationship is still remarkable. Moreover, as we shall see, Frank resisted having his daughters restricted by prevailing social conventions.

The letters set up a marvelous contrast between military and domestic concerns, visible even in a placid town like Brimfield. While Frank had shed the heavy religious beliefs of his Puritan forebears, he retained their sense of duty. As he carried out unfamiliar responsibilities far from home, he attempted to manage the home farm by remote control. Inevitably, Rebecca became more and more involved in daily operations, made more challenging by wartime economic dislocations. Perhaps somewhat reluctantly, Rebecca grew to meet her new responsibilities. Soon she was willing to offer strategic advice to the Union generals, something most women would not have ventured to do before the war. Separation tested Frank and Rebecca's relationship, and in the end the strong sinews of that relationship brought them successfully through the crisis.

An Unexpected Treasure

In the multitude of diaries and letters that have been published almost since the Civil War ended, there are usually two parallel stories. First and most obvious is the narrative of the original writer, serving whatever purpose he or she had in mind. Wrapped around that is usually a separate story of how later individuals came to edit and prepare the original material. I suspect that very few people set out to edit a Civil War manuscript in the same way one might decide (as I have done on other occasions) to write a book on a particular subject.

The element of surprise is almost as necessary in this category of literature as a murder is to a mystery, and that was certainly true with the Lincoln letters. In the center of Brimfield, overlooking the town's Civil War monument, stands the Hitchcock Academy. Started in 1855, it served as a public high school for a century before being converted to a community center. One room on the second floor, the Memorial Room, houses the former academy library and has become a repository for an accumulation of historical material. A committee of volunteers, of which I was a member, set forth bravely to inventory and organize this collection for the first time in more than 30 years.

Almost always this sort of project turns out to be more demanding than anticipated, but the treasure-hunt aspect compensates for the extra work. One day, entirely unexpectedly, the Lincoln letters appeared. They were found with materials associated with Mary Anna Tarbell, for many years the unofficial dean of the academy and town historian. No documentation explained why the letters were in that room, but the most likely surmise is that they passed down through the Lincoln family to Mabel Brown Peirce, who was married to Frank and Rebecca's grandson, Charles Lincoln Peirce. Mabel Peirce was an original member of the Brimfield Historical Society when that group was formed in 1962, and for several years it met in the Memorial Room. Mabel Peirce died in 1968, and the letters presumably remained in the Academy after the Sherman Room was set up in the town library to house historical materials and the historical society itself disbanded in the late 1970s. It is also possible that the letters were placed in custody of Anna Tarbell much earlier (she died in 1933) and came to the Academy by that route. However it came about, we are fortunate that our predecessors recognized that these letters were worth preserving.

My wife Koren and I set out to sort and transcribe the collection of letters, which proved to be easier than is often the case with this type of material. Although the overall size of the collection made the work time-consuming, it was enjoyable and revealing. As we read further, we not only came to know the Lincolns but became ever more convinced that their letters deserved a wider audience. We were by no means looking for another project, and we had no illusions that producing this book would be rewarding as a commercial venture, but we were driven by a feeling of obligation, much like Frank Lincoln's sense of duty.

When we began, the letters were out of order and our initial task was to put them in proper sequence. Where sheets had been separated, we tried to rejoin original letters, relying on clues such as continuity of text, condition of the paper, and the way it was folded. Still, it became evident that some letters were incomplete, while the text indicated that others were missing entirely. Their loss is regrettable, but it is apparent that the overwhelming majority of the letters are present.

Editing manuscripts of this kind forces a profusion of small decisions, and there is seldom an absolutely perfect solution. Mere consistency is often difficult to achieve. Generally speaking, our inclination was to interfere as little as possible with the original writing. Frank in particular used relatively little punctuation, seldom breaking his letters into paragraphs and not always into sentences. We modernized the punctuation in the belief that readability mattered much more than literal accuracy. In most cases we tried to retain odd or obsolete spellings, though some examples have probably been lost unintentionally due to the dominant word processing program's assumption that it knows what the user wants better than the user. In our notes and commentary, we resorted to modern spelling and forms of names such as New Bern.

We hope and expect that this book will appeal to specialists, but it is intended for the general reader, and thus we define terms such as sutler that a Civil War specialist would consider elementary. Similarly, we felt that it was important to let the reader absorb the tone of that era's writing. For this reason, we deleted very little from the letters and have added considerable supporting material or quoted extensively from contemporary sources in our notes. My own interest in the Civil War is fairly strong but does not approach the all-consuming intensity it holds for many people. By coincidence, however, I already was familiar with the 46th Mass. as a result of having edited the diary of an officer's boy in that regiment, which was published in *Springfield Fights the Civil War* (Connecticut Valley Historical Museum, 1990).

There has never been a regimental history for the 46th Mass., and it is unlikely that there ever will be, because its service was relatively brief and undramatic. This book does not claim to be a regimental history, but it is at least a contribution in that direction. Likewise, it does not purport to be a biography of Frank Lincoln, but it is probably the closest approach we will see. We also hope this book will make a significant contribution to the history of Brimfield and to a lesser extent the surrounding towns.

In our notes and explanations, we relied extensively on several main sources. Rev. Charles M. Hyde's *Historical Celebration of the Town of Brimfield* (1879), the last full history of the town, was essential for identifying people mentioned in the letters and sorting out family relationships. The area of North Carolina where Frank served was a relatively obscure theater of the war, but several books give a useful description of events there. We relied on John C. Barrett, *The Civil War in North Carolina* (Univ. of North Carolina, 1963) and the more recent *Ironclads and Columbiads* (1989) by William R. Trotter. Both of these draw heavily on the standard official source *The War of the Rebellion, a Compilation of the Official Records of the Union and Confederate Armies*, especially Series I, Volume XVIII, "Operations in North Carolina and Southeastern Virginia, August 20, 1862 to June 3, 1863," which we also used directly. For context on the complex and challenging subject of the war's effect on women, we followed Nina Silber's *Daughters of the Union* (Harvard Univ. Press, 2005). Silber was intrigued by Rebecca's letters as an example of the issues women faced and cited several in her book. David Stick's *The Outer Banks of North Carolina* (Univ. of North Carolina, 1958) was useful for its descriptions of places Frank visited.

Additional supporting documentation was found in the Brimfield Public Library and the Brimfield town clerk's office, as well as in local newspapers. The library contains original rosters and orderly books for Frank's company, which we cite extensively. Information on individual soldiers, mainly from this roster, is compiled in Appendix A.

We are grateful for the generous assistance provided by Joyce Beaton, Sherman Room librarian at the Brimfield Public Library; Laurie Prescott; Judy Reid Mathieu; Jill Reid Lukesh; Brimfield Town Clerk Pamela Beall; Tom Kelleher; Hitchcock Academy Director Sue Gregory; and Helen Morris and other members of the Academy Memorial Room Committee.

—Larry Lowenthal

INTRODUCTION

Frank's letters do not begin until he arrived in North Carolina. By then his regiment had a history going back three months, and these beginnings need to be summarized in order for the letters to be fully appreciated, without at the same time attempting to review the entire war to that point.

By mid-1862 the delightful illusion that the war would be a glorious adventure, a flag-waving triumphal march, had long since evaporated. Like a pact with the devil, the illusion was gone, but the war ground on, far more horrible and costly than anyone had imagined. On August 4, 1862, acting under a law that allowed him to call up state militias, President Abraham Lincoln issued a call for 300,000 militiamen to serve nine months, presumably to hold the Union position until a longer-serving force of volunteers and draftees could be organized. Conscription was authorized if enough volunteers did not come forward.

The situation was complicated because a month earlier the president had called for 300,000 three-year volunteers, so the towns were trying to recruit simultaneously for both kinds of service. The demand for three-year troops was divided among the loyal states according to population, and in Massachusetts apportioned among every town and city. Brimfield's quota was 20 men. By then 40 Brimfield men had already volunteered, motivated by patriotism and a craving for adventure, since it is hard to imagine that a private's pay could have been much of an incentive. Enlistments were slow, even though the federal government now offered a bounty (bonus) of $100. Brimfield, "fearing that the pay and bounty offered by the Government may fail to persuade this number in due season, therefore for the purpose of encouraging Enlistments and as an additional inducement therefore," began a voluntary subscription to give each volunteer an additional bounty of $150.[1] Subscription forms were circulated around town, and residents pledged to donate a certain amount for each soldier. Frank Lincoln signed for $1, which would have totaled $20 for the town's quota of recruits.

Fear of being drafted undoubtedly made it easier to recruit nine-month men, but the congressional act encouraged bounties and the town felt that this was necessary. Recalling the patriotic fervor that had sustained them in the War for Independence, the townspeople declared at a meeting on August 28, 1862, that "we believe it to be more in accordance with the spirit of our Institutions, the dictates of Patriotism, and the past history of this town, that the quota of the town of Brimfield should be filled by volunteer enlistments, rather than be selected by arbitrary military draft," and resolved to offer a $150 bonus to the nine-months' recruits, as well as to furnish "aid and assistance" to sick or wounded soldiers who needed "care and attention, that is not, or cannot be furnished by the Government." Despite the

---

[1] Original subscription forms in Brimfield Town Clerk's office.

jealousies, rivalries and religious and political differences that divided all towns, a strong residue of the Puritan sense of community must have remained, and so the townspeople explained the bounty as remuneration "for the loss incurred by so abruptly leaving their business avocations, also to enable them to provide for the present and future necessities of their families and friends dependent upon them for support."[1]

As with the three-year recruits, the quota for nine-month enlistments was passed down to the states and municipalities. The Massachusetts adjutant-general determined that the towns of Brimfield, Holland, Monson and Wales would be responsible for filling a regular company of 100 enlisted men. In Brimfield, Frank Lincoln had apparently been a leader in inspiring the town to meet the demands of war. Hyde reports that in the early months of the war it was on his motion that the town voted to borrow money for the support of men who had enlisted.[2] He must have assumed the main responsibility for recruitment in Brimfield, if not the other towns, and it was he who sent the completed enlistment roll to the adjutant-general.

On September 9, 1862, men who had enlisted from the four towns met in Brimfield to organize and elect officers. In recognition of his efforts, Frank Lincoln was unanimously elected captain, with 82 votes (not all recruits being present). This was clearly a tribute to Frank, since Monson's population was substantially larger than Brimfield's. Spreading the honors among the other towns, George H. Howe of Monson was chosen first lieutenant and Julius M. Lyon of Wales second lieutenant.[3] Another requirement was for the selectmen of each town to furnish a "Certificate of Moral Worth" for the officers, affirming that they were "proper persons to be commissioned."[4]

September 16 was a day full of symbolic meaning in Brimfield. Early in the day, members of the old Brimfield Rifle Company, which had disbanded in 1840, gathered for a reunion. Organizations like this were usually more social than military, and indeed it was reported that "If they had forgotten some things in connection with their regular drill, they were as near perfect in their dinner drill as any company we ever saw."[5] Nevertheless, one of the former officers, Gen. Fitz Henry Warren, was then commanding a brigade in Missouri. In the afternoon Capt. Lincoln assembled his recruits for two or three hours of drill, after which they adjourned to partake of "a splendid entertainment, provided by the ladies." Possibly the evolutions of the old militia company had been inspirational; more likely, Frank had studied a military manual such as Hardee's.

---

[1] Quoted in Charles M. Hyde, *Historical Celebration of the Town of Brimfield*, (1879) 331-332.
[2] Hyde, 330.
[3] Hyde, 333. A report in the Palmer *Journal*, Sep. 13, 1862, says that the volunteers met at Monson Sep. 10 to elect officers. There may have been meetings in both towns.
[4] Form in Brimfield Town Clerk's office.
[5] Palmer *Journal*, Sep. 20, 1862.

Brimfield August 22 1862

We whose names are hereunto affixed severally enlist in a company of volunteer militia in Brimfield and vicinity, subject to orders of the Commander-in-Chief and all laws and regulations governing the Militia of this Commonwealth, and agreeing to serve upon any requisition of the Government of the United States issue during the present year, as a militia man for the term of nine months consecutively, if orders therefor shall be issued by the Commander-in-Chief of the militia of Massachusetts, Provided the town of Brimfield or individuals shall pay to each man Enlisting as above the sum of One Hundred Fifty Dollars when he is mustered into the service of the United States and also that the full Quota of men for the town of Brimfield under the order of the President for Three Hundred Thousand men for the period of nine months dated Aug 4th 1862 is filled by bounty Enlistments

Francis D. Lincoln — William H. Sherman
Francis E. Cook — Byron W. Charles
Thos J. Morgan — Samuel C. Earle
Cheney Newton — Charles E. Alexander
Edward Bliss — Charles E. Loomis
Charles Upham — Abner H. Stebbins
George C Homer — Lyman T Parker

The names of Francis D. Lincoln and Thomas J. Morgan are prominent on the list of Brimfield men who signed up to join the volunteer militia regiment that became the 46th Mass.

Orderly Book, Company G, 46th Mass., Brimfield Public Library.

Brimfield's Civil War monument, with Hitchcock Academy beyond. The monument, one of the earliest in the state, was erected with town funding in 1866. Silas C. Herring, proprietor of the Brimfield Hotel, provided the elegant cast-iron fence. The hotel stood on the corner across from both the academy and the monument. Showing its continued interest in its monument and its veterans, Brimfield in 1882 accepted four Parrott guns, which had become surplus because the army was switching to breech-loading artillery. The monument occupies a conspicuous position in town, at the eastern end of the Common, which extends to the Congregational Church in the west.

The recruits for what had been designated the 46th Massachusetts regiment left Palmer September 24 to begin training at Camp Banks in Springfield, located along Boston Road in the vicinity of the present Mass Mutual headquarters.[1] Captain Lincoln's company was designated Company G. After a week in camp, it was reported that the men were in excellent health despite some chilly weather, but that they had not yet received uniforms and "'trainin' without guns is rather dull business."[2] This time in camp was a valuable transition period in which the men became accustomed to military life while maintaining vital connections with home.

The 46th Mass. was composed almost entirely of men from Hampden County, and Camp Banks was centrally located. The Palmer newspaper described the recruits feelingly as "the flower of the youth of the Connecticut Valley; the bravest and best of our mountain yeomanry; the true, loyal sons of puritan New England." Palmer people visited their company at the camp "carrying with them a supply of eatables and choice dainties which will cause the boys long to remember the donors," and a Brimfield delegation made a similar visit the following day.[3] As the time for departure drew closer, the "ladies of Brimfield" presented Captain Lincoln with a fine sword, sash and belt, and George C. Homer, one of the men who had enlisted from the town, gave him a Smith & Wesson revolver.[4] Gifts of this kind seem to have been common, if not expected, and once one town made the gesture others could hardly refuse. The women also gave each volunteer from Brimfield a "'housewife' well supplied with necessaries."[5] In November the regiment left for the South, and its story is continued by Frank's letters and other accounts.

A Proud Heritage

Frank Lincoln did not need a certificate from the selectmen to confirm that he belonged to one of Brimfield's distinguished families. His father, Asa, it is true, was not a native, having been born in Taunton, Massachusetts, in 1782. He was the oldest of nine children and, according to Hyde, had hoped to study law; but his father determined he should be a physician. Medicine in those days was taught by essentially an apprentice system, and Asa studied with doctors in Sturbridge and Brookfield, teaching school to support himself. When his studies were sufficiently complete, he set up practice in Brimfield. Later, he tried to pursue his original inclination as much as possible by becoming active as a justice of the peace.

In 1809 he married Sarah, the daughter of Brimfield's famed general in the War for Independence, Timothy Danielson. The general, however, had died in

---

[1] Palmer *Journal*, Sep. 27, 1862.
[2] Palmer *Journal*, Oct. 4, 1862.
[3] Palmer *Journal*, Oct. 18; Oct. 25, 1862.
[4] Strangely, Frank never mentions these accoutrements in his letters.
[5] Palmer *Journal*, Nov. 1, 1862. A "housewife" was a basic sewing kit.

1791, and in the following year his widow Eliza married William Eaton, who went on to an illustrious military career and considered himself a general. Among other exploits, Eaton conducted one of America's first interventions in the Muslim world, capturing a town in what is now Libya. By 1811 he had drunk himself into an early grave and would have been no more than a vivid subject of conversation in Asa Lincoln's family.

Dr. Asa and Sarah Lincoln had ten children, all of whom lived to adulthood, an unusual accomplishment at the time. All of the children were given the middle name Danielson. Sarah died in 1830 at the age of 40, and the doctor may have felt remorse over the possibility that her early death was related to having borne ten children in less than 20 years. Out of respect for her memory, he never remarried and made a practice of visiting her grave on the anniversary of her death.[1] Francis D., the sixth child, was born September 30, 1821, and was thus less than nine, a particularly vulnerable age, when his mother died.

There are suggestions in his Civil War letters that Frank endured hardship in his youth, and probably this was true. William Eaton had squandered the remaining Danielson fortune, and the practice of medicine was not as lucrative or as respected as it became later in the century. Trying to support several young children with no mother present would have been a difficult undertaking. The obituary of Frank's next younger brother James reports that he was sent to live with a relative after his mother's death, and Frank may have had a similar experience. James would have liked to become a physician, but "circumstances" led him into a business career.[2] Another element of strain afflicted the Lincoln family in the mid-1830s when the oldest daughter, Mary D., espoused Perfectionism, one of the more extreme expressions of the religious ferment that bubbled in those years. The Perfectionist episode in Brimfield, which could be the subject of a separate book, caused an angry division in the Lincoln family.

All of the Lincoln children were intelligent and would have been capable of pursuing careers in the professions. With three older brothers, Frank's chances of following such a course were limited. Like several of them, he became a schoolteacher. After teaching in several other towns, he took a job in Walpole, Norfolk County, Massachusetts. There he met Rebecca Cox, and they were married September 28, 1848. They had two daughters: Rebecca Maria, born November 7, 1849, and Henrietta Frances, called Etta, born July 2, 1853. There was obviously no interest in replicating the huge families of the previous two generations.

After his marriage, Frank returned to live on and manage the Danielson-Lincoln farm in Brimfield. The family dynamics that led to this decision could be fascinating but are not known. Asa Lincoln was still living—he did not die until 1854—but may have been in declining health. Additionally, the last three Lincoln children, although they had reached adulthood, died young during this period:

[1] Hyde, 174.
[2] Palmer *Journal*, June 8, 1906; obituary probably written by Mary Anna Tarbell.

William D. in 1846 at the age of 21, Charlotte D. in 1847 at 20, and Elizabeth D. in 1849, not yet 20. After that, Frank was probably the only one of the children who remained in Brimfield; his four surviving brothers were all well launched on successful careers elsewhere. Within the Brimfield sphere, Frank's abilities earned respect and he held various town offices. As far as can be determined, he seemed well settled and integrated into the life of the rural town.

Leaving Brimfield

Looking back from the early 1930s, with the terrible sacrifices of the Great War, soon to be renamed World War I, already beginning to seem like a tragic waste, an unidentified author described life in Brimfield in the mid-1850s, when the Hitchcock Academy was founded. With the loss of some 30 million lives and vast amounts of the world's accumulated wealth fresh in mind, he or she observed:

> [L]et us see if something cannot be said in favor of the peace and quiet of the Brimfield Common in the middle nineteenth century and the quiet living of its God-fearing, church-going inhabitants, in their finely kept homes, their homely virtues and their moderate amusement requirements in contrast to the turmoil of activities in which most of us are living today.
>
> Therefore, in fancy let us go to Brimfield in the late summer of 1854, and we shall find the breezes blowing through the beautiful trees, the singing birds, the humming of insects, and the drowsy atmosphere, just the same as it was when we entered the Academy for the first time at the beginning of the school year. . . .[1]

Allowing for blurring by the golden haze of memory and exaggerations such as the prevalence of church attendance, this was essentially the Brimfield that Capt. Lincoln and his troops left in 1862. The population of the town had peaked in 1830 at just under 1600, which was probably the maximum that could be sustained by an agrarian economy and a number that would not be attained again until late in the following century. In the 1860 census the count had fallen to 1363. Many of these were descendants of families who had first settled the town, beginning in 1731. There was a mill village in East Brimfield, relying on the waterpower of the Quinebaug River, but most of the townspeople depended directly or indirectly on agriculture and local industry.

Brimfield looked like a secluded, bucolic hill town, but it was not completely isolated or backward. Although sheltered by hills, it lay on a main road, the ancestor of present Route 20, connecting the Bay with the Connecticut River. Especially in its center, the town contained an active group of intelligent, forward-

[1] Hitchcock Free Academy Board of Trustees, "Honour Roll of Donors", commemorative booklet, 1932.

looking citizens who believed in the value of education and exemplified the traditional New England impulse toward improvement. They formed the backbone of church, school, and town government, and they lived close enough together on good roads to visit easily. With their farm on the main highway and secure in their illustrious ancestry, Frank and Rebecca Lincoln fitted solidly into this cluster of rural gentry.

For North Carolina

Federal strategists apparently decided that the nine-months troops would not be sent into places where intense combat was likely. The militiamen were even less well trained than ordinary soldiers and would not be in service long enough to benefit greatly from experience. Moreover, since entire units came from the same area, heavy losses could damage support for the war. Thus, these regiments were generally assigned to garrison duty, holding positions already won, although in Louisiana some saw pretty heavy combat.

One such position was the coast of North Carolina, which became the destination of the 46th Mass., as well as its sister regiments, the 44th and 45th. The strong Union presence there was a product of the "Anaconda Plan," named for the fearsome South American snake that killed by constriction. Recognizing that it would be extremely difficult to conquer the vast land area of the South, the Anaconda Plan proposed to use the North's overwhelming naval superiority to choke the enemy's ability to wage war, while the federal army gradually reduced its perimeter. Over the long course of the war, the strategy proved effective, though it did not remove the need for massive invasions and battles.

With its multitudes of inlets, sluggish rivers and small harbors, coastal North Carolina offered ideal conditions for Confederate blockade runners and commerce raiders, creating a nuisance that the North could not long tolerate. In addition, this territory formed a back door to Norfolk and Richmond, and capturing it would restrict the Confederacy's freedom of action. A combined army and navy attack by Gen. Benjamin (later "the Beast") Butler and Commodore Silas Stringham seized the Hatteras forts in late August 1861. The Confederates then withdrew from the outer banks to a stronghold on Roanoke Island.

The anaconda tightened another coil in February 1862, when General Ambrose Burnside, a Rhode Islander, led a major expedition against Roanoke Island. After a severe battle the Confederate fortress fell, and most of its garrison was taken prisoner. Burnside then regrouped and on March 11 attacked New Bern, the largest town in the region, with 11,000 men. After another hard-fought battle, he entered the town March 14. Later in the month he moved south and captured Beaufort, and in April Fort Macon, which had defended Beaufort, surrendered. Burnside celebrated with a victory parade in New Bern on April 26. These North Carolina battles, while not on the scale of the main engagements in Virginia, were major conflicts in their own right. Burnside demonstrated effective command, and his troops performed with courage and efficiency. The outcome of these battles was by no means certain, and Confederate mismanagement cost them a chance for victory on several occasions.

A Brimfield soldier, Pvt. Joseph H. Snow, serving in the 27th Mass., fought in both the battles of Roanoke Island and New Bern and described them in the following letter to the Brimfield hotel keeper. Snow's account is plain and straight-forward, devoid of artificial literary flourishes.

[*Addressed to George Monroe, Brimfield, Mass; postmarked New York, Sep. 4, 1862. Letter written on two sheets with different stationery; apparently on different days.*]

Newberne N.C. Aug 10th [1862]

Friend George

Dear Sir

Yours of July 22d came safe to hand and right glad I was to hear from you. Hope I may hear from you often and I will answer if I am situated so that[I] can.

I find myself well at this time. I have been sick two days the 6 & 7th. I was in the Hospital quite sick but I am all right now. We have quite a pleasant place here for an encampment, it being the Fair Ground formerly used by the Rebiles[sic]. When we first came here we found the Rebel Tents just as they left them in their hot haste to get away from the damned Yankees. We found the darkies here with mule teams carting off the goods as fast as they could. Our officers soon stopped that. We Boys then went in for whatever we could find. We did not find much money but plenty of Blankets and clothing Tobacco & Pipes & other articles to[sic] numerous to mention, some of which we sent home. I have sent John several things Over Coat & Blanket and a Knife which I got at Roanoke Is[sic] the place where they said I fell out. As it happened I was there and saw as much fighting as any one of the co[sic].

It was a very good slaughter yard the Rebels had fixed up for us but they got whipped. It was because I did not go on after the Fighting was over was what started such a story. One fellow in our Co started the story and I got square with him in the last Battle. I watched him & when the fire was the hottest he <u>skeedadled</u>. I laughed at him and asked him if he remembered Roanoke. He denied every word.

At this Battle here at Newberne we had a hard time marching through the mud 14 miles and some of the way dragging a Cannon. Slept on the ground in the rain only about ¾ of a mile from the Enemy. Early in the morn we were formed in line and mached[sic] on a short distance. Then our Regt[sic] filed off to the left into the woods. Soon we came in sight of the Rebels peeking over their breast-works. All you could see of them was their hat & head & Gun. Their flag we could see very Plain for they waved it saucily up and down as much as to say come on we are ready for you. In a moment the order came for us "Ready—Fire." About two thirds of the Guns went [off], the rest missed fire owing to the rain the night before. My rifle missed the first snap but I tried it again and then it was off and I suppose down came a Rebel (I cannot say as to that).

The next thing was that troubled me my ramrod stuck fast in the gun stock. I got a comrade to help pull it our and then stuck it up in the ground beside me and went in. Load and fire as fast as possible was the order. <u>Oh my</u> how the Bullets did whistle. Cannon Balls and shell grape and canister cutting of[sic] the trees and mowing down our men. Horrid work. I tell you people can stay at home and talk brave let them hear the Bullets whistle & see the wounded dead and dieing[sic] that I have seen and by that time they'll see enough of war.

[next folio]

We fought the Rebels an hour and five minutes and then we got out of amunition[sic], most of us having used our 40 rounds. We then fell back about 25 rods another Regt takeing[sic] our place. Our 2d[sic] Lt[sic] was killed at the 2d or 3d fire from the enemy. Tom Pepper[1] was wounded—a Bullet hit a fellow on top of the head. He was close to me and I shall always remember how it sounded. It knocked him down & I supposed it had gone through his head but on examination I see it only knocked of[sic] a little piece of his scalp and made the Blood run freely. It was probably a spent Ball. I could tell you Incidents enough to fill a newspaper but time will not permit.

Of the doings here now there is not much that would interest you. Our Regt is hear[sic] to help hold the place and do picket duty. We go out scouring the country once and a while. Sometimes we are successful and capture some of the Rebels. Two Co of our Regt went out the other day and surprised a party of them, killing two and capturing 10 prisoners & 20 Horses. No one hurt on our side.

Lightning struck one of the Tents in Co A killed one man and stunned 3 others. It was about 4 oclock in the morning. All were Laying down at the time. I was up and looking in that direction at the time—and it was only about 8 rods from me. "I guess I heard it." I have to send you some of our Newberne Papers once and[sic] a while. They will keep you posted on our affairs.

[1] Pvt. Thomas O. Pepper, of Brimfield.

About the Boys here I have but little to write. They all behave themselves well. I will mention the sick. Sergt[sic] Wm[sic] Nye[1] is sick and I am afraid he will never be any better. His disease acts like Consumption. He is now at Beaufort. Harrison Robinson[2] is there also though not dangerously sick. Harrison was close beside me in the fight here at N & I shall always remember how he sweat. In fact we all sweat. I never sweat any worse in the hayfield (<u>you may tell Wm Janes that</u>).

[paragraph deleted]

I will not attempt to write a lengthy epistle this time. It is nearly time I quit now & I think I will. With my best wishes for your welfare.

I Remain Yours &c &c

J.H. Snow

[1] William A. Nye, of Brimfield.
[2] Pvt. H. Wilson Robinson, of Brimfield, died at New Bern Apr. 25, 1863.

The Lincoln family homestead in 2006.

The Lincoln homestead around the turn of the 20th Century. The exact date is unknown, but the photo must have been taken before 1907, when trolley tracks were laid along the main road (present Rt. 20). The Lincolns walked or drove along this road countless times, but the mature elms that lined the road have long since succumbed to disease.

Photos courtesy Judy Reid Mathieu and Jill Reid Lukesh.

THE LINCOLN LETTERS

Capt. Francis D. Lincoln

Illustration courtesy of harpersweekly.com

New Berne, Oct. 10, 1862,

Dear Rebecca

You will like to know all about our passage and how we are after the voyage. Well we left the "roads" Monday about an hour before sundown.[1] It was as pleasant as anything could be all the eve. Monday mor[sic] When I got up we were between Martha's Vineyard and some and some[sic] other island, which remained in sight some two hours and was last land we saw belonging to New England. Each day of our passage was pleasant and very much like the other with two exceptions.

One day was a little windy and the vessel pitched and rolled about so as to make quite a number of the boys seasick. Tom Morgan*[2] & a Monson boy suffered more than the rest. Tom did not get over his till we landed but is quite well. The other exception was when we got off the coast of Virginia. It became quite warm and the atmosphere felt pretty much as it does in New England in the first of Sept. You will think perhaps it must be delightful to glide over the ocean with just a gentle perceptible rocking motion about such as the mother would give to the chair when the baby was nearly asleep. And for a little while it is delightful, but to have four or five days in succession of this gentle rocking is enough to give a nervous person the "fragetts". Then again to have the sea always look so smooth is very far from being pleasant. The day I enjoyed most was the same that made so many of the boys sick.

We came on as I have described seeing only now and then a sail and nothing else except the ocean and a few gulls till Friday morning, when we hove in sight of light houses off Cape Lookout [North Carolina] and being soon after the land. Had the boys been in prison a month I don't believe they would have been more glad to have had their liberty than they were to see land once more.

Two hours more the Capt of the boat said when we pulled the pilot aboard would bring us on the dry land but in this we were all disappointed, for the pilot ran the vessell[sic] aground when within a quarter of a mile of the wharf and she stuck fast in the mud. The other vessells passed by ours on either side, much to our mortification and their joy, for you will understand there is more or less strife between captains about which shall land first. Provoking, was it not, to the capt as well as us to be beaten by both the other vessells through the carelessness of a pilot. Well, we lay there till the Missippi[sic] has taken off the Forty-fifth[3] and the Saxon have pulled in by her side with the seven companies of our reg. And then (about six o'clock pm) the Col. sent a steamer and took off the Merrimac, put us on the Missippi to stay till morning.[4]

---

[1] Road or roadstead: the protected shipping channel into Boston, now called President Roads.

[2] * Asterisks indicate men in Frank's company. For information about them, see Appendix A.

[3] The 45th Mass. Infantry, another nine-months regiment, which accompanied the 46th.

[4] It has not been possible to find further information about these vessels, which were probably merchant ships chartered for the purpose. U.S. Navy ships with these names were elsewhere during this period. (*Dictionary of American Navy Fighting Ships*, http://www.history.navy.mil/danfs/).

Saturday before sunrise, we tumbled on the wharf at Morehead City, packed bag & baggage aboard the cars for New Berne.[1] On we came with the speed of lightning through a country fit for nothing under the sun but to keep the water off more decent land. The whole distance from Morehead City to New Berne 38 miles is a poor bone waste[?] of swamp & brush as far as one can see on either side, and with the exception of Beaufort, which is near by Morehead. Think of riding through a country for more than 30 miles and not seeing a single spot where a <u>Yankee</u> would try to get a living.

But I must close for we have an order from the Col. to strike our tents immediately and move to our own ground. Tis a God-forsaken country covered[?] with Negroes at New Berne. At some future day I will send more particulars. So good by. My love to all. Your father.

F.D.L.

There is confusion about dates in this letter, as the correct date for the voyage to North Carolina should be November 10. "Monday" is also used for two different days in the first paragraph. The letter is noteworthy for showing Frank's initial reaction to the landscape around New Bern, typical of the impressions recorded by most northern soldiers on seeing the South for the first time.

[1] "The cars" was a common expression for travel by railroad.

Board Ship   November 11th 1862

Dear Etta & Mother

I suppose you have read in the paper that we have had to wait till after the storm was over and gone finally in three vessells[sic] instead of two, but still perhaps you will like to know all about it, so I will tell. I wrote you that the steamers we were to go in were not fit for the purpose & that I had been on shore to see Rebecca & was coming back the next day. Well I came and found the men in very bad shape. Wrote back to F.W.B.[1] to see the Gov. and try to have things changed. At the same time the Col. of the 45th went, and among them they got the Gov. to send a boat & bring the 46th back to Boston. Sunday night in the storm we all came back to Boston and stayed in Faneuil Hall all night, the city furnishing food & coffee for the men and the proprietor of the Hancock House feeding the officers.

Monday morning we went about the city a few at a time to get a few things we wanted. G.H. Howe[2] & I took breakfast at the hotel. About noon it was decided that I should take my own company & half of Capt. Cromwells[3] and got on board the Merrimack. Capt. Spooner[4] with the other half of the company on the Missippi[sic] and the other seven companies go on the steamer Saxon (not Swan as the republican says)[5]. So we came out of the Hall down in front of the market & they treated us all with apples and then we came board the vessells & started for sea.

It was as beautiful afternoon as ever you saw and the weather and novelty made it delightful. So we steamed on all night. This morning when I got up (a little before sunrise) we were all off Martha's Vineyard and about nine we bade farewell to old Massachusetts and have seen nothing that looked like being inhabited with human beings except the three other vessels and one sail in the distance. It is very pleasant and we glide smoothly along with a gentle rocking of the boat just enough to have you feel that we are in motion. How queer it seems to stand on deck & look all about and find no land.

Nov 12th. Up to this morning our boys have been well except poor [George E.] Stacy* who had been at home sick some time before we left camp and whom I tried to persuade to stay at home. But he was so anxious to come I gave way and the

---

[1] Francis W. Bird of Walpole, MA, a paper manufacturer and prominent abolitionist, who was influential in the Republican Party and later a candidate for governor. Frank Lincoln's obituary (Palmer *Journal*, May 17, 1901), almost certainly written by Mary Anna Tarbell, mentions their friendship.

[2] George H. Howe, 22, of Monson, a lieutenant in Company G. Frank was not yet in the habit of referring to men by military title.

[3] Probably Capt. Russell H. Conwell of Worthington, commander of Co. F.

[4] Capt. Samuel B. Spooner of Springfield, commander of Co. A.

[5] The Springfield, MA, *Republican*. The reference shows that, even this soon after arriving, Frank had access to recent home newspapers.

result was that we had to leave him at the Hospital in Boston to be sent home the next day. Poor fellow. I can but feel we shall see him no more on Earth. But to day the waves . . . .

[*Page(s) apparently missing; continues across salutation, first page.*]
I told Rebecca she must not go to school this winter against the desire of Dr. Witter[1]. Now Mother, see to it that she does not. Better to go to Dorchester so as to be away and return day after Thanksgiving. Give my love to all. Kiss for Mrs. Th… & Charley.

Yours
Frank

[*Below*]Write.

An unidentified person who perhaps had accompanied the 46th wrote the following account, published in the Palmer Journal, November 15, 1862, of the distressing experience the regiment endured when it first attempted to depart Boston. If there was any value in this ordeal it was to prepare the men for the greater discomfort, loss of privacy and other hardships of military life they would soon encounter.

The 46th regiment, which left Camp Banks on Wednesday, last week, did not sail for Newbern on Friday, as expected. They waited until Friday for a gun-boat to convoy them to their place of destination, when a driving north-east storm set in, which rendered them very uncomfortable. They were packed on the steamers as thick as pigs in a rail-car, and the severity of the storm kept them between decks, many of them being forced into the hold, below the water line.

Seasickness prevailed extensively among them, and the ships became filthy in the extreme. The wind blew so hard that it was almost impossible for them to receive succor from the shore. On Saturday afternoon, however, the Governor sent Gen. Schouler[2], Quartermaster Reed, and Surgeon Dale, to look after the men. After examining into their condition, they approached Fort Warren[3] in the steamer Nantasket, with the intention of making arrangements for landing the men there; but the guard would receive no communication from the boat, ordering it off, with a threat that it should be fired into if it remained. The soldiers on shipboard consequently spent Saturday night and Sunday in the harbor, rocked about by the force of the wind and waves.

[1] Dr. John Witter succeeded to the medical practice in Brimfield of Dr. Ebenezer Knight, who died in 1857.
[2] Massachusetts Adjutant-General William Schouler (1814-1872).
[3] Located on Georges Island, Fort Warren was the main fortification defending Boston harbor.

On Sunday evening they were taken off, sent up to the city, and quartered in Faneuil Hall, where, for the first time since their embarkation, they obtained rest. Some of them were sick and had to be carried in the arms of their comrades. On Monday afternoon, seven companies of the 46th embarked on the steamer Saxon, and three on the Mississippi and Merrimac, and the three steamers, accompanied by the gunboat Huron[1], sailed about sundown. On Tuesday morning, they were seen opposite Chatham, off Cape Cod, making good headway out to sea.

Col. Bowler, of the 46th, did not, we understand, share the suffering of his men in the harbor, but safely quartered himself at a comfortable hotel in Boston. There has been considerable complaint among the men concerning Col. Bowler, and we presume not without reason.

The diary of Addison H. Watson, an orderly in Co. K, supports this chronology. On Wednesday, Nov. 5, the regiment started for Boston about 9:30 a.m. and arrived 4:30 p.m. Watson said they "were cheered at every corner we passed in the city." On Thursday they were aboard ships anchored in the harbor. They were still in the harbor Friday when the sea became rough, making a great many of the men sick. The storm passed on Saturday, but the men remained on ship until Sunday, when the Nantasket took them off. They returned to Faneuil Hall, "where there was a good supper waiting for us." On Monday, Nov. 10, they left for the boat at 2 p.m. and sailed around 4. (Diary edited by Larry Lowenthal, Springfield Fights the Civil War [Connecticut Valley Historical Museum, 1990], 97-98.)

[1] A Navy ship of this name, a schooner-rigged screw steamer launched in Boston September 1861, was on duty with the Atlantic blockading squadron and may have been detached as an escort (*Dictionary of American Naval Fighting Ships*, http://www.history.navy.mil/danfs/).

Dear Rebecca

  I was a little disappointed yesterday in not receiving a letter from some of my friends at home, for I had written two to you & Etta one to Rebecca which I supposed you must have seen, besides one to Charles and to the Whiskey Club, also one to Esq. Wyles.[1] And being in the city when the mail came and seeing two big wagon loads of mail matter from the North thrown off at the P.O., I could but think a part of it must be for me, but as it proved not a line came to any of the Brimfield boys but George H. [Homer]* & William Stearns.*

  Well, we did not draw the the[sic] conclusion that the rest of us were forgotten so soon, but rather settled down on this, that you hardly knew where to send a letter. You must know all the news, for a letter is of little value but for news. We landed safely Friday night. Saturday came to New Berne and I found out as soon as we were fairly stowed in our tents where the Walpole boys were. Went over to see them, had an hour's chat or more with Ed Ridge, Jim H., Rob Duff, Charley Gray, Henry Fuller, and L. Clap's wife's boy. Saw & spoke with several others, who recognized me whose names I never knew.[2]

  They are all well and in very comfortable quarters, barracks as they are called, which means long sheds something after the style of our wood shed externally except that they are long enough to hold a Reg. divided into rooms, one for each company with an out side door in the center of one side and nearly opposite a window and an oppen[sic] fire just one side of the window. On the right & left of the window and door are the bunks built against the walls of the barracks, with one near the floor, another above, leaving room enough for a person to sit up between the two and another still above with the space between it and the second, the same as between the second and 1st.

[1] John Wyles (1792-1875) was one of Brimfield's most prominent citizens. He is described in Hyde's history of Brimfield, 195-197. He lived in a large house on the south side of Sturbridge Road, just east of Town Brook (the brook that drains Sherman Pond). The "Whiskey Club," must have been an informal group of friends. If nothing else, the name showed a lack of sympathy for the prohibition movement that had gained many adherents.
[2] Frank and Rebecca retained many connections with Walpole, and his friendship with the influential Francis W. Bird originated there. The soldiers Frank mentioned were members of the 44th Mass., another nine-months regiment, which had arrived in New Bern about three weeks earlier. Those who can be identified are Robert H. Duff, 18; Henry C. Fuller, 33; Charles Lawson Gray, 19; and Corp. Edward (Edwin in one source) B. Ridge, 27. There were four men named Clapp in the regiment, none of whom were from Walpole. "Jim H." could refer to at least six men in the regiment; the likeliest is James E. Hutchinson, 25, of Co. K. All the Walpole residents in the 44th belonged to Co. K, just as all the Brimfield men in the 46th were members of Frank's Co. G.

In the middle of the barrack is a hall about ten feet wide running the whole length, making quite a dancing Hall. I said they were comfortable quarters, but you might think that Brussels carpet and papered walls were preferable to rough boards but I declare that the fireplace heaped with wood even in this rough shanty are[sic] more pleasant to me than the palace with the stove to heat it.

Sunday afternoon we removed from the tents we had occupied to the ground we are to occupy until our barracks are finished. Pitched our tents in the rain on a cold clay soil (about like that at East Walpole) and lay down to take our rest in the mud with nothing between us and it but our blanketts[sic] & yet the men generally slept well. I did not wake but once during the night and then I found that the <u>orderly</u> had, instead of covering the Capt. as you know the army regulations require him to do rolled him . . . .

[*Missing page(s); concluded on first page.*]
See to it that Rebecca does not go to school against the Drs[sic] advice. With much love to all

Yours
Frank

This is another incorrectly dated letter. Presumably, it should be dated November 23.

It is probable that some letters written by Frank and Rebecca during this period have not been preserved. After arriving and setting up camp at New Bern, as Frank described, the next several weeks were devoted to establishing rules and procedures to create reasonable military efficiency. The following entries from the company orderly book, preserved in the Brimfield public library, show some of these regulations. It must have been a difficult process, since there were probably few officers in the 46th Mass., or its sister regiments the 44th and 45th, who had significant military experience. They would have had to rely on regular officers at the brigade and division level, in addition to published manuals and general orders. Initially, the 46th was attached to the 3rd Brigade, 1st Division, Dept. of North Carolina.

Order No. 1

Head Quarters 46th Regt M. V. M.
Newbern N. C. November 19th 1862

The duties of the Camp will be conducted as far as practicable, in the following order

Reveille	6 o'clock	A. M.
Roll Call	6¼ " "	
Breakfast	7 " "	
Surgeons Call	7¾ " "	
Guard Mounting 1st Call	9 " "	
" " 2nd "	9¼ " "	
Company Drill	10 " "	
Dinner	12½ "	P.M.
Battallion "	2½ " "	
Dress Parade 1st Call	4½ " "	
" " 2nd "	4, 4,0 " "	
Retreat	5½ " "	
Tattoo	7½ " "	
Taps	8 " "	

By Order
Col. Geo. Bowler
James G. Smith
Adjt.

Copy

Regimental order No. 1 set out a typical day's routine for soldiers in the 46th Mass.
Orderly Book, Company G, 46th Mass., Brimfield Public Library.

Special Order No. 3   Newbern   Nov. 18, 1862

The Guard of this encampment will be careful to pass no man across the lines without a permit from the Colonel commanding, except it be a commissioned officer or a fatigue party under charge of a sergeant. Men will not be permitted to pass for wood or water except with Sergeant in charge of the squad. No person will be allowed to pass between the Retreat and Reveille without a countersign.

The Guard will be particular in the care of their Arms and see that they are clean at all times and in good order for Inspection.

The sentinels will attend strictly to their duties, not indulging in conversation with each other unnecessarily or with any soldier without the lines.

By order, Col. Geo. Bowler

Regimental Order No. 2   Newbern   Nov. 22, 1862

From and after date passes to town will be allowed to only two privates from each company in one day, excepting only the postmaster and newsboy of the Regiment.

Each soldier receiving a pass will be required to return it to headquarters and report himself. Otherwise the company to which he belongs will be considered as holding a pass for the ensuing day.

Regimental Order No. 4   Newbern   Nov. 26, 1862

Commanders of Companies will at once proceed to instruct their commands in the different firings, viz. By files—By platoons—By Rank—and By Company, taking care that the men do not spring the hammers, but simply go through the motions.[1]

Special Order No. 5   Newbern   Nov. 28, 1862

The Guard on coming off duty will be taken by the old Officer of the day to some place off the camp for Target Practice. The Target to be at 80 yards distance, not more than two rounds will be fired. The soldier making the two best shots will be excused from guard duty on his next turn.

---

[1] The men were being instructed in the manual of arms, but without firing. If they had pulled the trigger, thereby springing the hammer, it would have risked damaging their musket. Live firing was ordered on Nov. 28, but only two rounds per man were allowed. It is a telling illustration of how little practical training the men received.

Special Order No. 6   Newbern   Nov. 28, 1862

         The captains of companies in this Regiment are hereby charged with the duty of preparing a Roll of their Companies which shall designate the name of every soldier, with his place of Residence, the name and Residence of parents or friends who should be notified in case of sickness or death, the Blanks for such remarks as need be made in reference to them, which Roll will be carefully preserved with the Books and Papers of the Regiment.

Special Order No. 7   Newbern   Nov. 28, 1862

         Fatigue parties for wood will not hereafter be sent from the companies, the wood cut by the pioneers[1] being brought to camp by the teams belonging to the Quartermaster's department.

Regimental Order No. 5   Newbern   Nov. 30, 1862
[Forms ambulance corps.]

Regimental Order No. 6   Newbern   Dec. 1, 1862

Officers and Soldiers having business with the sutler[2], must transact it before the Sabbath, as no business will be allowed to be transacted by them on that day.

Regimental Order No. 7   Newbern   Dec. 1, 1862

         Greater attention must be given to the duties of the Guard. It is therefore strictly enjoined that the officers of the Guard shall not allow the reliefs to go out of hearing, that particular attention be paid to saluting and that the Guard be called out on the approach of the Officer entitled to that honor—and that the whole time of the guard and its officers shall be given to their duties and not have any conversation while on the beat or to be wandering about the camps when off their beats.

[1] Pioneers were men who performed construction or engineering work, including wood-cutting, often in advance of troop movements.
[2] Sutlers were civilians who sold items such as special food, stationery, and various personal articles that the soldiers could not obtain by other means. They usually operated from a wagon, or sometimes set up a temporary store.

Regimental Order No. 9   Newbern Dec. 5, 1862

As the articles of food sold by peddlers to the Soldiers are, in the opinion of the Surgeon, injurious to health, it is hereby ordered that no articles of food shall be sold by the negro peddlers on the camp with the exception of Fruits and Vegetables.

Regimental Order No. 10   Newbern Dec. 7, 1862

    Captains will inspect their Companies every Sunday morning at 9 o'clock. No soldier will be excused from Sunday inspection, except the Guard, the sick and the necessary attendants in the Hospital.

Regimental Order No. 12   Newbern Dec. 8, 1862

As it may be necessary for the Companies of this Regiment to be employed as skirmishers at any moment, the commander would enforce upon the officers in command of the various companies the necessity of attending immediately to such drill as will make them efficient in this department and especially, as we are the only Rifle corps, and consequently more liable than any other to be detailed for the work.[1]

[1] This implies that the 46th was armed with rifled muskets and that other regiments may have been using obsolete smoothbore weapons. According to a diary kept by a private in Co. I of the 46th, his company was armed with the "Windsor" rifle, which he termed "quite a solid musket and considered next to the Springfield musket." (Beryle C. Doten and Gertrude M. Lyons, transcribers, *Memorandum and Journal of Samuel Chapin of South Wilbraham*, Hampden, MA, Historical Soc., 1987.) The "Windsor" rifles were Model 1841 percussion rifle-muskets manufactured by Robbins & Lawrence in Windsor, VT, and modified by Massachusetts authorities. (See George D. Moller, *Massachusetts Military Shoulder Arms, 1784-1877* [Lincoln, RI: Mowbray, 1988], 86-90.)

The Military Situation in Eastern North Carolina

The fighting in eastern North Carolina was conducted as a sideshow of the primary action in Virginia. When things were relatively quiet in Virginia, more troops could be sent to North Carolina; but when a major campaign was planned in Virginia, it drew manpower away. When Burnside held his victory parade in April 1862, he had a force of approximately 17,000 and was preparing a move inland against the railroad town of Goldsboro. This could have posed a severe threat to the entire Confederate position, but just then Burnside and two of his divisions were ordered to join the drive up the peninsula toward Richmond under the leadership of his friend George C. McClellan. The remaining forces had no choice but to dig in on the defensive, though New Bern, with its mild climate, was not a bad place to be stationed. "New Bern, crowded as it was with soldiers and Negroes, was considered by many 'to be quite a pleasant' town."[1]

Although the federal forces in coastal North Carolina had been successful, their position was inherently precarious. There was always a possibility that the Confederates could accumulate an overwhelming advantage before the North could send reinforcements. To reduce this danger, federal strategists sent additional troops, and it was this consideration that brought the 46th Mass. into the region. In *Ironclads and Columbiads*, Trotter writes that "Most of the reinforcements, however, were newly raised volunteer regiments from Massachusetts, and some of the companies were so raw that the men didn't know how to load their rifles." (p. 165). This was undoubtedly an accurate description of Frank Lincoln's company G.

Brig. Gen. John G. Foster, who had replaced Burnside in North Carolina, launched a sizable expedition from Washington, North Carolina, into the interior on November 2. Foster, a New Hampshireman, had been a friend of Burnside's at West Point and had commanded a brigade under him. Trained as an engineer, he proved to be a dependable, competent field commander. Undoubtedly, one of his motives for the expedition was to rub the shine of newness off some of his troops. Afraid of being cut off as he ventured further inland, Foster began to withdraw on November 5. The 46th Mass. had not yet arrived and therefore missed this opportunity to gain field experience. The 44th Mass., which included Frank's Walpole friends, had arrived in time to participate in this march, and its members must have seemed like hardened veterans to the bright green troops of the 46th.

For the 46th, the first real campaigning began on December 11, when Foster launched the expedition toward Goldsboro that Burnside had intended. On the scale of fighting in this theater, it was a significant force, with 10,000 infantry,

---

[1] John C. Barrett, *The Civil War in North Carolina*, 132.

640 cavalry, and 30 cannons.[1] Foster understood that he did not have enough troops to capture and hold large territories, but he meant to keep his foes off balance. The danger of the situation had been highlighted only a day before (December 10), when Confederates attacked and drove the Union garrison out of Plymouth, North Carolina. Although Foster's expedition must have been planned considerably earlier, the attack could only have reaffirmed his belief that he needed to remain active. The firing drills described in the orderly book were part of the hasty preparations for the expedition.

After tiresome marches and some sharp fighting, Foster's expedition reached Goldsboro and succeeded in destroying the railroad bridge on December 17. He then decided not to attempt to capture the town and turned back toward his base at New Bern. Supply problems may have been a factor, and the general may not have had full confidence in his new troops. It had been a well-managed campaign in many respects, though of little lasting consequence, and cost the Union 92 men killed and 487 wounded. In combat, Foster relied on a few seasoned regiments, of which the 46th Mass. was not included.

Written soon after the troops returned, Frank's account of the Goldsboro expedition is one of his most valuable and compelling letters, and it is regrettable that part of it is lost. With his strong powers of description, he captures the novelty and excitement of his first taste of war. For him, as for most others, the pageantry of flags and masses of men on the march are dramatic, but before very long practical considerations tarnish these gleaming images. For a middle-aged family man like Frank, the glimpse of the deceptive grandeur of war is quickly tempered by his ability to foresee the consequences—a perfect example of why men his age seldom make bold soldiers.

[1] *The War of the Rebellion*, a Compilation of the Official Records of the Union and Confederate Armies (USGPO, 1887-; hereafter, *OR*), Ser. I, Vol. XVIII, 54 (Report of Gen. Foster). In launching this drive, Foster wrote that he had to borrow troops from elsewhere, as "My present force of infantry, consisting of 9,000 men capable of marching and fighting, 6,000 of whom are new—nine month's men—is too weak to give a good support to my forty pieces of artillery and to afford a fair chance of success against the older troops of the enemy in front of us."

New Berne   Dec. 22 '62

My Dear Family

Well do I know how anxiously you have waited to receive this letter, for you must have feared the worst, knowing as you did that we had marched to the field of battle. I have felt each day how anxious you must be to hear from us & how you would wonder why we did not write. You will believe me when I say that the thought that we were going to be able to answer all this anxious inquiry gave more joy to me when I recd[sic] the word that our expedition was at an end than the consciousness of being relieved from danger did.

I wrote you a week ago Wednesday that I expected to go on an expedition and on the envelope wrote that we were to march Thursday mor[sic]. Now if I have time before the mail closes, I will give the main incidents of the journey. And I wish you to preserve this letter, as I may not make out another as full description.[1]

We started from camp on a chilly morning, the fog so thick that you could not discern anything but a few feet from you. Went to the parade field and there waited for the other Regiments of the Brigade to be formed and join with us, and for the trains of Baggage, trains of artilery[sic] and Regmts[sic] of cavalry that belonged to the two Brigades that were to precede us to get on the way, we being the third Brigade, composed of the 27th, 25th, 46th, 3d & 5th Mass. Regiments in the order I have placed them, preceded by Riggs Battery which we [were] to support at all hasards[sic].

Long before we were ready to move the sun shone forth in all its splendor, seeming to wish to smile on us all and promise success. It was a grand sight as you could possibly imagine to see the broad highway for a mile or more filled with armed men clad in their uniforms all nearly new & alike, to see the bright bayonets glistening in the sun with here and there the flag of our country floating proudly above them: I must say that I had never beheld one more glorious. And yet as I looked & meditated I could but reflect that with all this splendor we were going on an errand that must send sorrow to many a heart, and the still more sad thought would come to me that perhaps the hearts of those nearest, dearest to me might be made to go on through life in sadness from the effects of the very adventure we [were] about starting on.

---

[1] Evidence that early letters have been lost, but also the beginning of the policy of saving most letters, so that the correspondence becomes much fuller after this date.

Well after waiting till everybody in our Reg. was nearly out of patience we marched slowly along, halting and waiting every few minutes to that extent that, although we started at 7 in the morning, at 2 ½ PM we had not advanced more than 3 miles. Now the teams have all passed the swamp and we begin to move quite steadily. On we go, tramp, tramp, tramp, sometimes through mud and water over shoe, sometimes in loose sand as deep, halting and waiting whenever the teams crossed a place where the load went hard, on, on, on through daylight and darkness till nearly ten o'clock in the eve[sic] when we came to the camp—so weary that we were hardly able to throw off our things.

It is not in my power to describe the camp in the eve. Language must fail any man in attempting. 14,000 troops spread over an open field with a bonfire for every 15 made of rails from the fences, they seated about the fires cooking each for himself a cup of coffee, with their arms stacked before them, their equipments hanging on or lying about them.[1] The bayonets glisten in the light of the fire. With the darkness of midnight skirting the field, it seems as though all <u>animated</u> nature had been gathered for a feast and the God of the Light sat without to protect.

That night we learned that the enemy had filled the road with trees to prevent our passage and we felt that we were in an enemy's country. On go the troops of pioneers with axes and teams, and before or by the break of day the road is cleared of the obstructions and the advance moves on, our Reg. occupying its old position.[2] We move about 8 A.M., having had pretty good sleep and supper & breakfast of hardtack[3] & cold meat which we brought with us.

The next day's march succeeds to the first, the only exception being the surprise of some Rebel cavalry by ours, in which they had three killed and as many wounded and we have two wounded (cavalry). And during the day lost 4 as prisoners. This began to look like war, the dead & wounded lying by the side of the road as we passed. This day we march till 12 at night, and really it did seem as though the men would give up an hour before we halted. That night Tom & George, Bill S.[4] & I camped in the woods and had quite a pleasant time of it, the chaplain lying by our fire.[5]

[1] Frank's estimate of the number of troops is exaggerated beyond Foster's official report of 10,000, but represented more troops, and probably more people, than he had ever seen gathered in one place. According to Foster's report, his expedition covered 14 miles on the main Kinston road on the first day.
[2] Foster confirms that he "had the obstructions removed during the night by the pioneers." (*OR*, Ser. I, vol. XVIII, 54).
[3] The dried unleavened biscuits that formed the staple army food, figure in countless reminiscences of the war, and march in the title of a classic account of Civil War army life, John Billings' *Hardtack and Coffee*.
[4] Sgt. William H. Sherman*.
[5] Frank does not identify him by name; the regimental chaplain was George W. Gorham of Holyoke, who had left a good parish to enlist as a private.

Next morning the boys were anxious that I should let them go to get chickens & pigs for their breakfast. I argued with against[sic] till they finally left out the case to the Chap., and he decided that it was entirely right, so out they go. I take a towel and go to a little brook in my shirt sleeves to wash. Pretty soon I see them after a pig pell mell, & the fear that they might loose[sic] it and the argument of the chaplain, one or both of these, so completely overcame my consciencious[sic] scruples that I went after the pig & caught it. Our good friend Paige might say we were prone to evil, but no matter about that now.[3] We got for our Co. three pigs, 5 or six chickens, a hive of honey. And the negroes with the company killed a yearling & took one quarter.[4]

On we go again about three miles & are separated (7 companies of us) from all the rest of the army except one Battery to act as guard to the Baggage traveling about a mile. When the cavalry had met a force of Rebs that had fled before them, we were drawn up in the line of battle had our arms stacked and lay there in the warm sun till four, when we were treated to some whiskey, ate some crackers and continued on our march again about sunset. About nine were halted in the thick forest, the men requested not to have any loud talk nor to light a match, but to keep in their places. And we stood for more than an hour in the wet road, fearing that something was wrong, dreading what it might be. By and by the adjutant came to me and whispers the trouble. The men flock about to inquire, but though I knew they would imagine it all the worse for my refusing I did refuse . . .

Frank's account extends through only the first three days of the expedition, and the remainder of letter is apparently missing. Foster's official report, dated Dec. 27, places Frank's experience within the larger context of the expedition: "On Saturday, the 13th, we again started, leaving the second main road, the one I was on, to the right, and leaving at this intersection the Forty-sixth Mass. and one section of the artillery (24th of New York) to hold the position and feint on the second main road."

[3] Deacon Paul W. Paige, a respected Brimfield resident, identified by Hyde as a strong abolitionist (pages 214-17). He lived on Paige Hill Road.
[4] Interesting testimony that local blacks, probably escaped slaves, accompanied the expedition, where they would have performed valuable service as guides.

Orders issued soon after the expedition returned suggest the commander's dis-satisfaction with the slow progress and the supply problems Frank described in this and the following letter:

Regimental Order No. 13   Newbern   December 25, 1862

       Commanders of Companies will resume the drill of their companies To-morrow Dec. 26th and will devote particular attention to the skirmishing drill. The order and daily exercises will be resumed tomorrow as it was practiced before the late Expedition, with the exception of Company, Battalion and Brigade drill, the first two being from 9-30 to 11-30 A.M. and 2 to 4 respectively. The latter will be omitted and it is earnestly enjoined upon the Officers of the Regt. that they hereaf-ter lend their earnest efforts in sustaining and assisting the Field Officers in enforc-ing discipline in the Regt. The commanding officer hoping by their cordial coop-eration to bring up the military standard of the Regt. to a point of excellence to which he regrets it is now far below.

       Other orders issued at this time instructed company commanders "to ascertain the number of guns, quantity of ammunition and Equipment that have been issued to them since the organization of the Regiment" (Special Order No. 18) and to immediately turn over to the regimental quartermaster "all Horses, Mules, Carts, Waggons, and other property of whatsoever nature or kind seized or captured during the late expedition" (Regimental Order No. 14).

New Berne   Dec. 29 62

Dear Rebecca

     I had not intended writing you again so soon, thinking you would have reading matter enough in my last to keep you busy for two weeks at least, but being a little out of tune I have given the command to the Lts. for the day at least, and perhaps may as well spend a part of the time in scribbling, though it be to no other effect but to scribble.

     We came home from the expedition weary & lame, many of [the] boys having their feet blistered, and of course not able, nor have they been required, to do duty till Saturday. I think it would have been better for them to have done something before, as too long a rest becomes irksome and is thereby detrimental to the efficiency of a Reg. The old adage that the Devil finds labor for idle hands is as true of soldiers as of others. As a general thing, the less they have to do the more discontented they are. Men must have something to occupy their time, especially when far away from home, otherwise they imagine their trials greater than they are. I would not have you think that we have no real trials, on the contrary that we have enough of real ones not to torment ourselves about imaginary ones.

     Our march was hard, very hard, to bear. I wonder that so many of the company stood it as well. Still, the long waiting without any real labor to perform has made it appear like a mountain to some who really appeared as well when they returned as when they left. I flatter myself that if we go again (and I expect we shall go before many days) our position will be such as to make the march much less fatiguing. We went, you know, as reserve, that is, in the rear. You will understand how much more fatiguing it must be when I tell you that the advance generally bivouacted[sic] about sunset while we did [not] manage to get in till ten at night and several nights till after midnight, and yet we of the Reserve were on our feet most of the time.

     You want I should explain how it could be so. Well, I will try. Our whole line would fill the road when they were in regular marching order two miles or more, in the train a thousand horses. Well we start off, go perhaps a mile, come to a watering place and the first team stops to water. We stop too; the horses drink, wasting perhaps ten minutes. That team moves over and keeps right on; of course they will gain on the next team a distance of a good many rods. We in the rear march just the length of the second team and halt for them to go through the same that the first did. They pass over and go on. Of course they will gain a like distance on the third that the first does on them and so on to the end, when all the teams on our route are two, perhaps four miles behind.

     Then again, perhaps the passage is such that only one or two of the men can pass at a time without wetting their feet. And here comes another halt for the men. You will understand that down here they do not have bridges over such brooks as the one by our house but the teams pass right through the wet and one side, sometimes on both, there is a log across for foot passengers.

Lincoln Bridge
An early 20ᵗʰ Century postcard shows the bridge on the highway (present Rt. 20) in front of the Lincoln house. The Congregational Church stands prominently in the background.

Then there is another obstruction to our steady marching: in many places the roads are bad and the teams will be wallowing through at a snail's pace for rods. Some teams stop and have to be unloaded and reloaded. And of course the forward trains must gain when they get over on those in the rear & all of them on us. Now, remember that in all these delays we have to be on our feet moving a few rods and then halting so that with the trial to ones patience & all it really is more fatiguing than it would be to keep on a steady march during the same time. More than once when we marched fifteen or eighteen miles at three o'clock in the after noon we were no more than five miles on our road and then have to wait for the horses to drink before going into camp.

I think I wrote you that I stood the march as well as any man in the regt[sic], but each night it did seem to me that I should not be able to go on. Next morning would find me in pretty good shape. I think I told you something of how we lived. Perhaps the ladies of Mass. would not have relished our food much, and I am quite sure the exempts[1] would have fainted at the sight of our meals, even if they had been able to have dragged their crippled carcasses over the days march. For the first two days we lived from our haversacks. After this we drew bread, coffee and sugar from the teams and we took what meat we could get, and of sweet potatoes we had what we wanted.

After adopting two or three different ways, I hit on the following. Along in the after noon I would detail two men to look out for some meat, watching for an opportunity they would fall out of the company and be on the watch for

[1] These were men exempted from the draft but who might have still been eligible to volunteer. Mocking them as unmanly is a persistent theme of his letters.

game. When they had a good chance, they would shoot one or more hogs & report to me. I would then detail enough men to carry the game, the rest of us taking their equipment. Some nights we had plenty, others very little. Two hogs with all the waste in cooking after the fashion we have to, would about supply us for supper & breakfast. Their mode of operation was to shoot the pig, cut the head off, cut it into quarters and carry it in this shape to camp. When in camp the quarters were skinned, sliced up and fried in our tin plates. Quite an interesting spectacle it was to see the several squads about their fire cooking their _____ crock & _____, sticking their black fingers into the plates each for himself after a slice and devouring it in a manner which left no doubt of the state of their stomach.

Had you met the company some mornings you would hardly have recognized old friends at the first glance. Many of the boys in the reg. did not wash them[selves] during the whole trip, though I think most of our boys washed & combed their hair each day.

We can hardly believe that you have snow on the ground. Why, here to day it is as pleasant as you ever saw it in Apr., and for three weeks it has not been cold enough except two or three nights to freeze the ground.

Had you not better pay Mr Wyles his note if you have money, also a note H[enry] Brown has of Mrs Morses.[1] Tis better to pay such debts when you have the means, for there is no telling what bank bills may come to. I have had no pay yet. When I do think I may send some hence—you must write to Charles or have Rebecca write to Mary[2] & explain in person you did not visit them while at Roxbury. My love to all the widows—particularly Mrs Tom & Charles.

[*Overwritten on first page.*]
Keep a good account of your money matters and don't think because you have a little extra money that it will always last. When I come, if we have the means, we will visit the western country with the children. Write, let us know what the pigs[?] _____ & all about the hens & chickens. Have Rebecca give my respects to her teacher.

Frank

---

[1] Sophia Parsons Morse, wife of Rev. Jason Morse, the pastor in Brimfield, who died in October 1861 when only 40 (Hyde, 112-114). They were neighbors of the Lincolns, in the next house to the east. The "note" was a loan from one individual to another, part of the informal financial system that prevailed before banks became heavily involved with personal loans.
[2] Frank's oldest brother Charles, who was employed in Boston, had a daughter, Mary W., born 1843 (Hyde, 176).

The letter illustrates the random damage done to property and livestock by a horde of men marching through enemy territory. Frank does not notice a contradiction between concern about the care of his own livestock and his approval of casual but unavoidable looting of southern farmers who were by no means wealthy. In northern eyes, the fact of southern "rebellion" justified such actions. Both armies had regulations against this kind of foraging, for the valid reason that it increased the hostility of enemies and created animosity among friends. Nevertheless, officers in the field winked at the practice, as the regular supply organization was often unable to provide sufficient quantity or variety in a timely manner. Soldiers played along with the game of deception and rationalization, explaining that rebel pigs had to be killed because they refused to take an oath of loyalty. For a fuller discussion, see William C. Davis <u>A Taste for War</u> (Stackpole, 2003, 46-61).*

The closing paragraphs illustrate a vital wartime dynamic, in which northern women, by necessity, assumed responsibilities that were new and disturbing, even in a marriage of relative equals like that of Frank and Rebecca. Using them as an example, Nina Silber writes in <u>Daughters of the Union: Northern Women Fight the Civil War</u>*, "From the time when men first left for the war until the moment they returned, financial concerns were a central preoccupation in their wartime exchanges with women at home," (Harvard Univ. Press, 2005, p. 48). The vast majority of Civil War soldiers, perhaps 70%, were young, unmarried men, but for those who were married, the war made challenging new demands on their wives and had lasting effects on their marriages.*

My Dear Family

I wish you a happy new year, well are you able to judge how heartily I wish it. And although you may fear that it is a hopeless wish, I can but think that much more of joy than sorrow is in store for you all.

Your letters show not alone great anxiety, but a degree of despondency which your second better thought will teach one wrong to indulge in. The anxiety I had expected, and when I saw the article in the Republican about the fear there was and the probability of our being cut off I did not wonder at your depression. I had seen before enough to show me that the Editors north write most of their articles on the war without having any well known facts to base their theories on. I do not wonder that it is so. A hundred times a week I am bored by being asked if I have heard such and such news, most of which, though it be most absurd, is still quite generally believed. Much of the same kind of stuff is written home and many times gains credence by being announced as coming from an officer in such and such a Reg. in confidence with the commander of the Post. Knowing these things I first warned my friend Paige some days before leaving, and you just before going of what I supposed we were about to do and also not to believe a word you might see in the papers about our success or failure until it was confirmed and recon-firmed. In a single point I failed to speak, and that was that you must not expect to hear from us till we returned.

Now let me say one word on the point for your future consideration. Most of these expeditions are made exclusively through an enemies country where is no chance of sending letters if we had time to write them. We go with what is deemed necessary for the entire event[?] and if what we take fails us there is no other way but for the entire force to return, for (you can see) being in a country filled with rebs, everything has to be strongly guarded, particularly army stores. And were we to send back a force sufficient to protect what we might want, there would or might not be force enough left to protect those remaining. We did send from Kinston a party of cavalry to take the the[sic] guns back that we captured, but they did not, nor were they expected to, return to us.

Col. Bowler[1] left with this force and left for home immediately after our return to New Berne. I hear there is an impression at home that he became fright-ened at Kinston and feigned sickness in order to get away. This can not be so. Col. B. has been unwell, or claimed to be so, from our first coming here, as the prayer

---

[1] Col. George Bowler, a minister of Westfield. The reasons for Frank's animosity toward him are unclear and may have dated to events before the regiment reached North Carolina, such as the incident described earlier, when the soldiers were trapped below decks in Boston harbor by a storm. Bowler returned home for a 30-day furlough (Springfield *Republican*, Jan. 1, 1863) and did not rejoin the regiment.

uttered night and day by many in the reg. has been that he would remain so until he had recd[sic] sufficient punishment to pay him for his course in relation to the surgeon. I know, for I heard the order of the Gen. read that he was ordered to return[?]to the Gen. his sword[?] when we left and Col. Shurtleff[1] had from the first the command of our reg.

There [is] considerable sickness in the camp, nothing alarming, mostly bowel difficulties. I have been somewhat troubled the past week, not with the dysentery but diarrhea. There seems to be something in the atmosphere or water that produces it. My supposing is it is the latter, for while I was on the march I had nothing of it, and although the weather would seem to indicate the same atmosphere the water was entirely different & what confirms me in the impression is that as soon as we arrived near enough to the city to get the warm water there is in all the springs in this reg. the same difficulty came on to most of the company.

I intend writing Dr. Witter today to send (if there should be a Post sent from Brimfield as some of the boys say there is talk of there being one) some medicine for those diseases which border on the cholery[sic], particularly that medicine which he furnished Tom, and which he had the misfortune to loose[sic] just at the time he most needed it. As for myself the surgeon and assistant are very attentive, particularly the latter who is ready to give anything he can, come and see any that ask him to at turn. In a single case (that of Byron Charles*) the surgeon took a devilish mean course with him, and I told him so in the presence of the Lt. Col., after which I fancied if he was not particularly obliging to me. There is however no confidence on the part of our boys in him and but little in the Reg. as far as I am able to learn.

George has written his wife that he is happy to learn that the home guard are so debilitated as not to be able to propagate the race as the cowardice of their fathers is sufficient to damn as many as three generations should they leave no children. Really Rebecca sad as [I] know the lot of the wives of our volunteers to

[1] Lt. Col. William S. Shurtleff, 32, a lawyer of Springfield. In his report on the expedition, Shurtleff says that "Colonel Bowler accompanied the expedition until after the affair at Kinston, but was unable by reason of indisposition to assume command, and felt constrained by increasing illness to return to New Berne on the morning of the third of the expedition." This report provides a full account of the 46th's activities during the expedition. Shurtleff, who had practical command throughout, agrees with Frank that the men returned "very foot-sore and weary, otherwise in good condition and spirits" and concludes that "from my careful observation of the men under my command, both under the trials of toilsome marches and the excitement of anticipated engagement with the enemy, I believe you have in them a body upon whom you may with confidence rely should occasion require you to use them in any of the ways that the exigencies of the service may require." (Report to Col. Horace C. Lee, Commanding Third Brigade, First Division, Dec. __, 1862; *OR* Ser. I, vol. XVIII, 88-91).

be, much as I feel for them all, I still can rejoice that they do not stand in the position of those women of the town, many of whose husbands are physically as well and in other points better able to come as some who did.[1]

Mrs. Tom asks why, if I am so sick of the war and the part I have taken I do not resign: a pertinent question surely, but if she and the rest of the war widows are anxious I should I will bring the matter before the company and should they coincide it will then consider the matter. But I have written much more than I expected when I sat down. I wish to have you understand that it is probable that we may go again before long. Should we I will try to let you know before and then you must wait patiently till you hear from some of us, believing that nothing bad has happened until you do hear. Should a box be sent to us you may send some dried apple if you have it, some ginger or cayenne pepper.

Next time I write will try writing more particularly to the children—they must write me at any rate, tell all about the school—any little things. Hope they will improve their time this winter and am certain they will give my friend Woods no trouble, for I know he will do all in his power for them & it would [give] me much satisfaction to hear from him that they assist him all they could.

[*Upside down on first side page 2.*]
continue to direct to New Berne.
Your Husband & Father
Frank

Although relatively new to military life, Frank had already gained a keen awareness of the prevalence of pernicious rumors in the army, the inevitable result of lack of information about the "big picture." His observation on the causes of the widespread sickness in camp, characteristic of all armies at that time, is also on the mark. More soldiers died of these miserable camp diseases than in battle.

[1] Another example of the vicious scorn Frank poured on those men who had not joined his company.

Dear Frank

We received your long letter tonight and I can not wait a moment to tell you how much we prise[sic] it.

Dear little Etta could not consent to get ready to go over to Sam's[1] where she was invited to <u>dinner</u> (so the note said) with Sissy and the Warren girls to eat Duck till I had read "a little, just a little, mother, to see if he is really alive and not wounded."

Almost every one takes an interest in my letters, so when you have any chiding or advising to do you must do it on an extra slip of paper. It is all around about any large letter. I presume I shall be overrun with interest now. Tom and Charley's wife have been in already to read it and I assure you it is a pleasure to me to have them.

Sunday eve.   It is nearly a week since I commenced this and I thought then it would go the next morning, but some one came in before it was finished and so here it is, for I have had my hands full ever since, with company, callers and getting Sissy ready for the exhibition. She did finely; the performance was a success, but but[sic] there was not very pleasant feelings behind the curtain. Mrs. Wyles started it, and so wanted all the say, and was rather mean beside showing so much vanity. No one knew her children were to appear till they were put on stage as angles[sic] and they were stuck in whenever it was decent and when it wasn't. Everyone was disgusted with her actions.

Tim Bliss was buried the past week. Aron[sic] has been sick ever since before thanksgiving, looks badly, does not go out. Sissy and I called there yesterday. Hattie was at home and wished her to come.[2] You know she always makes a great deal of Sissy. Had a very pleasant call.

They are going to send off a box Tuesday and I want to send you something, but do not know what to send. There is to be a cheese and I pay for a quarter. If it gets there safely and you remain there any length of time, just let us know what would be acceptable and it shall be sent.

Mr. and Mrs. Hitchcock have been in and sat a little while with us. I suppose they came to hear your letter but Luvan[3] carried it home today. Mrs. Charles is a sad looking woman. She remains in the same state of mind that she did when you went away. Mr. Herring received a dispatch yesterday that Fred was

[1] Probably Samuel W. Brown, who lived across the road.
[2] Brimfield residents: Timothy Bliss, born 1783, died Dec. 31, 1862. "Aron" is probably Aaron Bliss, born 1814. He had a daughter Harriet, born 1840.
[3] Luvan, born 1842, was the daughter of Abraham Charles, who lived in East Brimfield.

killed in the last battle.[1] He goes tonight for the body. William is here now. He got so low while away that he had to sleep out of doors, so now he is at home and their man gets what he wants, that is segars and such things. They do not let him have a cent.

Mr. Hitchcock says the President has given the South a hundred days more to come back into the union; don't hear what will come next.[2] I dreamed the other night that Jim came running in with your valise in his hand, and says the war is over, Rebecca, and here is Frank. I turned round, saw you in the door, screamed and woke up. Do be as careful of yourself as you can and not expose yourself too often to save the men.

[*Continued on top margin, first page.*]
Hardly a letter comes I guess from the boys but they bless the Captain. We do not succeed in selling either of those cows so we are going to get some hay of Paige. Write how the boys spend their time and how they appear since their expidition[sic].

Every body is in bed but me.
Rebecca

This is the earliest surviving letter from Rebecca and also marks the beginning of the practice of self-censorship by Frank, so as not to offend anyone in his wide circle of admirers. While some of his characteristic pungency of expression may have been lost, the new policy increased the odds that the letters would be saved.

[1] Sgt. Silas F. Herring, Co. L, 15th Pennsylvania Cavalry (Anderson Cavalry), a unit composed largely of Philadelphia men, was killed at Stone River, TN, Dec. 29, 1862. He was the son of Silas C. Herring, a safe manufacturer originally from New York City, who lived in Brimfield and owned the hotel. Contrary to Rebecca's information, another account states that the soldier, who was probably called Fred to distinguish him from his father, was buried in the National Cemetery at Nashville, TN (http://www.pa-roots.com/). The death was reported in the Springfield *Republican*, Jan. 14, 1863. Subsequent information, published in the Palmer *Journal* Jan. 17, showed that Sgt. Herring had died a hero. When most of his regiment mutinied over trivial causes, he announced that he would go into the fight if he went alone. He persuaded his company to follow; this was the only entire company to go into battle, and he was the only one of the company killed. Perhaps Rebecca was thinking of him when she wrote on Jan. 18 "all the noble hearted ones gone."
[2] His interpretation of the Emancipation Proclamation, which freed the slaves in the seceded states. It was promulgated by President Lincoln Sep. 22, 1862 to take effect 100 days later, Jan. 1, 1863.

Dear Rebecca

I suppose you receive this at the same time you do a letter. I wrote some ten days since and also a letter to the children a week ago today, besides one you will see to the War Widows, addressed to Tom's wife, for I am told that Gen. Foster forbad the P.M. to send any mail north just after I first wrote & that the injunction is not yet removed. Much as I feel the loss of your letters to me, I regret still more that you should have to wait for mine. We do not open your letters with trembling hands when we receive them, nor do we feel when there is any delay that you are in trouble or taking any special risk by going on expeditions, whereas we know that you must be extremely anxious about us when you fail to hear somewhat regularly.

But I am not disposed to complain for I can see that much trouble might arise by suffering the mail to go its regular trips, especially when troops are arriving here constantly and there is an expectation that we are to move on some point. Had the mail been sent the morning we left for Goldsboro & by any chance fallen into the hands of the enemy, he might thereby have obtained information which would have cost us many lives and entirely changed the result of the expedition. So I say I am not disposed to complain of the regulation though I look upon it as a sad necessity. It is evidence to me of the sagacity of our General.

We have been in doubt ever since I wrote whether we were to go the next time troops were called or not and are still in the same doubt. Sometimes I rather hope we shall, for I am fully satisfied that we are to do fully our share of the fighting and I think the sooner it is done the better. Then again I fall into the same train of thought which prevails in the company, that the longer we put off the day the less liability that we are called at all. Situated as we are here now, there is nothing but the absence of our families that is bad to put up with.

Tom, George, Ira & I mess together, they drawing their rations from the Gov. and I buying butter & cheese, sugar, crackers, oysters, fish, sweet potatoes, and such things as the Government either does not furnish at all or not in sufficient quantity, which Tom or George cooks and from it all we not only have enough to eat but quite a variety. I hardly think however that we any of us shall so fall in love with the mode of living as to refuse to sit at your table or relish the food set before us when we return.

I wonder not that you were depressed at the defeat of Gen. Burnside, for it must have seemed to you that the last hope was gone. For a time everyone I met here seemed cast down, I might say hopelessly sad over the defeat, but we are getting somewhat over that. But we all wonder still why it should be that we should be beaten by Virginia always and as almost as uniformly successfully[sic] elsewhere. There is a mystery hanging over it I can in no way explain.[1]

I do not however wonder that Burnside was defeated in the battle at Fredericksburg. It would have been a wonder if he had succeeded. No man need hope to be victorious when all his leading men have no hope. Burnside might have been beaten had it been otherwise, but defeat was certain as it was.

You say that you have heard that I have written to Smith Gray[2] that I was heartily sick of the war and regretted having enlisted. Now I have written to no one in Walpole but Frank Bird to whom I wrote an acct[sic] of the expedition and in reading it over I saw that he might conclude from the narration of fact that I was heartily sick of the job & so wrote him in conclusion that it was no worse than I had anticipated and had I known of things that I then knew should still have done as I did.

I see Jim H., Ned Ridge, Rob Duff and other Walpole boys every two or three days. They all went except Tisdell to Goldsboro. Rob (so Ned says) caught at Readville what no boy ought to bear.[3] I was so provoked when Ned told me of it that if I had had the fellow in my hands I would have pitched him into the sink. You need not fear of my writing Smith Gray. [*Two sentences about Walpole matters deleted.*]

I learn that you are to have a rail road to drive the cows to pasture on. What is the impression in regard to the matter.[4]

[1] This refers to the battle of Fredericksburg, VA, Dec. 13, 1862, in which the Union Army suffered a catastrophic defeat. Gen. Burnside had been given command of the Army of the Potomac, in part owing to his splendid performance in North Carolina, but at the head of the main army he proved inadequate to the task. He had replaced George C. McClellan, who had been sacked by President Lincoln for his lack of aggressiveness, barely a month earlier and felt obligated to take the offensive immediately. Frank's question as to why the North was successful almost everywhere except in Virginia has occupied military historians ever since.

[2] Smith Gray was another Walpole resident. Walpole vital records show that he married in 1836, so was some years older than Frank. The soldier Charles Gray, mentioned earlier, was not his son. (http://www.walpole.ma.us/hhisdocvr).

[3] "Tisdell" is probably Corp. Francis A. Tisdale, 20, of Co. K, 44th Mass. The other Walpole soldiers in that regiment were identified earlier (see Oct. 23 letter). The reference to Rob's acquisition at Readville (the camp near Dedham where the 44th was trained) is almost certainly to venereal disease. Frank's lack of delicacy in mentioning this, uncharacteristic of the age, testifies to his forthright relationship with Rebecca. It is possible that Rob and some of the others were Frank's former students, which would account for his disgust. Sink was the soldiers' term for privy or latrine.

[4] The war should have been sufficient diversion, but railroad mania continued to flourish. The town of Brimfield already had a railroad station, on the Boston & Albany RR in West Brimfield, but access was so difficult that it had little value to people in the center of town. A railroad had been chartered to reach nearby Southbridge from the east, but it was not completed until after the war. Frank is referring to a proposal to build a line from Palmer to Southbridge, which would have passed through Brimfield. (See Larry Lowenthal, *Titanic Railroad* (1998), p.40). A survey for this line had recently been completed (Palmer *Journal*, Jan. 3, 1863). Frank's dismissive comment indicates that he didn't think a railroad would be much use to the largely agricultural community. Again, he shows that he values Rebecca's judgment, a contrast to the prevailing idea that women should not be concerned with matters outside the domestic sphere.

George was made quite happy a few days since by the news that he had had a son born to him.[1] I like George much better than I ever expected to. He is much more of a man than I ever thought him to be, is really a great help to me. He & Tom are with me most of the time. Tom's letter to his wife is nearly finished.

[*Overwritten across front page*]
Give my particular regards to Cousin Patty's folks, be sure to write also my regards to Mr. Hyde, say to him I recd[sic] his letter and will write as soon as I have anything new to write about.

Frank

[1] George C. Homer's first wife died in 1856, and he married Adelaide Adams in March 1862. A son, Carroll, was born in December, but lived less than two years.

Brimfield   Jan. 11th 1863
Friend Lincoln,
  I offer no apology for writing to you. I have nothing new to write, but I am going to write a letter nevertheless. I presume you get all the news from home worth hearing. Time passes here much as it has in times past, except we miss the cordial greetins[sic] & genial faces of some of our friends, but though they are gone, they were never more thought of or spoken of than they are now. We lose something in their absence, but we feel that we have no cause to complain. They are risking all for our good, as well as theirs. Our common country is in danger & no one can do a nobler act than to volunteer in her defence.
  I am almost surprised at the heroism of those ladies whose husbands have gone. As far as I have known, they are hopeful and confident and do not complain. I think some of them would as lief hear that their husbands were slain in battle as to hear that they were coward.
  It is generally understood here that everything depends upon the army now in the field. If something decisive is not done during the nine months service, it will be difficult to raise another army. Our progress is slow, & we here[sic] some complaints, but I do not think I have any right [to] criticise[sic] the doing of those in authority, for I cannot know the circumstances as well as they.

We hear from rebel sources that you are about starting on another expidition[sic]. We hope & pray that you may be successful & return in due time to your families & friends to receive the honors & rewards so dearly bought.

I have thought some of detailing to you some school affairs, but I presume you have no time or inclination to hear them. I commenced with 40 scholars, but two or three of them have been sick most of the time. I am doing considerable in school, but am not succeeding as well as I could wish with some. Others are doing exceeding well. Oscar Brown[1] is not doing nearly as much as he ought. He is <u>lazy</u>.

It has been a hard task to manage so as to keep them in good order. I cannot afford to spend one half my time in flattering a school, nor have I any inclination to get down on my knees & beg of them to do what they know to be their duty. I have punished one of the largest boys for disobedience & another for gross immorality.

Generally the school has been very willing to obey any rules I made & I have had no real trouble, though some trials. The fact that you & others were willing to entrust your & their children to me has stimulated me to an effort that I never made before. I hope some of the fruits may be visible to you when you come home.

Your children are doing finely. Rebecca is progressing very thoroughly, if not rapidly. I am not sure she has the physical ability to apply herself as some have. I admire her as a scholar, for she never says "yes sir" to what she does not understand. Etta is so impatient to proceed that she is hardly willing to spend time enough on a proposition to fully master it. I am afraid that she will get so many new ideas that she will forget some. I may be mistaken, but if she does not she has remarkable power for one so young.

Our term is now one half gone. I will not trouble you with any more on school affairs, except to say that they are most of them doing well. My man John Robinson was wounded at Goldsbury[sic], but I have not been able to hear how badly.[2] He was in the 27, Co. I.

Please remember me to neighbor Morgan and others of your Brimfield Co.

Respectfully Yours   J. L.[?] Woods[3]

---

[1] Oscar F. Brown, born 1850, was the son of James B. and Harriet Tarbell Brown.
[2] The information about Pvt. John Robinson is correct. It is not clear why Woods referred to him as "my man."
[3] The writer was presumably an elementary school teacher. Frank may have had something to do with the selection of Woods, who writes as a close acquaintance. The fact that both Lincoln daughters attended the school was another factor, of course.

Yesterday morning I attended church again to hear Mr. James who preached a very good discourse bearing mainly on the Proclamation of the President.[1] I judged by what he said or rather from the manner in which he spoke of Sumner, Beecher & W. Philips that he had had but little sympathy with what we call Abolitionism. But he urged upon his hearers the necessity of acting on the Proc. in good faith, considering it the supreme law of the land, hoping and believing that it would be the means of assisting us in putting down the rebellion. It seemed strange to me to hear a minister say that although he would not have been ready to have left his home & friends to come here to sustain such a Proc. as a philanthropic measure, he was ready to lay down his life to sustain it as a measure deemed by the highest military authority of the land one of military necessity. Such a declaration would perhaps become one whose life is to fight, but a minister of the Gospel of Peace, it seems to me should manifest in his words at least a little different spirit.

I again saw the little girls of whom I spoke last Sunday. They were at church with their father & mother and I learned they were the children of the Rev. Chap. Clark. I declare if I ever meet those children in the St.[sic] I will kiss them, whether they are willing or not. The eve.[sic] I spent at Lt. Prouty's, had a very pleasant time.[2] Mrs. P is a very pleasant woman & it did really seem like home to be there and have her sit on the hearth, crack nuts with a flat iron, giving one each to her mate & myself then taking one, so keeping up the rounds till all were gone.

Do you wonder that for a little time I beguiled myself into the thought that I was in N.E.? Not hardly that either, for the thought would come that <u>my</u> wife & family were far away, wondering where I was and what I could be about and perhaps indulging in the pleasant dream that the time would come that I should be with them again to spend the Sabbath eves more pleasantly than ever before. What a distance between us, yet how close the communion of feelings. Sometimes I fancy that I can see you of a Sabbath eve sitting about the stove, each intent in thought and wonder feeling for the moment that I am <u>near</u> and then counting up the months, weeks, days, oh the hours & minutes even before we can be together and fancy seems to hear the sigh that it should be so long.

---

[1] The Emancipation Proclamation, which took effect Jan. 1, 1863, freed the slaves in the rebellious states. As this and subsequent letters reveal, the proclamation heightened the long-running debate about abolition and forced every federal soldier to define what he was fighting for.

[2] 1st Lt. Merrick Franklin Prouty (1829-1898) of the 25th Mass. His wife was the former Ann Elizabeth Jenks. It is not clear how Frank became acquainted with Lt. Prouty, a native of Spencer, MA, who had entered the army almost a year earlier; however he was the nephew of a John Prouty who lived in Brimfield. John Prouty's daughter Marietta was a classmate of Rebecca Lincoln. Another possible connection is that Frank's brother Charles was married to a Maria Prouty (Hyde, 176).

Console yourself with the reflection that I have tried to do my duty, for if any step in my life was honestly taken my enlisting was the one and I have that faith in the Eternal justice of Heaven that it cannot doubt that the result will be best for me, best for us all.

Write me, about the things on the farm, if Lewis[1] needs any instruction &c. We are all physically better than we have been since coming here, except Baxter Bennett* of H.[Holland], who is sick of a fever at the Hospital, of whom I have some fear. My love to all.

Yours. Frank

Monday eve

Dear Frank

All is quiet and as it is not quite nine I will commence my next letter.

As a general thing we have breakfast at half past seven, the children do the breakfast things and I work, busy as a bee, till about two in the afternoon, then dress and rest a little and it is tea time, so goes the days one after another varied with more or less callers. This afternoon I rode down to Charlie's but Lizzie was not at home. I came back did up some things to put in the box, and took them over to Mr. Brown's. He is packing it. Found Lizzie and Tom's wife there but they all seemed sorter[sic] blue, so I made a short call and came away. Found Sam there.[2] He was smoking some tobacco, got in and drove me home. Found Sissy at our gate and she screams "That'll never do mother Lincoln riding out with the gentlemen, now you have got to go with me Mr. B.," and so he went a little way.

I do not know but you will scold at my sending in the box as you told me so many times not to, but I could not bear to have it go and not carry something

---

[1] Lewis, the hired man who managed the farm in Frank's absence, was such a routine figure in the household that the letters do not offer much information and he remains unidentified. There is circumstantial evidence that he may have been Lewis W. Benson. After Frank's return Benson, then 18, received a bounty of $198.66 and joined the 2nd Regiment of Heavy Artillery Sep. 3, 1864. He later transferred to the 17th Mass. Infantry and served to the end of the war.

[2] Probably Samuel Watson Brown. Born 1822, he was nearly the same age as Frank.

for you. But as you have never spoken of wanting any thing there was but little to send, and if you do not want it, give to those who do.

Tuesday eve. It is raining hard, the children have just gone to bed, Lewis has not come in, so I will talk with you. The papers are full of fighting tonight, and consequently of hope. I expect every night to see that you have started on another expidition[sic], but shall take it for granted that you are untill[sic] I see that the rebels have had at least three weeks' notice.

Mr. and Mrs. Peck called today.[2] They had heard that Ira was sick, so I read your letter to them and they concluded they would not be frightened till they heard again. Mr. P— sent his respects to the Capt. She said he sent them as often as he had a chance.

Tom's wife drove up to the door tonight, had been to carry Charlie's wife home. She went home with her last night. Lizzie must be made of something stronger than iron or she would give out, or it is easier work to visit than I have ever found it to be.

The visiting club are going the rounds. Perhaps they don't know there is any war. They were at A[lfred]. Converse's last week, at Mrs. Witter's today, the same old company. I will try and make some calls as soon as this thaw is over and see if I cant find some news.

The children get tired as death of Woods. Sissy say[sic] he is a fool only he happens to know a little rithmetic[sic] but that is all he does know or ever will.

It is too bad we sent the box yesterday and today your letter came giving some idea what you would like. This letter is not very full but I will send it so you can have what little news there is before starting on another jaunt. I wish I could command the army a little while. This fighting in one place at a time. Why can't they attack the Rebels in half a dozen places at once.

Since the Union generals were not doing especially well, opportunities were created for armchair strategists. In a larger sense, Rebecca's willingness to comment on the military situation illustrates the wartime tendency for women to take greater interest in national affairs and become freer to express opinions on matters that had been reserved for men in most families (although New England women were traditionally better educated and more outspoken).

[2] The parents of Sgt. Ira Peck in Frank's company.

[*Undated fragment from Rebecca.*]

It is Sunday night dear Frank and one of the worst snow storms we have had this winter. It was quite pleasant this morning but grew cold and raw till finally it commenced storming and the first thing tomorrow morning we shall hear Lewis's haw and gee.[1]

Mr. Perkins preached today.[2] It was unexpected to me as I heard a Brookfield man was to preach, and the sight of Mr. P and associations, one thing and another, brought you so vividly that I have had a day of suffering such as few dream of. You do not have as many such things to go through, and keep all to yourself, and then be told that you grow proud and haughty, so Mr. Wyles told me, and some of the children told Sissy, some that were to meet on <u>business</u> for the band of hope, they were afraid of me.

Mrs. Morse and I went to Palmer Wednesday. I spent twenty dollars and only got half what I wanted, got R. and Etta each a pair of shoes, 20 yd. Of 25ct cloth, 5 yds of two shilling three of cambric, 1 doz. goblets, 1 doz. custard glasses, sewing silk and three hats. Now in <u>old times</u> I could have got full as much again.[3]

Called on Mary Foster.[4] She expressed a great deal of pleasure at seeing us, also at Dr. Vails, and saw an old lady who claimed cousinship with you. Her name I think was Nicols. [*Some additional local news deleted.*]

Friday we went to the vestry to work for the soldiers. In the evening Eunice[5] came over and wanted to know if I wanted to make that visit in Thorndike that I promised to as long ago as last summer, so we went yesterday. It was on a minister by the name of Tuck. Mrs. T. and Eunice were room mates at school. Found them very agreeable people with four children, and the evening before they had been to a silver wedding at the next house, and they described the elegant things. They said they had a friend in your company and showed me his picture but I do not remember the name. So this ends the week. Haven't I been tolerably busy, but I never go on a visit and return at night but that awful feeling will come that no Frank will be there to meet me and that ache you can not have, though you may wish ever so much to be at home again.

The children have just come in from evening meeting. Etta was very anxious to go because Mr. Hyde gave out that it was the evening for especial prayer for our country, but <u>she</u> <u>didn't</u> <u>see</u> as the prayers were any different from what they always were.

---

[1] Lewis giving commands to the ox team engaged in clearing or rolling snow on the town roads or around the yard.

[2] Identity uncertain, as various ministers conducted services after the premature death of Rev. Jason Morse.

[3] Evidence that wartime inflation was becoming noticeable.

[4] Possibly the daughter of Rev. Festus Foster (1776-1846), a prominent resident.

[5] Probably Eunice Knight, daughter of Dr. Ebenezer Knight (1792-1857), who was about the age of the Lincolns. The doctor had resided on the north side of the Common, and the family may have remained there after his death.

Lewis has sold the black cow and a little bossy for $35. Have let Spaulding have the oldest calf, and we have one he is going to raise from the Wales cow.[1] The pigs are doing nicely, four. [*Sentence of news about unidentified people deleted.*]

I am very anxious about the box we sent. The bill says all boxes with

[*Continued across top margin, opposite side.*]
liquor will be confiscated. There is none for you in it but for Charley and C. Alexander. I do hope there will be a letter for me tomorrow.

Your Rebecca

[1] P.F. Spaulding was a butcher and grocer, with a store on Main Street.

New Berne   Jan 17th '63

Dear Rebecca,

The mail goes in the morning and although it is a little in advance of my promise & I have but little to write, still I will just say a word, for every mail from the north is worse than none to me unless something comes in it from home. So I suppose you must feel when letters come to our friends there, unless you get something from me.

I have your letter written a part of it after the box was ready. There is a large amount of express matter at Morehead for this Reg. I am told. A few small boxes have come here one to [Ira] Peck* and Lyon each, but whether the box you sent came in the same steamer we, of course, do not know. I think but little of the practice of sending things of this kind to the soldiers, but as the other boys all have them it creates a desire on the part of Brimfield boys to get them. And I own that I am not entirely free from the feeling. Not that we need the things. God knows I can not in honesty say that we actually need anything but a Dr. and him not as a cure but a preventative, for we are most of us as well as we should probably be at home.

I wrote H.F.B.[1] that all are comfortably well. I should have excepted Baxter Bennett, who is sick of a fever at the Hospital, whose brother I got the Col. to excuse from duty that he might see him as often as he liked and whom some of the commissioned officers visit daily. I think he will get along. He certainly has good care as he could have at home. Everything at the Hospital is in as good shape as it could possibly be made. I know nothing of the skill of the physician except what I am told (which is that he is an excellent Dr.) but it is a great relief that we can feel that the sick have experienced nurses and that our sick (I mean those that are really very sick) are removed from the influence of the fellow who plays surgeon to our Reg.[2]

The expedition is about to start I think for Wilmington [North Carolina]. We are not probably to go. I say not probably for I have heard from the Col. that he had had assurance that it was not, and what convinces me of the fact that it is to stay is that we have done nothing to get us in readiness. Gen. Foster keeps his counsels to himself or at least from his Col's and had I no better means of getting information than through [him] I should never attempt to predict any movement. But I have and although I do not wish to disclose it, still I am generally appraised of the destination of any considerable body of troops before they [start] moving. In this case I judged of the fact of our not going from certain circumstances in which I may fail but think not.[3]

[1] Henry F. "Boss" Brown, holder of many town offices.
[2] The regiment was listed as having two surgeons: James H. Waterman, 27, of Westfield and Thomas Gilfillan of Cummington.
[3] A large federal force had been assembled, originally to take the Confederate stronghold Fort Fisher, guarding Wilmington, NC. Later, the government changed the objective to Charleston and Port Royal, SC. Foster led 10,000 men to Port Royal but returned to North Carolina in late February. (John C. Barrett, *The Civil War in North Carolina* [Univ. of North Carolina, 1963], 150-152.)

Our boys have received their pay to the 1st of Jan. from the time of enlist-ment. I did not get mine because I refused to take the pay master's construction of the law for paying officers, he claiming that they were not entitled to their pay only from the time of their being mustered, nearly two months later than the men drew theirs from. It may be so but I don't believe it. At any rate as I did not need the money and it is perfectly safe as it is to get as much as they offered to pay me I thought I would wait. *[Paragraph of family news deleted.]*

I have written the Crawford girl in answer to her letter.[1] You remember she wrote me somewhat more than two weeks ago. We were not a little amused at the description of your celebration though we did not think that muslin was the only thing wanted to make the little girls angels. What kind of wings would the mother need to make her an angel! Ah well there are grades of all kinds of beings that I am acquainted with and perhaps there are of the kind you tried to represent.

Tell the children I can not listen to a word of complaint of my friend Woods, for whatever they may think of some of his notions, he will do everything for their improvement that can be done. The only word from home, I have been sorry to hear, was that of complaint of their teacher. It is wrong—very[?]. Remem-ber my children that the teacher's life is one of trial. Your duty is to assist him all you can, you can not do this without kind feelings towards him. I know Mr Woods is doing the best he can for your good and have felt all winter that it [is] a great advantage you had in attending his school.

[Overwritten on first page.]
Will write again in season for the next mail which I trust will not be delayed as they have been the last month. Charles sent a box by the Schooner Frye. I have not recd[sic] it yet.

Yours
F.D. Lincoln

As a former schoolmaster, Frank displays sensitivity to any criticism of his friend Woods.

[1] Unfortunately, the identity of this person remains unknown. There was no one named Crawford in Frank's company or from Walpole in the 44th Mass., and the name is not familiar in Brimfield.

Brimfield   Jan 18th

Dear Frank

It seems of little use for me to try to write tonight for I am altogether too sad, and if you ever receive this you need not in reply tell me to have courage &c for you know the news of a battle from the first of the war has always made me faint and sick. This you may call weak, womanish, whatever you like, still I think the same we have no right to cause such suffering. Oh how my heart aches, not alone for you, but for all those poor wounded suffering boys in Vir. And Tenn. Deas. [Deacons] Paige and Brown called today. The latter was strong in the faith the Lord would let us triumph yet, only we must pray more earnestly. But dear, what will the country be good for, with all the noble hearted ones gone, for it is of the warmhearted impulsive class that we find volunteers.

Etta went home with Dea Paige tonight from meeting. Dell is not very well, and our school does not keep tomorrow as Woods wants to visit schools. She has a letter written for you, but I do not know where it is. I presume the most important fact is that Lewis has made her doll a cradle, and a more delighted creature I have not seen lately, for Etta has been very quiet this winter. If it were not for Sissy I believe we should all grow dumb, but she jabbers from morning till night and she neither lacks in wit nor common sence[sic]. She is not very well today. I don't know whether she has over done or what it is.

It has been rainy nearly all the week. Mr. Wyles came and brought Sissy her Album with his picture on the last leaf, and if she moves it he says he shall take it away from her, and yours for the first picture, so she thinks she has it nicely commenced and ended.

We took tea at Mrs. Morse's Tuesday afternoon. It is the only place I have been to sit any time since you left.

I had a hen killed yesterday & Lewis took off 9 ounces of fat and there is nearly as much more that rose on top of the water I boiled it in. [*Paragraph of news of Walpole people deleted.*]

Tell me all about how the boys acted when they got the box and what was liked best and if your things were mussed up any. Well I must close but how I dread this. It does seem as though I have suffered all I can.

Rebecca

On a short and gloomy Winter day, Rebecca's feelings were certainly understandable. By then the war had touched almost every family, and no end was in sight. In <u>Daughters of the Union</u>*, Nina Silber observed that "The war made domestic life a source of anxiety and loneliness" (p. 92).*

Dear Rebecca

It is now settled that the 46th is not to start with the famous[?] expedition, though it is not so certain to me that they will not be called to assist in the fight before it is finished. As near as I can learn, our folks are expecting to accomplish their purpose this time without drawing very heavily on the Infantry; relying on their heavy siege guns and the gun boats.[1] But it is more than probable that they may meet a force of infantry that will require more force of the same kind to gain a victory. And I think more would be taken now if they had transports to take them.

For two days past I have been off on a visit, the first I have taken to myself since coming here. Being at Lt. Prouty's a few eve's[sic] since, he gave me an invitation to go down to Moorhead [Morehead City] and see the grand fleet before it started on the expedition and I concluded to go. And am very glad I went, for although the fleet is nothing wonderful for one who has ever seen the shipping in Boston or even Providence, I learned some things in relation to the movements of the army that can be but interesting to my friends as well as myself should the time come that I can sit with them and talk it over.

You wonder that the movements of the army are so <u>slow</u>. I well remember with what anxiety we waited for a movement to be made when the papers had hinted that something was to be done, how day after [day] we searched the paper to find the consummation of the act till our patience was nearly exhausted. Sometimes time dragged on till we lost interest in the move, and I doubt not that you are now wondering why the much talked of expedition of General Foster's is not made. And many a loving mother who has never for once raised her voice against the rule of <u>one</u> man, is now ready to shoulder broomstick against the whole Government for suffering such delay.

To me <u>now</u> it is no matter of wonder; I am rather surprised that they should be in readiness so soon. For there are such a multitude of changes to be made for the success of each new expedition, to say nothing of delays occasioned by storms, that with the utmost exertion a long time is consumed in getting ready. Were it necessary to move nothing but infantry delays would be in a measure inexcusable, but to move heavy artillery with all the armaments necessary is a job one not acquainted with the business can hardly appreciate. Knowing what I knew about the matter, it was a complete surprise to me to see the amount of labor to be done. Even Gen. Foster who has been in the army from his youth, it seems has but a faint idea of the time necessary to fit out an expedition like the one he has undertaken. I <u>know</u> that the men in charge have worked nights & Sundays to satisfy his impatience & that that has not been sufficient. Doubtless there are officers in

---

[1] This was after the objective had been shifted to Charleston, where the Navy was expected to have a prominent role.

command who do not exert themselves to accomplish what he is expected to do, but it would require some better evidence than the mere fact of delay to prove to me indifference on the part of any of them.

I do not now recollect if I have written that 2 companies of our Regt. have been detached for picket duty. They are stationed on the RR about half way between here & Morehead City to guard the RR. On my return I stopped to see them. Staid with Capt. Spooner and his men that night. They are in log cabins, each having an old fashioned fireplace made thereby not only comfortable but to me seemingly pleasant, & although I would not care to occupy their position I would be glad if we had the log huts with those fireplaces. How vividly it brings back the scenes of my youth! How happily I spent the eve. The war and all connected therewith was forgotten for a time as I sat gazing at that cheerful fire and meditated on the happy days of childhood. Happy am I that the reflection on the past has so little of sorrow, so much of joy.

Next day I visited the pickets. They are stationed from a little distance from the camp to the distance of a mile, those at one point having little shanties of some kind, convenience for a fire, seats etc & c. One stands continually on the watch relieved at the expiration of two hours by one of his comrades who in his turn is relieved by a second. So they take their turns through the whole day & night, all being relieved on the next day by another squad. No one is suffered to pass there in the daytime without a pass, in the eve without the countersign. Should they be alarmed in the night or day the one on duty fires. If the fire is repeated it alarms the whole camp. So you see that even a hog that can not well answer the sentinel's challenge may at midnight alarm the whole camp. Once they have been thus alarmed and once again by a ___ cow. How provoking & yet how laughable.

After visiting Cap. Spooner's men I went with him to see Lt. Stewart[1] who has thirty men with him on what is called Bogue Sound. He too has pickets out and a kind of fort which they call a block house with one six lb gun. With him is Jason Lewis.[2] Could one have his friends I can understand how pleasantly he might spend his time where he is on the sound (just far enough from the ocean), a beautiful sheet of water as ever you or anyone saw skirted on either side by evergreens. The sound and its surroundings has that quiet loveliness that one is impressed with the idea that God had made expressly as a retreat where all animated nature might repose in safety. What a strange contrast to the scene in our camp! Lt. Stewart was very glad to see me and inquired for all the folks at home. Sent his love to all—wished to be remembered particularly to Etta.

When I returned I found quite a commotion among the men turned[?] about a report that we were in danger of an attack from the Rebel Gen. Jackson; how much there is in it I know not, but there are indications that Gen. Foster is

[1] 2d Lt. George M. Stewart, 23, of the 46th Mass. Although a resident of Wales, he was in Co. K, along with several enlisted men from that town.
[2] Possibly Jason Lewis, 21, of Co. A, a Springfield resident.

suspecting that some Rebel Gen. may attack us after the expedition leaves. At any rate he has moved the most exposed Regs. (ours among the number) to a safer position and is busy in throwing up breast works for our defence[sic]. We are now in a safer and in other respects more pleasant position than we at first occupied. I do not think the Rebs mean to attack us. Should they, God give us the pluck to give them H—. I mean their just deserts.

[Page numbered 4; presumed continuation of this letter.]

Some ten days have gone by since we had any mail from the north. And the chaplain is inquired of continually when we are to have ours. You would think to hear the anxious inquiries that they thought him somehow to blame, and that if he did not do better they would have another P.M.

For a week or more we have had unpleasant weather, but today it is beautiful again. This morning the little birds chirped as they do in those warm smoky days in Apr. at home. There is no mistake in calling this the sunny south in the most delightful sense of that expression during the more disagreeable part of a N.E. season. By the way, some of the officers of the 46th talk of sending for their wives to come, should the prospect be that we remain here. If Lt. Lyon[1] sends for his wife, shall I send for you? Prouty's wife will go home probably in May so you would if you came have good company home. I am told that there is a probability of excursion steamers running from N.Y. here and returning on which it is proposed to take passengers for $25.00. Should this be the case one could come & be able to return at almost any time they might like.

Tom & Bill have gone for a few days to Newport to get out lumber for the Reg., Tom going as commander in chief of a squad of ten soldiers and as many negroes. I did not like to part with them, but the Quarter Master wanted Tom, and he Bill & knowing that it would break the monotony of their life here, I could not deny the request, though I felt and still feel that we shall be somewhat more lonely without them. Have Lewis write if he needs any instruction, and if not let me know how he thinks he is getting along.

Yours. Frank

Special Order No. 48   Newbern   Jan. 25, 1863
[Details six men for duty at sawmill near Newport. Sgt. T. J. Morgan and Sgt. W. H. Sherman from Co. G.]

[1] 2d Lt. Julius M. Lyon, 34, of Wales.

Frank may be responding to a missing letter from Rebecca in which she commented on the slow movement of Foster's Goldsboro expedition. He provides a good description of the routine picket duty that made up a large part of soldier life. Sgt. Thomas J. Morgan was not only Frank's closest associate but was probably the most useful member of the company. Having gained experience operating saw and grist mills at Little Rest, where he also manufactured nails, he represented the rural Yankee type that could fix anything and make it run.

Hereafter the wood for camp fuel will be deposited in one common pile in rear of the tents of the line officers and must be there cut and prepared for use by those entitled to use it; and all persons are forbidden to cut, chop, or split wood in any place about the camp in front of the rear line of the sutlers kitchen, as now established.

Each company is required to keep in order and cleanliness that portion of the Camp between the front line of its street and the rear line of its tents, extending from the Color line to the rear line of the street in rear of the tents of the line officers.

The swill or other refuse from each cook house must be deposited in a covered barrel, and as often as the barrel shall become full must be removed to some suitable place beyond the limits of the camp.

Any person using any part of the camp ground, except the sinks for the purpose for which the sinks are provided will be required to do guard duty at the post nearest the sinks for three successive days.

The commanding officer hopes, now that the Regiment are newly established in a spacious and cleanly camp, that a proper self-respect and regard for the credit of the Regiment will induce everyone to endeavor to establish for the Forty Sixth a well deserved reputation for order, cleanliness and gentlemanly deportment.

Exhortations like these were routine in the Union Army. In camp there was powerful temptation for soldiers to relieve themselves away from the thick stench of the "sinks" provided for that purpose. Perhaps such appeals to decency were more likely to be heeded by militia soldiers from small towns in Massachusetts.

Dear Rebecca

I wrote somewhat in a hurry to you on Sunday and had not time to give those particulars in regard to the things which I suppose you would like. I think I wrote you that we had a box from Charles and also one from the Whiskey Club and gave a slight description of them, but I know you will desire a complete list of the things and I give it. Charles sent about 4 lbs. of crackers, a bottle of Raspberry vinegar, two bottles of Whiskey, a jar of current gell[sic], a bottle of gerkins[sic], and some nice apples all very good and came safely. The boys sent 2 lbs of tea, two tin jars of Quince, one of Tomatoes, three of chocolate, a pack of dried apples, a dozen lemons, six boxes of sardines, two lbs ginger, one of Cayenne pepper, two bottles of Whiskey, and four of French brandy, three lbs of tobacco. Now then mix these together and what a feast for soldier boys.

And you may believe that our mess counted them quite an addition to the things recd[sic] from home, though there was not that pleasure in receiving them that there was in getting them, that each of us had in the things which we knew came from our own households. You would have hardly thought that such veteran soldiers would all at once become so completely boyish as we all did on receiving the several packages from home. I can imagine nothing but seeing you all that could affect us as much. Not that we were in want of food nor that we could not get things of the same kinds here, but that does not satisfy. It seems to me now that I would give more for one good meal of biscuit and butter such as we have at home than for all the food we have in New Berne.

You must not think that our whole or principal thought is of what we shall eat or drink, or what method we shall be clothed, but we all do at times remember the good things at home. But you can send few things that will be of use and those of the kinds I wrote you about in my last. My boys from Monson made me a present a few days since of a very nice hat, which cost them about eight dollars, a little the best one I have seen here.

Today is the first day we have had which has seemed like a N.E. winter. Yesterday was a beautiful May day. Last night we had a thunder storm and today it has hailed most of the day, so we have now slush enough to keep the farmers of the field from doing anything but to sit in Boss' shop and debate the cause of the nation.[1] Here we have to use our time in making out papers of some kind.

---

[1] An unidentified member of Co. A. reported to the Springfield *Republican* "Tuesday morning, the 3d inst., the rain and sleet commenced falling pretty freely and soon turned to snow, and continued till about noon, falling about three inches in all; but to-day it has all disappeared, having rained for the past twenty-four hours. This weather made the boys think of home in old New England, and many a one expressed himself as suffering more, standing on guard, than ever before at home, when the snow was four feet deep, or less, and the thermometer twenty degrees below zero." (Feb. 12, 1863).

Col. Bowler has resigned, and his resignation has been accepted by the authorities and hailed with joy by a great part of the Regt.[1] If the old rat don't get his pay for the part he has played in this Regt. there is no justice in Heaven. You know I do not have much faith in the Hell of some of our good folks, but really I don't know where such negligents[sic] will get their just desserts but in some such institution.

Boys in the company are well except those I wrote you of before, Brimfield boys particularly so. Byron[probably Byron Charles*] looks the healthiest I ever saw him and our boys will average to weigh some ten lbs more than usual. Charley, Tom, W.[illiam] Stearns*, [Israel C.] Earle*, all the boys are as fat as cubs, and even the sedate old gentlemen like George, Lum [probably Charles Lumbard*], C[heney] Newton* & myself are quite corpulent. We have three men in the Hospital, 2 from Monson, one from Wales, Eli Thompson*. I hope to get a discharge for Eli this week. The man taken of a fever at the time poor [Marcus H.] Chaffee* was is better and the Drs. think he will get well.

[*Written across salutation, 1st page.*]

We have no news to write. The expedition has not been heard from.

Yours
Frank

Give my respects to S.W.B.[2] My thanks for the food recd, tell him if there be anything to write about I will write—Frank

---

[1] He was replaced by Lt.Col. Shurtleff, who was selected by a vote of the officers on Feb. 6, according to a report from a member of the regiment in the Springfield *Republican*, Feb. 12, and confirmed in Watson's diary entry for Feb. 6.
[2] Probably Samuel W. Brown.

Dear Frank

We received your letters last night, and like Annie Hutchinson over Etta's picture, so did I over them, that is had a good cry.

I do not know whether to be glad or otherwise, about your remaining at Newbern, for I think from the papers, the Rebels may make it rather warm for your comfort; but I suppose you will be free from the fatigue of marching.

As for your sister Maria[1], you know very well, Frank, her staying away has been to gratify some fancy of her own, as I have made her two visits since she came to see us, and on each of those visits I asked her to visit us, but she has not seen fit to do so for seven years. Well, I have got along very well without her for so long a time, and as for sympathy now, I do not wish for it; neither do I wish for them to lay this oddity to our not inviting them here, for they know it is a lie. They are beginning to feel a little ashamed of their actions, and are trying to soft soap it over; but as that is an article I don't use, they may stay away another seven years, if they wait for me to write long letters and make polite apologies.

Rebecca will write soon, but she has every moment taken up out of school, and Mr W. does not allow it in school. She and Etta wash the breakfast dishes in the morning, and as we do not get up till seven, they barely get them done in season for school. Then at night they clear away after tea, and commence practicing, but hardly ever play and sing as long as they want to before there is a rap.

The other night Mr Wyles came a little earlier than usual and heard them singing as he came in the yard. When he got into the room, he says, where is your company, I heard them singing, so they may as well make their appearance, and would not believe it was the children till they sat down and sang the same piece.[2] They do sing finely. Sissy has been very free from a cough, so they practice every night, and not singing at all at school, they enjoy it very much.

[*Paragraph of news about unidentified people, probably from Walpole, deleted.*]

This is the first time I have commenced writing in the day time, but I am having boiled victuals, so after I got them on I sat down a few minutes, but it wants a quarter of twelve, so I must spread the table.

It is a beautiful day, good sleighing, sun shining bright, no wind. Lewis is drawing logs, yoked the little steers and hitched them on. The oxen didn't seem very well pleased when he started.

---

[1] Frank did not have a sister Maria. He had a sister named Mary, who had been involved in the Perfectionist controversy of the mid-1830s, but she was dead by this time. He had a sister-in-law Maria, Charles' wife.

[2] Etta became noted for her beautiful singing voice.

New Berne   Feb. 5 1863

Dear Rebecca

I have thus far made a practice to write to some one each time I am placed on duty as Officer of the Day and have whenever I knew a mail was to go out, and to follow the practice I write you today though I think I sent a letter but two days ago. Your letter of the 25 came this morning. With you, I wonder what the lady Lyon finds to write about and have wondered ever since we came. No mail comes but he receives as many as four and sometimes seven letters. You may however be mistaken about the ability one displays in writing so much and often. I know nothing of hers but do know that some of the boys in camp that can't spell one word in four rightly nor frame a single sentence in good English, write letters all the spare time they have, and I should hardly conclude from that fact that they were gifted like Bancroft.[1] Father[2] used to say that a man of common sense could put on a half sheet all that could be made of interest under ordinary circumstances, a little strained perhaps as were many of his expressions, yet I think one can derive a lesson from it. I would not have you take a hint from it, for you will remember that he was speaking of the state of matters in times of peace, now we have grim <u>war</u>.

We understood that the mail did not go North for some time, as the steamers were wanted here, and I knew that after they started the one with our letters was delayed at Hatteras a number of days on acct of the storm, but long ere this you have the mail, giving the joy to so many and oh what sorrow to some.

Today we have placed in the schooner Frye the remains of Chaffee.[3] The same vessel that came freighted with so many tokens of love from home! You will receive this before the body arrives and if the weather and your health should be such as to make it prudent, I would like to have you attend the funeral. I have written his father all I felt like writing. There are no services performed here over the body of one that is not to be buried. The undertaker goes to the hospital, takes the body in a government coffin to his shop, seals it in a tin case, and it remains there till there is an opportunity to send it home.

---

[1] George Bancroft (1800-1891), born in Worcester, the most famous American historian of the time.
[2] Frank's father, Dr. Asa Lincoln (1782-1854), a man of strongly marked personality traits and opinions.
[3] Cpl. Marcus H. Chaffee of Wales died Jan. 30, 1863, of malarial fever, the first of Frank's company to die. According to a report from a member of the regiment in the Springfield *Republican*, Feb. 10, Chaffee and a "private Bradbury" also of Co. G "appeared on drill in the forenoon, were both taken sick in the afternoon, were raving maniacs through the night, and Corp. Chaffee died Friday afternoon." "Bradbury" is probably Rodney Bradway of Monson, who was listed as discharged from Foster General Hospital April 7.

The sick at the Hospital have all the care one can have away from their friends & I think perhaps better care than most could have at home, for there is every convenience for them there and no lack of experienced nurses, besides good Physicians. The men I have had sick have had some friend to visit them each day, and I have made it my business to go myself or send one of the Lieuts each day to see if there was anything we could do for them. Baxter Bennett is so much better that I sent him half of the sponge cake you sent. Today I saw him and found that the Dr. was willing he should eat it in small quantities and he is so well pleased that I shall keep the remainder of the loaf for him.

We have now four in the Hospital besides Baxter. Wm Foskit* [Fosket] was taken today, is quite sick and I have some fears for him (I think his mother is sister to G. Bacon). I have made out the papers for Eli Thompson's discharge but fear the surgeons will not grant the request. Tis but little use to try to do much in this matter of discharges—If the examining board are satisfied from their examination that they can be of no use to the government they will discharge them, otherwise it [is] of no use to beg. I have spent two whole days for Eli and have sent George and Lyon over and now they tell me it is doubtful if he is discharged.

I heard Tom read a few lines from his wife's letter (that is a lie, Frank, you read it yourself) to the effect that the war widows were left out of the ring in the

[*Written at right angles across front page*]
parties held this winter. Oh dear, what can the matter be. Think you would feel better to go visit more. Have the children get all the music they can and not interfere with their other lessons. We have had two days of Winter weather quite like New England. Feels as much so as I like in that particular.

My respects to all,
Yours, Frank

The swampy region of eastern North Carolina was considered unhealthy, and during the warm months residents who could afford it fled to the mountains or to the Outer Banks. Natives dreaded a poisonous vapor called miasma, which they believed caused the fatal fever physicians diagnosed as malaria. (David Stick, *The Outer Banks of North Carolina* [Univ. of North Carolina, 1958] 95).

Dear Frank

One would suppose that that[sic] you had been away long enough for you to be done with the idea that I could see you any where, but today I went into the dining room to the west window and Lewis had got the boards laid for rolling in the ice. I stood a moment thinking about it as though you would appear in a moment and you may imagine my feeling when that idea was banished by Lewis bobing[sic] his head out of the ice house door. They are to get ice tomor-row.[1] L. is going to have his father and one of the Dunham boys to help him.

Things go on about the usual way. I was to have Eunice and Mrs Witter to tea and commenced doing my work in a hurry to get done so as to do a little cooking. Well before I got the chores near done Mrs Dunham[2] came and sat a long time telling her joys and sorrows and had but just gone when the old lady Lumbard[3] came and staid til dinner time. Well then I thought I would do the best I could with what I had as it was only them, but when they came Mrs Hubbard came with them and Newton came to tea. When he came it was hard work to bear up, but that wa'n't all, for he says as he followed behind me to the dining room "well, have you got used to being alone." I didn't say yes.

The Hubbards stayed the evening and Mr Palmer, Mrs Goodell[4], and Mary came and they all stayed till nine, and we had a nice time. Mr Paige and Mary were in last evening, also Tom's wife. She was feeling pretty low-spirited. I felt bad for Charlie's mother today. Lizzie is gone all the time and where it makes no difference. Jim Warren, Dea Brown, Sam, Tom, Mrs Morris staid there several days and helped her some about the house. I don't know your idea but I think she would look better at home.

Mr Wyles has gone to New York, so we shan't have him to call. Don't you think people do well in the calling line. Almost every one has called but Mrs Wyles, but she is all done up in the minister and the souldier's[sic] aid society.

Bridget wanted her money so Henry looked over the account, made it $42, so I paid her.[5]

Well, the success of the war seems to depend on that portion of the army in N.C. now, and every one says they thought they knew what it was to be impatient but they have found they didn't.

---

[1] January or February was the usual time for harvesting the year's supply of ice. Eaton's mill pond, a good source, was located only a short distance from the Lincoln house.
[2] Possibly Lucy Sherman Dunham, widow of Seth, who was then about 66 years old.
[3] Prudence Willard Lumbard, Charles' mother. She died later in the year. The Lumbards were neighbors immediately to the west.
[4] Nathan and Lucy Goodale had a daughter Mary, born 1839. They lived a short distance up Warren Road, within easy walking distance of the Lincolns.
[5] Bridget is not otherwise identified and may not have been the person's real name, but it appears that the Lincolns were sufficiently well-off to have an Irish hired girl part-time.

Sunday eve.

This is the first Sunday evening we have spent entirely alone but it is quite into the evening and no one has come. It is very muddy. I went to Mrs Morgan's yesterday and had to walk my horse nearly all the way. Her father and mother were there, everything seemed pleasant as need be. I did not get your last letter before leaving Newbern till Thursday. It is too bad you have not got my letters, not that they are of much account, but perhaps better than nothing. This is my fourth since I came home.

Well, I have had my company.

[Continued on top margin of front page]
Boss Brown and A. Converse[1] . Not a word of news from either. Mr Brown has all he can do this winter. I have let the town have $150.[2] If you have not got my other letters you may not know where this came from. The Shaws have paid our three hundred. Who takes care of your money from the government. You have never spoken of it.

Rebecca

[1] Alfred L. Converse, born 1824, son of Marquis Converse, a prominent resident.
[2] The Selectmen had authorized an enlistment bounty of $150 to volunteers, and Rebecca may have been loaning or donating money for this purpose.

[Undated letter from children]

[In Etta's handwriting]
Etta sends love and will write next time.

Brimfield

Dear Father

Etta always begins her letters first and if I lisp a word that I am going to write she writes it first, so when I get ready I don't have a great deal of news. Last Sunday evening old Mr Hichcock[sic] and his wife came and spent the evening. While they were here, Mr Wiles [Wyles] came but did not stay long. Monday, mother invited Mrs Witter and Eunice Knight to spend the afternoon here and in the forenoon Mrs Dunham and staid ever so long. After she went away Mrs Lumbard (Charley's mother) came and staid an hour. Of course mother was very glad to see her as she comes so seldom. In the afternoon they came and Mrs Hubbard was at E's and so she came with her. Just as we were going to have supper Mr Hubbard came after his wife. He had been at Mrs Knight's but she was not there. He staid to tea and in the evening Mr Palmer, Mrs and Mary Goodell, 9 in one day.

I suppose if you have read mother's letter you know that they are going to have an exhibition and [space] and[sic] that I act in it. In one I represent Spring. I am dressed in white trimmed with green leaves and hemlock. Marietta Prouty is Summer, Hellen[sic] Emerson is fall, and Calvin Ward, Winter, and in a sharade[sic] I am a young lady. Oscar Parker is my <u>father</u> and Julia Brown is mother. Orvill Bliss is my leov[sic], and Ellen Warren my maid. I can't write any more. Mother and Mr Brown are in the parlor all alone which I mistrust is Dangerous especially as he has been here a great deal since mother got that money.

[*Signed Sissy in mother's handwriting*]

[*Continued by mother*]

We are very impatient to know from you of the battle, how you felt and all that. Oh I am so impatient for the coming week to see what effect the proclamation.[1] God grant us deliverance from the sheding of any more northern blood. What think you of the slaves as to their serving? Are there intelligent ones enough to do anything? I am reading, "Among the Pines" it is called, it represents them as belonging to a secret society more extensive, it says, than the Golden Circle, and there is no doubt of their rising at the right time.[2] If the time has not come, when will it?

We killed the beef Friday. It is very good. Mr Paige does not take but a quarter, so we shall have plenty. It is after nine. Old Mr Warren and his wife have just gone, said he met Jim in N York[sic].[3] [*Sentence of news about unidentified people deleted.*]

Charlie's wife staid here Wednesday night. Sam has given me a Tribune to send to you so you will see the war news at Goldsborough & c.

Mary Knight remains in Troy [N.Y.][4] She has had some very fine presents, but Eunice is lonesome enough this winter.

Every one speaks of the children this winter. They think I take good care of them, but can't say the same for me. Sissy since we came home has been the best I ever knew her. Her throat troubles her some, but not as it did last winter. There is no singing in school and she is not used as an assistant. She has been over taxed with such things.

---

[1] A somewhat tardy reference to the Emancipation Proclamation, which took effect Jan. 1, 1863. The final form of this document authorized the recruitment of blacks in the Northern armed forces.
[2] *Among the Pines; or South in Secession-time*, by Edmund Kirke, a pseudonym for James R. Gilmore (1822-1903). Gilmore/Kirke, a northern journalist, spent considerable time in North Carolina. He reproduced the African Americans' dialect and reported their sentiments. Interestingly, he may have been in eastern North Carolina during the period the 46th Mass. was stationed there. (Victor T. Jones, Jr., comp., "New Bern in Fiction: Works of Fiction about or Mentioning New Bern Area," (http://newbern.cpclib.org/nbccpl/pdf/nbfic, 2006).
[3] John M. Warren (1797-1868) was the father of James J., born 1822.
[4] Mary T. Knight was Eunice's younger sister. She later married Rev. Charles M. Hyde, author of the Brimfield town history.

Brimfield

Dear Father

I don't suppose that I shall have much to write, but I will write a little that happens every day. Sunday—we went to church all day, and in the evening, Mr and Mrs Ward[1] called, and he showed me about a piece of music, which a few of us girls are going to sing, at the Band of Hope exibition[sic]. And in the last part of the evening Mr Merrick Warren[2] made us a short call.

Monday—We went to school as usual, and after school went to Lizzie Munroe's, to reherse[sic] a dialogue, staid there untill past five, then went over to Mrs Chamberlain's, and could not possibly get away untill dark, went home in the slush, and rain, then asked mother if I might go over to Ellen Warren's to meet the girls about that dialogue, but she said No. I asked Lewis if he would harness the horse and carry me and come after at eight. He said yes, if mother was willing, so she let me go. Etta spent the night with Alice Bacon.

Tuesday—of course we went to school. In the afternoon Dr Hall came into school to vaccinate all the schoolars[sic] (Oh, I forgot to tell you that Mrs J-G- Brown has got the smallpox). Etta & I were vaccinated. Etta's is going to work, but I don't think much of mine. Well, Mr Woods let the schoolars do just as they had a mind to, except to go out doors, and as Dr had so many to attend to, he had to stay a good while. Mr W— let out school at quarter to four.

Mother was into school the other day, and the classes all recite on seats in front of the school. We told mother that he had us there because there we could not make fun of the scholars, nor anything they did, only of him, and Mother said after we got home that we looked sitting there for all the world like pictures of Piggirs[pagans?] sitting around a missionary.

Wensday[sic] evening I went to the singing school. Saturday we went down to Mrs Lyons, had a very pleasant time, came up to Pen[uel]—Parker's and up to Mr Paige's. When we got home, we found a letter from Anna P— saying that she would be here in 3 weeks. Mother has said three or four times it is time to go to bed.

Rebecca

Dear Frank, When I receive your letters I think what a blessing is ink and paper, but when it is my turn to use them, they are but miserable tools, for one to think & feel so much, and yet express so little, but if ever you return you will find me the personification of selfishness, as far as you are concerned. And you may make up your mind to be tied to my apron string the rest of my life, "for where thou goest, there will I go," and I often think and ask myself should it be so, and why were we made of such natures that the abence[sic] of one, only one, all the remaining the same, and yet we be so miserable. No, I should not say all else the same, for every one is so kind and attentive.

[1] Probably Calvin M. Ward, born 1820.
[2] John Merrick Warren (1797-1868) and his second wife, Charlotte R. Burley.

Try, Frank, and feel as kindly toward all here as possible, for I have wept after men have gone away at the feeling they have exhibited over your pictures, and Calvin Ward in particular, it was all he could do to command himself. If they have not all the manly courage to go as you have, they have shown to your family that they have hearts that can feel for us.

Dr <u>Vaill</u>[1] preached here today. This afternoon, he had the same text he preached from the first time he ever entered this pulpit. He said he was speaking with some one about it, and they asked why he didn't preach the same sermon, and had told them because it was so green. He had it with him and held it up, and it looked pretty yellow.

[Written across salutation, first page]
Do you think there is any truth in what the papers say about the suffering of the Rebel troops. If there is, I should think if we have one honest Gen., we might be victorious by and by, but we will hope on hope ever. And may our heavenly father guide, guard, and direct thy every step till he brings thee home.

Amen

Rebecca

[1] Rev. Joseph Vaill (1790-1869), then pastor of the Second Congregational Church in Palmer, had been a long-time minister in Brimfield, serving from 1814 to 1833 and again from 1837-1841.

New Berne,   Feb 11th 63

My dear family

                    To day the whole camp was made glad again by the receipt of a mail. Tis difficult to imagine that more anxiety could be had on your part to hear from us than is manifested by the boys here to get news from home. We generally hear two or three times that a mail has come to the City before one comes and each disappointment but sharpens the anxiety to have one. Finally one comes and the chaplain informs the camp that a big mail has arrived in the city and then ten times in an hour some one will put his head into my tent and with a hopeful look will ask "Capt. is there a mail in?" "I understand the chap. Said there is." "Spose[sic] it will be up tonight?" "Well, really I can't tell: twill[sic] depend something on the size of it, I 'spose."

                    The last mail we had the news of its arrival at the city about sun down. So impatient were the men to receive it that I went down to see when it would be ready. And on returning told them that it would probably be up at 10. So they waited till 11 & reluctantly retired. At 9 the next day it came, and although the company drill commences at that hour I ran the risk of a reprimand from the Col. that the boys might read their letters.

                    Well when distributed all but Charly and myself had one or more, some as many as six. I went through the tents to get what news I could, but no one of the boys was disposed to let me read one but Henry Lumbard*, who handed me a scrap of paper with a "Here, Capt., seeing you did not get a letter you may read this". I took it and read a pretty printed note from his little boy. The boys are now disposed to have a little laugh over my disappointment but Charles, who felt a little too much as I did, for sport. I had just come to the wicked resolve to be certain of getting letters in future by not sending any home for a time when George came in and said there were two bags yet to be distributed. So hope revived and in the course of half an hour I rec'd the letters from you & George Etten & one from H. Brown. Well, they were all I wanted one letter from home and that as late as any rec'd I value as much as four or even a dozen. Tis all I desire, but that one I can not do without, that is, I am not sure how I can.

                    The days that I have long feared have finally come: for some time I had noticed the sickness prevalent in the regts about us with a fear that ours would be the next. We have lost within ten days 4 men in the reg. and have many more sick, how many I do not certainly know, but Co G has eight men in the Hospital and although I do not consider the case of either of them very bad still I would that I able to speak of the Co as I could a month since. Foskit is the sickest man we have and he is no worse but rather [better] than he has been. Charles Alexander* is the only one of the Brimfield boys. I wish you to go immediately to see his mother and tell her that Charles was taken of a fever on Thursday of last week. Friday was worse and we took him to the Stanley Hospital. The next day he was no worse and Sunday seemed better and has improved each day since. Say to her that I visit him each day when it is possible and send George each day, that he is as well taken care of as he could possibly be at home having the best medical attendants there are in the city (and there is as good here as anywhere), the best of nurses, a good easy couch and everything a sick man could want. Were I to be sick I could not desire to be placed in better hands, and would rather trust my life in the care of the directors of this Hospital than any where else. Tis true that one had rather be at home, sick or well, and most people especially if sick, but after all that I do believe that there is not one home in a thousand where such care is possible [as we] have here.

The Sisters of Charity visit this Hospital: everything is kept as neat as possible; few of the best conducted houses in N.E. are kept neater. I fear that most of the housewives at home would be ashamed of their bed rooms were they to visit the rooms where the sick are. They furnish to the convalescent every delicacy which the city furnishes at their expense. Say what we will of the catholics, I must believe that the order of "Sisters of Charity" is the most truly benevolent organization in the world. Let us not be disposed to find fault with their superstition, rather let us thank God that there are those who, for the purely religious desire of doing good, should spend their all. In the other Hospitals the sick have good care, very good, but do not have that sort [of] sympathetic attention which woman alone can give. I said that I did not know to what extent the disease prevailed in the reg. The only facts I know bearing on the matter are that we have in Co G more men fit for duty than any other company has, and the Col told me that the Dr. said that it had the best care of any of the companies. Say to Mrs. Alexander that I will write in regard to Charles every mail until he is able to write.

Have just returned from a visit to the boys [at the hospital]. Found them all as well and they think better than when I saw them last. Spent as long time with them as I though[t] best. Talked with Charles some time. Told him I was writing to his mother. He begged that I would not write any thing to alarm her. I told him I should tell his case exactly as I thought it was. He seemed anxious to know, then, what I thought of it and I told him, with which he seemed satisfied. I asked him if he wanted any thing & he said he would like a lemon, and after consulting the nurse I procured some for him. I charged him to obey implicitly the requests of the nurse. He is just beginning to have a desire for food and said they did not give him half as much as he wanted. This you will of course understand. I think they will all recover, as most of them have the same fever, which has proved fatal in less than thirty six hours if at all.

You will not think that we are a sickly feeble set because there are so many in the Hospital, for the rest of the Co. with the exception of H. Lumbard who is troubled with rheumatism & a Monson boy are as rugged as bears and most as fat, for proof look at the picture of Charley L.[Lumbard] which he sends in this mail to his wife. I went to the city to have one taken of the Capt but found the saloons [salons] all filled, so returned without one. If you desire it I will try again, though I assure you that the last time I saw his face he looked as natural as a basket of chips—at least I can see no difference except that he is a little fuller in the face and has a crop of ugly looking bristles on his upper lip which if I remember rightly he did not wear at Camp Banks. Then again he is evidently proud of wearing a nice hat with a splendid bugle in front which they say the Monson boys gave him.

Ned [Edward] Bliss* and myself have been quite unlucky in the way of shirts. I had a squaw wash mine for a time and they grew no bigger each time, till one day she brought one of them back so badly shrunk that it was difficult to draw it over my head and when on, the wrist bands came where the elbows used to and the neck band needed about three inches to make it meet. You will probably guess that there was some twitching and pretty considerable amount of talk not entirely complimentary to the squaws, or niggers in general, all to no effect so far as making the shirt any bigger.

Next trial with it was to give it to the man who does the washing for the company to see if by any coaxing it would give way any. He returned it and I pulled till I got it on. Then came another pleasant talk and twitching & yanking till I tore a big hole under each arm, but not a bit would the cloth give except it gave a little more than necessary. You would hardly think it possible that such soft pleasant amiable disposition as the shirts up to this time had shown could all at once become so stubborn and unyielding. I dare bet to the half of my pay that a yoke of oxen can't make the collar yield a hundredth part of an inch. Well I must wear it while my other is being washed, for it is Sunday and the other is already wet, so a string is to be made of woolen yarn about four inches long to hitch the ends of the collar together and on it goes.[1]

In the mean time Ned had washed his and hung it on a pole to dry but being so much taken up with the prayer meeting in the eve he forgot the command to <u>watch</u> as well as pray and thereby lost his shirt. Well Tuesday he comes into my tent with a "Capt, I have found my shirt on one of the nigger boys here." "How do you know it is yours?" "I know tis by the looks of the cloth." "Is it like the one you have on?" "Yes, and there are more on the ground like them." "Where did you get the flannel?" "At the depot." "Beg your pardon, Ned, but I know of some eight or ten like the one you have on in this company, however bring the boy in here."

In came the culprit; tells his story, "He took his two shirts to be washed and the wash woman gave him this to wear till his was dry. He knew nothing about where she get it. She give it now sure." I looked at the shirt and at Ned's. They were alike so far as I could see. "Was your shirt marked, Ned?" "Yes" "Where & how?" "On the flap, my name is on it, or was." "Pull off the shirt, boy." Slowly, with a repeat of "I knows not where she got it but she gave it to me sartin" he pulls it off. (What a scene in the Capt's tent.)

[1] Clearly, Frank's shirts were made of wool, and the washerwoman's boiling of the laundry, commonly done as a precaution against lice, was not improving the fit.

I take the shirt, it has Ned's name on it. Poor nig is now frightened and tells the story again. "Never mind, my lad, you bring the wash woman here and that will clear you if you tell the truth." "She won't come." "How do you know?" "Cause she lives way over the Trent." "Well after drill is over I will go with you to see her. I will keep the shirt." Ned objects, "I don't want the shirt, let him pay for it." "Well, Ned, you have heard of the proverb of serving the beggar." A new thought seems to strike Ned. "What do [you] call the shirt worth, Ned?" "Two dollars." "I will sell the one I have on my back for one." "I will give it" and pulled out his money. I pulled off the shirt, glad enough to part with it, went immediately to the city and bought one for 3.50, quite a fancy thing made of Loden cloth. Guess I shall have to learn to cross & overstitch to keep it on my back. After drill the nig was no where to be found. So ends the story of the two shirts, very interesting, ain't it? I hope none of you will have to suffer as I did for a day or two from the feeling that the shirt is too small.

You say that the people at home manifest a good deal of kindly feeling towards you and ask that I should not lay up anything against them from which I conclude that some conclusion may have been drawn from what some of us may have written in a careless way about the exempts. It would hardly seem necessary for me to express to you a favorable opinion of the people of Brimfield generally, for you have known for years how much I regarded them. You know too that I sacrificed the society of friends such as few ever have to come to Brimfield because I had a feeling for the people there that I could have for no other. I can hardly think that anything I have written would induce you to believe that I had lost my feeling for them. Tis true that certain insinuations that I learned from the boys, some of the folks at home made in regard to the motive which influenced me in coming; this kind of talk that I should or expected to make a good thing of it, did provoke me some, and I would like to see the man who would bear such things with complacency from a <u>brother</u>.

Of all the men whom I have claimed as friends there is not one who I feel has done what he should be ashamed of except Jim B.[1] Nor do I entertain any feeling of bitterness towards him. Tis a pity that he should have suffered his name to be used by the party which voted for him representative last fall. And I don't believe I shall ever regret that he was beaten, for it was reaping a just reward for his actions. There are others in town who showed a mean cowardly spirit (not of my <u>friends</u>) but they were those of whom I long since ceased to expect anything honorable.

You are unable to satisfy yourself whether to be glad or sorry about our being left here instead of being taken on the expedition[sic]. I am in the same fix myself, not that I fear that an attack will be made on New Berne at present, but I desire to do the fighting I have got to do and have it over with. Gen. Foster has returned, and it is understood that he wants more force so there is a possibility that we shall be taken yet, and I think a probability for we are the Brigade held in

[1] Probably James B. Brown.

reserve here, having no particular post assigned us in case of attack. And it seems to me that should he take any force from here ours would be the Brigade.

Did I tell you that Tom & Bill were away on duty for the Regt. Well they are and I suppose they have fine times. Tom has charge of a gang of hands at a saw mill about thirty miles from here, and I am told that he tries to make up for the loss of society of his wife by using the Negroes. Don't blush now; I mean <u>male</u> Negroes. I am going tomorrow to see him and shall be able to tell more about it when I return, and although I might tell a pretty good story from hearsay, I prefer waiting and giving the facts as I see them. Say to his wife that I am doing the best I can to keep him in the way of virtue, and I rather guess if she does all she can to help, he will come out all straight.

You speak of my pictures, as I sat looking at Etta's which is constantly before me when at my desk. I wonder if the same feelings of fear & hope, of sorrow & yet of gladness comes over your spirit in looking at mine. She seems to say to her father wont we have good times when you come home. Yes, my darling, it shall be the happiest of my life.

[*Written in top margin of preceding page.*]
Tell Henry B. his letter I have recd[sic]—will write ere long. Give my thanks to Mr. Bates[1] for favors.

Yrs[sic] FDL

Frank has produced one of his richest and most revealing letters, full of observations that tell us a good deal about himself, as well as the situation he was in. Since the troops had been in a semi-permanent camp for over two months, camp disease, one of the great curses of the Civil War, was becoming prevalent. Much of it was due, as Frank suspected, to poor sanitation, but the cause and the remedy were not well understood. The situation pulled the ties between home and camp even tighter, as Rebecca was assigned the duty of relieving the anxiety of a soldier's family. This would be an unlikely occurrence in the regular army and illustrates vividly the strengths and defects of hometown militia units called to duty in a serious war. Frank's description of mail call displays the easy camaraderie that existed between him and the enlisted men, not at all like the rigid class structure of the regular army; but this closeness and solicitousness also made the loss of any of the men harder to bear.

*Having absorbed a lifetime of anti-Catholic sentiment, Frank found it difficult to concede grudging admiration for the Sisters' nursing efforts. His conclusion was shared by others; Nina Silber notes that "Catholic nuns, so many doctors believed, showed a greater willingness than Protestant women to accept male authority." (*Daughters of the Union*, 213).*

---

[1] Unidentified.

This is the first letter in which Frank begins to address at a personal level the overarching issues of emancipation and the status of African Americans. "Squaw" was a disparaging term for the black women who performed necessary services such as laundry around camp. At other times they would have been called camp followers, and in this situation they probably had little choice. Most likely they were slaves who had escaped into the Northern lines. For want of a better classification, such people were initially labeled "contrabands of war," because, with slavery still legal, they were considered to be someone's property; moreover, most of the regular army officers had little interest in freeing slaves. With the Emancipation Proclamation in effect in the seceded states after Jan. 1, 1863, the former slaves would technically be free, but had no way to support themselves other than working around the fringes of the Northern army camps.

In his first approach to the subject, Frank depicts the blacks he encounters in an amused and condescending manner. Like many northerners, James Gilmore being a well-known example, he is fascinated by the black dialect and attempts to reproduce it. As time goes on, his understanding deepens and he displays a more nuanced and sympathetic attitude toward the former slaves. Content aside, he shows a strong narrative gift, making it easy to imagine him writing a descriptive book like Gilmore's. The idea seemed not to occur to him, and it is only now, almost a century and a half later, that the book he might have written is finally appearing.

New Berne   Feb 18th

My Dear Family

I went on Saturday morning with George, Frank [Cook]* & [George] Barnes* on a visit at Newport to see Tom & Bill, and will give something of an acct[sic] of our journey. Newport is on the Rail Road some thirty miles from New Berne on the Route from the latter to Morehead City & is what they call in this country a right smart place. Yet every building there is in sight from the Road. (They have no Depot nor even a platform, so that one getting into or out off[sic] the cars here has to step up on a sort of stirrup hung on the side of the car about three feet from the ground.) One finds little dwelling houses which were in their best days about like Dunham's[1], with this exception. Neither of them was ever guilty of using any paint, four <u>stores</u> and a hovel, where once a blacksmith thrived. Near by there stood not long since a <u>southern</u> church, but that has gone the way of all the world.

Nor is there any village or collection of houses any where within ten miles [of] this "right smart place." The dwellings will not average one in a square mile for a distance of eight miles around. We spent some time however visiting the stores, which are kept in buildings of the size of the "City Hall" of Brimfield, each containing a little of "everything." About them will be found some thirty loafers in the shape of southern gentlemen of substance drinking ale[?] and conversing about the war and the price of turpentine, which is the prime article of trade here and is seen lying on the ground in large quantities about the shops.

The people come here to trade for twenty or thirty miles, most of them with an apology for an ox team, consisting of a yoke of cattle a little bigger than the average size of our yearlings hitched to a skeleton cart; that is, a pair of wheels with a couple of round sticks about six feet long fastened at either end and having some three or four stakes on each side about two feet high, laden with one or two bbls of crude turpentine. The driver does not drive, but leads this brave yoke of oxen with a rope on the horns of one sometimes on both of them. Laugh now and say tis a lie, but not only is it true, but they were actually incredulous about the power to use cattle by the haw and gee power which we use, and they speak always of the cattle that Tom & Bill use as "them cattle that they drive without a rope" and all the men in the vicinity have been to see the wonderful performance.

In one of the shops we stood for some time conversing with the clerk, a very pretty female, and vied with one another in entertaining her for an hour or more. And I dare not predict how it might have ended had she not taken from her pocket her snuff box and swab and rolling the swab in the snuff put it into her <u>mouth</u>!

[1] Although the Dunhams originated in a remote part of Brimfield, a section that became known as Dunhamtown, where conditions made agriculture unrewarding, a Dunham widow may have lived closer to the center of town, on Warren Rd. An old Mrs. Dunham was earlier recorded as dropping in on the Lincolns.

Well we did not need an invitation to leave; had the swab been a new one perhaps we might have fallen in love with the practice, as the operator was so pretty, but the thought that the self same swab had been rolled in the same box of snuff and then in the lady's mouth a dozen times a day (perhaps twenty) since the box was filled, some how took the edge from our desire to converse with her. I am told that the practice above mentioned is a general practice among southern ladies, lovely aint it! Don't mention it to any of the war widows for any thing. I know that could they have the least idea of the effect it has on their lords, they would loose[sic] all confidence in the power of their virtue to withstand the temptations with which they are beset.

We went down to the saw mill of which Tom has charge. Tis a steam mill and has the same appearance of neglect that everything else does in this country. Think of a saw mill in a country covered with the best timber in the world, with the whole machinery standing out of doors, not a particle of roofing or covering of any kind on the frame, just barely the frame absolutely necessary to keep the machinery together! God of heaven what shiftlessness! Remember that of all the apparatus for a sawmill, the engine & boiler are most expensive and that to preserve them requires the best only that a single day's work of the mill would saw boards enough to protect it completely; and yet that a man should be so shiftless as to spend five thousand dollars to get the necessary implements, and then leave them in such shape as to be completely ruined in a short time; when by a single day's work he could so well protect the whole! Tis enough to make the whole shiftlessness of the north cry out shiftless.

The mill is on the banks of the Newport, a deep stream, which Tom says is the most convenient river in the world, since the ebb tide the water runs one way and at the flood the other, so they have only to roll the logs into the river and they float to the mill and when the tide returns tumble in the lumber and it is floated to the rail road. Do you wonder that with such convenience the southern people are lazy!

Tom has a log house to live in, and quite a home he makes of it. For amusement after supper he summoned his darkies to dance, and we who had only seen sham Negro performances rolled and laughed till our sides were sore to see the real! Twould be useless to attempt a description of their antics, or music, a sort of sing song with a constant slapping the hands to beat time; the dancing, independent of nigger shines, is not to be beaten. No, not even by my friend Dr. Witter, and you know he is the most active man on the dancing floor in our parts. I honestly believe that the five nigs that danced to amuse us, would have so pleased Herod as to have gotten his promise for the whole of his kingdom.

It was Saturday and the game was kept up I rather guess till nearly midnight. Well the next morning we all started for the sound, Bogue it is called. Look on the map and you will see a long narrow island, stretching from the mouth of the river a long distance on the coast towards Wilmington. This is Bogue island, and the water between this and the main land is the sound. About half way down on the main land is a block house where Lt. Stewart is stationed with thirty men to keep a look out for and hail any vessels or boats that may attempt to pass either way so that nothing contraband may get up or down the sound.

To this point we make our way as soon as tis light enough to pass our pickets stationed between Newport and the sound. We found the Lt. at home enjoying his pipe by a roaring fire; was glad to see us. Anyone with a blue overcoat is welcome. At the picket posts, as luck would have it, the boats which are kept at this post had been used on an expidition[sic] and on the return the boys got sick of rowing against wind and tide and had left them some seven miles up the sound. So we were in a quandary—shall we go back & so loose[sic] the main object of our tramp which was to go on the island to spend the night; or shall we tramp seven miles through a suspicious country over the loose sand for the boats. After consulting I found all but Bill disposed to give it up.

Well after reflecting on the chances of capture, I concluded to go with Bill for the boat and we packed all our duds on our backs and started. On we go over a country fit only for wild bears to roam over—lonely enough to give Saint Sanguine himself the "Blues." On, on, on four miles through the woods without the first sign of a living creature, except now and then a busserd[sic] sailing high in the air, till we meet a native. "Sarvant, Captain." "Good morning. Can you tell us how far it is to the creek?" "Well I <u>reckon</u> tis smart three miles, Capt." "Do you know if the boys at the blockhouse left their boats there yesterday?" "Yaw, I reckn[sic] they did, Capt." (These fellows either commence or close every sentence with the title the man bears and never presume to make any conversation with an inferior in rank in the presence of his superior.) "Can you direct us on the route to the landing?" "Tis no difficult to find, Capt., keep right on till you come <u>up</u> <u>with</u> the church and then take the left Capt." "Good morning." "I reckon you don't get any news from the north do you Capt.?" "Nothing of any consequence. I understand they are making arrangements to raise another lot of troops." "Be they though, Capt.? How many do you reckon they will send this time Capt.?" "Don't know. Some three hundred thousand I suppose." "I hear there is right smart of them <u>that</u> <u>their</u> time is out this summer. Do you reckon that's so Capt.?" "Yes, some, but they mean to send enough to more than make their places good." "Do you reckon," but the devil take the fellow with his reckon. Bill & I must be going.

We "came up with" the church: you have heard of churches without a Bishop, but you can have but a poor idea [of] a southern church and its surroundings. This one stands in the fork of the the[sic] roads, is eighteen by twenty, two windows on each side, and a door on each end so that you can pass straight through without any convenience for _____ : not a house, with a single exception, in sight, nor one on the main road passing by it for two miles either way! Where the people ever came from to fill such a church one is at a loss to conjecture. But the lady in the shop at Newport, whom I saw again on my return assured me that "they used to have right smart meetings there!"

About a mile farther on is another building, which we took to be a school-house, partly because we can not conjecture what else it can be, and partly because it is in the most destitute looking place in this desolate country. Well by and by we came to a plantation, where there is an opening to the sound and we conclude that we are near our journey's end. And find on going to the house that the boat is on the shore "just over the pint yonder." Here are four men who they say are loyal, and I rather think they are, for they really look like decent men. But we can't stop to detail the talk we had with them.

We go to the shore, strip off our boots and stockings and wade out to the boat, and after a deal of pushing pulling and swimming finally get it afloat. And now for a row. On we go over the smooth water, for we were on the lee shore, for an hour or more. Tis a relief to row, bringing as it does an entire different set of mussels[sic] than we employ in marching into action, but seven miles of this kind of journey is no fun. Still we persevere and about three come back to the boys.

Tom is busy fixing a boat of an old log to go over the sound in, but tis not finished, and he finally concludes to let it go and try his luck with the one we have labored so to get—though he insists that he could fix it so he could go over the sound in it. Well I think he might perhaps, for he does most anything he attempts, but I rather guess Mrs. T. would think it rather risky to go over a sheet three miles wide in a trough.

The wind begins to rise and Frank is a little fearful about the trip in the boat, but after being assured by Tom (who by the way had crossed the sound once) that three fourths of the way the water was not more than waist deep he concludes to go, though twenty rods of deep water was full enough to drown any one. However the conveyance seemed to satisfy him and we set sail, or rather set rowing. Over the blue waters we go pitching and tossing, for the wind had risen and there is quite a sea. Sometimes a sprinkling of water over the side of the boat makes Cook open his eyes, but he is most of the time too much engaged in looking at the ducks to think much of getting ducked. We labor till the gun from Fort Macon assures us that the sun has gone and still are a mile from the point on the island where we wish to touch, for Tom is particular as is determined to land us opposite the hut of an old fisherman where he had before been. And I have enough dictating in camp to satisfy me, so am glad to suffer dictation when we are away, especially when it is by Tom, as his main object in it all seems to be to get one into a better situation than they would choose for themselves.

George sometimes uses a little strong language about his being so generous as not to be willing that others should enjoy themselves when they want to, but then George is a little fretful if he can not have his way, which is always the way that costs the least labor. Well by & by we see the boats and are all glad that our

Sabbath days journey is nearly at an end. By the shore sits the old man and hard by is his son in a skiff, which he pushes through the shallow water to take us one by one to the shore, for our boat will go no nearer.

We see the boat fastened and follow the lead of our host to his mansion. And such a mansion should satisfy even Sam Clapp. The island is twenty-five miles long and averages about a mile wide. There is or has been four dwellings on it, this one is the one farthest north, and nearest to the fort, which is on the extreme north end commanding the harbors opposite Morehead & Beaufort. I asked the old man if they could cook us some meat and give us a chance to lie on the floor, to which he replied "Why God damn it, if you will be satisfied with it, we will give you the best we have, but you see the old woman and I are in pretty snug quarters with seven little devils, Capt." (I will not try to put in the spice which he sprinkled in his talk but will simply say that he swore so continuously that not one of our gang has even been heard to say devil ever since.)

Snug enough, thought I as we came up to the house. I have so often spoken of the style these people live in that I am almost ashamed to detail another, but will try for this once only. This house is some 16 feet by 20, with not a single window in it nor any convenience to let in light except the cracks in the wall and chimney, unless the doors are open. There is a single room in it, no chambers. Three things in the shape of beds for a family of nine, a single table and sort of chest, and some five or six seats of one kind or another. In one corner is the ____. All they have is boys for you must bear in mind this is the only building they have. On the other side stands the table and chest; in one end are the three beds with just room enough between them to pass side wise. The chimney is made of four poles for a frame covered with boards, the fire place having large sheets of iron set up between the boards & fire. On the outside close by the chimney stands a ladder to use when the chimney takes fire (you see they run up the ladder and wet down the chimney.) Note: now aint this a house to live in.

The doors (one on each side opposite one another) have no convenience for fastening or latching except to put in a wooden pin as they used to in stable doors, so that no one can come into the house if the door be closed unless the pin be removed. Nor can one leaving it close it; but some one from within must both open & close. Tis of no use for the mother to scream to the departing one "come back you hussy and shut the door after you!" She must close it herself if it be done. What a convenience for children going out! What a contrivance to keep out unwelcome visitors!

Now look a moment at this family. A man who has seen considerable of the world has been a sailor in his younger days, has been as he says "round quite smart, been to NY & Boston!" is naturally rather bright has had a wife in his younger days & lost her, married another, and he told me in the presence of his whole family "that if he had been cunning and married an older woman he need not have been troubled in his old age with such a lot of little ones, but then you know Capt. that the old man desired a young woman."

This woman is possessed of more than average ability is quite a good looking woman does not swab out her mouth with snuff, is, or would be I think, quite tidy were she in a situation to be so, wears a dress made of bed ticking which I dare bet is the best dress she has, for who ever knew a woman who did not wear her best dress on Sunday. Frank Cook says the dress was made of an old tick but I did not scan it close enough to affirm or deny. Here are seven children, six girls and one boy. The boy say fifteen dressed in decent suit of clothes, the girls ranging from thirteen down to baby three weeks old, all clad in filthy rags, bright looking children as you see any where. Not one of them can read a word, have never seen the inside of a school house, the mother does not know how to read; all in all is that not a <u>home</u>.

We had some fresh ham for supper well cooked and after talking a while with the family, spread our blankets on the sanded floor and lay our weary bones down to rest. In the morning we arose with the firing of the gun and went over to the other side of the island to see once more the broad ocean and give one long look <u>towards</u> home. Returned to breakfast, had fresh shad. George says they dressed eight and we ate them all. I can only say that we ate as hungry soldiers only know how to eat. Went to the sea shore and picked up shells, a few only I have, and of little value except that they were picked up on Bogue Island. If I get an opportunity I shall send them to Etta.

We left the island about 2 P.M. receiving as a parting salute from the old fisherman "God damn you Capt., come & see us again if you can!" Pretty rough but hearty. Arrived safely last night, found your letters mailed the 9th waiting for us today.

I have been through the Hospital to see the sick ones. All improving but Foskit, and I think he is no worse. Say to Mrs. Alexander that Charles is decidedly better. George H. went with me and has written a letter to Jane, so I do not deem it necessary to write particularly but you had better let her know what I say about it, for the poor woman would doubtless like to have his improvement affirmed by all who see him. Lyman Parker* was taken sick last night after my return. Has a quinsy sore on the neck & I hope this will prove to be the whole trouble, but he has a little fever. If you can get word to them I wish you would. Should he be worse I will write his father.

Tell Dr. Witter that I found his friend right at the Stanly Hospital, that he was engaged in writing to his folks was so far recovered to be out in pleasant weather. He has all he desires, thanked me for the offer I made to get him anything he wished and said he would walk up and see me the first pleasant day. Say also to the Dr. that he is in the best Hospital in the city and has had the best of care. I would have written him had I time. Give my best respects to him & his wife.

[Overwritten across salutation, first page.]
You ask that I should tell what we say & do. Well really we talk most of the spare time we have with our dear ones at home, and think of them always and as for doing we <u>do</u> drill. Say to Mrs. Tom if she gets no letter from him that in consequence of my visit with him he did not get her last letter till today and that is the reason, that he is well and I guess thinks of her all he should.

Yours Frank

Frank again displays his narrative and descriptive powers in a detailed account that is particularly valuable because it was written while the impressions were fresh. The amount of time it must have taken to write this report with pen and ink under less-than-ideal conditions in itself testifies to the Captain's devotion to his family.

His observations reveal genuine and profound astonishment at many of the scenes and people he encountered and are typical of the reaction of educated northern soldiers on encountering the South. The accounts of Union soldiers, especially New Englanders, abound with descriptions of a backwardness and lack of care that they found appalling. Frank's emphatic use of the word "shiftless" is endlessly reinforced by others. Trotter in Ironclads and Columbiads *(159) observes that "If the New England troopers had a high opinion of the antebellum standard of living enjoyed by the upper and middle classes of New Bern, they were often bemused and mildly repulsed by the quaint folkways of the lower classes, the so-called 'poor white trash' that lived in the woods and along the tributary creeks all around the town." Women usually came in for special praise in accounts by northern soldiers. A corporal in the 44th Mass, who was a correspondent to a Boston newspaper, observed on his initial journey from Morehead City to Newbern that "The women are the most doleful and disgusting looking of their sex." (Corporal Zenas T. Haines quoted in William C. Harris, ed.,* In the Country of the Enemy, *(University Press of Florida, 1999), 75. This attitude was not restricted to northerners, and a Virginia soldier who was in the area around the same time described the inhabitants as "grossly ignorant squalid and such specimens of humanity [as] I have never met before in all my travels. . . . Children and pigs abound at every homestead and beauty among the ladies is unheard of." (John T. Ellis, quoted in Barrett,* Civil War in North Carolina, *158.)*

To some degree Frank's dismay can be attributed to unfamiliarity. Accustomed to the normal spatial layout of New England towns, centered on the meetinghouse, he considers the more diffuse southern arrangement as a violation of the natural order. Similarly, the deplorable inability of the Southerners to manage oxen may be due to the fact that horses or more likely mules, which the inhabitants were accustomed to use, had been drafted into military service. Oxen were not common draft animals in the South, as they do not work well in hot, humid conditions. Still, Frank's observations highlight the vast cultural differences between North and South and illustrate the fundamental paradox of the war: if most northerners, like Frank, despised the southern way of life, why did they wage such a determined struggle to restore the unsatisfactory relationship with their degraded former countrymen?

In venturing to the Outer Banks, Frank encountered people who were considered strange and colorful even by other North Carolinians. Northern troops who earlier in the war captured the Hatteras islands, further to the north but inhabited by similar people, registered astonishment much like Frank's. "Queer folks in this region!" exclaimed one, while others commented on women who never wore shoes (Trotter, Ironclads and Columbiads, *73).*

New Berne   February 23d

My Dear Family

In my last letter I gave a long and perhaps dull account of our visit to Bogue island, but do not remember now whether I spoke of getting shells or not. If not, you will now hear that I did get a few indifferent ones, and should I be able to get no better shall sometime send these. In this letter is a string of small ones for Etta which were gathered on the same shore. I am told that at certain tides larger ones of the same species are to be had, and I may be able at some time to get some. If I am certainly shall, as they are not only quite rare with you but are really ornamental.

There is a peculiar phenomenon on the island of which I made no mention in my last. Just on the shore which the ocean washes are high ridges of sand which the wind and waves have thrown up. Perhaps these ridges occupy a space ten rods from high water mark back, and are covered with more of less p_____ grass. The rest of the island is covered with wood, most of which is 15 or 20 feet high, but now and then a pine much taller. As you stand on the outer ridge of sand and look back on the island, you overlook the wood entirely and the sand has drifted in about the wood at its outer edge so as to cover the outskirt up to the top branches. Looking down upon it you can hardly believe that the woods are more than a kind of small bush spread out on a flat; you see the sand being filled in about the trees near you as you stand overlooking the whole, and the woods being so thick that the delusion is perfect. Pass down and through the top branches of the trees and you walk down a gradual slope of sand till you come to a land from which the trees take root. Perhaps I have not been able to describe it so as to give you any idea of its appearance, but tis the best I can do today.

As we stood there gazing over the broad ocean, heaving in her wrath with all her mighty power, mine I presume were the thoughts of the entire circle: would that my family were here to witness this scene. On the one side was a picture of the terrible struggle in which our country is now engaged. On the other was a beautiful emblem of what she was in days gone by.

You ask me to give the conversations we have and what <u>we</u> do! Do you remember Rebecca how many times you have asked to have me tell what they said at judge Brown's shop? And how little of it when I was urged to tell was interesting enough for you to listen. Now we have not much different grown by coming here. Every wife at home should be thankful should she be able to meet her husband <u>no more</u> than when he left. God helping me, my wife and family shall receive me as I was. I did not promise much more. I hope too that each dear wife in Brimfield may be made (& I believe they will) happy in the thought their husbands have trod the path where temptation and vice beset them at each turn with no additional scars on their souls.

Of what we <u>do</u>, you must know that most of it is the same round of duty we had at Camp Banks. And when we have anything extra I have written home so minutely about it that each letter has seemed to me so dull that I have been tempted to burn it, and nothing but the fact that it was my handwriting with my name affixed and contained the assurance that I was well and had still a dear longing for my home has prevented; but I must write something though it be dull & stupid and so keep on.

Now I am to give you an acct[sic] of a grand jubilee in which your friend took a prominent part. The Lieutenants have a man to do their chores, and for the sake of paying part for his services I have had him cut my wood and wash the dishes for my mess. We board him with a negro family close by the camp. Friday evening there was a wedding at the same house & Saturday they had the wedding party, to which Lt. Howe & myself were invited—or rather told that we could come if we wished.

Well we accepted the chance and about eight we, namely Lt. Howe, Tom, Bill, Cheney N., A. Newton[1], Frank R. Cook & myself, walked into the mansion of our sable brothers and were invited to take seats on the side of the room where they had blocked up a plank for the accommodation—at any rate it was for somebody's accommodation, and we used it.

One after another, the visitors gathered in, "some in rags, some in tags & some in velvet gowns," some in checks, some in stripes, Darkies in all shades of pants, vests, neck stocks, pins and rings, dresses for all seasons, some that probably had been cleaner, and a few that were decent, if not pretty. As a general thing I think that the girls were not of that class which any of the dear ones at home need feel jealous of. In the whole crowd only two that I took any fancy to: one of those was a woman who has had 12 children, has 9 living. By the way I have since engaged her to wash our dishes and clothes, by the advice and with the consent of Ira, Tom & George; the other a girl as handsome in the face as the Rider girl, Julie. Most of them were buxom lasses as could desire to see, and wore hoops of fair circumference. The Gentlemen darkies, I hardly think I should feel in the least jealous if I knew you were doing your prettiest to entertain them.

Well, after a long time, in which the ladies exhibited a fair amount of bashfulness at appearing in the presence of commissioned officers, the dance commenced. No mortal can describe the dance in words, but I think tis the very great essence of dancing. Of one thing there [is] no lack, and that is motion: from the crown to the heel, tis all dance. The figures are easily understood, simply enough. For musicians they had only two or three men to sing & spat their hands. Really now, there was something so exciting about the performance that Tom was soon the most excited of all the musicians and I was so stirred up as to dance one figure with the good lady with the small family of whom I spoke.

---

[1] Alfred Newton, according to a subsequent reference, though no soldier with this name in Co. G or from Brimfield is recorded.

They treated with wedding cake, which I called good. On the whole, we had a grand time and I think you will all understand how exciting the whole scene was and what effect it had on us weak mortals when I tell you that Frank R. Cook actually was so wrought upon as to call one of the ladies sister. And I actually caught him standing behind two of the girls who sat close together, with his head between them alternately turning his face to one & the other in such proximity to theirs that had his whiskers been as warm as they look they would certainly have had their faces scorched. Lt. Howe seemed to me to be the most completely in his element as anyone there, but at a time when even Uncle Cheney appeared like a boy of seventeen. Tis difficult to tell who is enjoying most.

We returned in good order, without the loss of a single man, after receiving the shot of their heaviest batteries for 4 hours of more, and feel that we are getting to be veterans. Now is not that just as good & better than to detail or try [to] detail the conversation we have. For the life of me I could not tell a word I said to any of them. I did not have any bad nonsense with any of the Ladies, nor do I know that any of the boys did, though one of the ladies said that my Lt. was courting the girls in the back room, but I guess he did not carry it very far.

If you really desire I will try to keep a memorandum of the talk for a single day, and I know one day's talk will be sufficient. For amusement we sometimes play a game of whist or some other game with cards. For matters of duty we have the necessary drill and camp duty and the sick to visit, for I make it a rule that some one of the officers shall visit the Hospital each day.

Both of the Lts. are ready and willing to do right for the comfort of the men, although I think Lyon takes most interest in looking after their welfare. He is, so far as I have been able to discover, a very conscientious man, of firm purpose in that which he deems right; is universally liked by the co. probably more so than he would be had he the entire command, though I think that if that was the case he would command the respect of all those whose respect is worth one's having. We get along very peacefully and the company [is] generally esteemed, if for nothing else, at least for its general good behavior. I have been frequently told that the field officers considered the company if not the best drilled worth more for duty than any other Co. in the regiment. I know that the surgeon thinks tis best taken care of. In spite of all the care we have sick men, eight now in the Hospital, no one of which will probably be able to do camp duty during our term of service. One that I feel never will see New England again (Foskit of Monson). The rest I think will, though Lyman Parker has been the sickest man in the regt. that lived, he is getting along as are all the rest but Foskit.

Now a word or two about the shirts. Tis no use to try to wear the wollen[sic] shirts here, as they are washed: the one that I bought is too short at both ends and too small every way. And I must have something. Alfred Newton has some made of a kind of Nankin which he likes and so do I. Will you go to Monson and get some of the same and find what shape they make them and make me some like his immediately. Send them in a box by express to me. Do it as soon as you can for tis a continual annoyance to wear these. Make the collar big enough. Send also a neck tye[sic], for this dog collar I shall cast off when it get[sic] a little farther along. If there is nought else to send anything you can send such other things as you like. Send no cooked food but cake however. Again let me ask you to do it quickly, for besides the vexation I have in wearing these tis getting quite warm and I think a little less wool would be quite as pleasant.

Another mail has come and no letter from home. Tis a little provoking, Rebecca, the third mail from the North since I came here with no letter from you. How is it every other man in the Co. has a letter regularly, I always have to wait. The next time I fail—well guess I wont say that.

Spring has already come and in the gardens are the Daffodils in bloom. I hope the spring will bring a relief to you. Am quite certain it will not to me, for when the time comes to sow the grain I fear I shall feel more like being in the field than in my tent. However I shall get along with as best I can.

[Subsequent page(s) apparently missing.]

Most northern soldiers had little previous contact with African Americans, and those would not have been recently released from slavery. Even among the relatively small number of northern soldiers who held strong abolitionist sentiments, few were prepared to treat blacks as equals or have social relationships with them on that basis. Thus, almost all comments on the subject by Yankee troops, even the more enlightened ones like Frank, come across as racist by today's standards of political correctness. In this letter, Frank, while still regarding the freedmen he encounters with a certain amusement, is more able to see them as fellow humans and individuals. From the black perspective, accustomed to generations of concealing their most meaningful activities from their masters, the invitation to northern soldiers whom they barely knew displays considerable trust. Confederate soldiers would have been horrified and enraged by the scene Frank describes.

By way of contrast, what may be a more conventional opinion was expressed by a member of the 46th in a letter to the Springfield Republican*. This unidentified correspondent declared "The soldiers are getting of the opinion that this is too much of a 'nigger war,' and if that is the case, ask why the lovers of the black race—those who clamor so loudly about their welfare—do not head their followers and lead them into the enemy's country to conquer or be conquered . . . and not stay at home and tell what they would do if they were down here. Further, if the desire is so very great to put down the rebellion, why don't government arm every black man able to carry a musket and set him forth to earn his and his brethren's freedom with the shedding of their blood instead of killing so many* *whites, whose blood is nearly as valuable.*"[1]

Frank shows some exasperation that Rebecca, probably searching for topics of conversation, keeps asking for accounts of his routine daily activities, while at the same time he is expending great effort to provide vivid descriptions of unusual events. There is also an element of sexual tension discernible in these letters. Even a mature couple like Frank and Rebecca, with a candid relationship, have difficulty addressing their physical longings openly and sublimate their desires in the form of teasing about flirtations.

[1] Feb. 10, 1863. The writer went on to assert that the war could not be won. It must have required great dedication to the ideal of a free press on the part of the editors to publish this, since they were generally strong supporters of the administration. As if to compensate, a more patriotic letter, with a more favorable estimation of the Negro regiments, was printed shortly afterward.

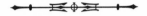

Brimfield   Mar 1st

My dear Frank

Does not the date of this letter seem nice? Only to think that we have really lived through the so dreaded winter. Yes I certainly think you all ought to feel proud of your noble darlings at home, that we have had ambition to keep out of the chimney corner and appear when among people worthy [of] the love of the noble ones who are away, however weak and womanish we may be now and then, when alone.

They begin to talk of a draft in April, but Jim seemed to think they could never do it, says things will remain pretty much as they are till another Presidential Election and then things will be patched up and slavery would remain as before the war and seemed very much surprised when I asked Sam Brown (he was talking with him) if he wanted peace on those terms? and he said no. Can it be that is the sentiment now in New England? and said he thought your opinion as regarded the slave had changed since you went South and quoted what you wrote to Charles respecting the conversation you had with some, on your return from Goldsborough.

I received your letters yesterday dated the 11th and 18th, so the first was a little behind in news. I had begun pretty sad about not getting any letters with the rest and do not think their length quite made up, for I heard through all that the Capt. was well and enjoying himself, so you must know I was rather unhappy, and it effected me so much that the first salutation of several was "What is the matter?

How pale you are, you sick"? What is the reason of some being delayed so and others coming directly through.

I am thankful you have a chance of improvement in the way of seeing different places but do not I beg of you be too risking about going on water or into the country without sufficient guard. I hope the time will yet come that I can enjoy some such jaunt with you.

Dr Witter has had an arrival at his house of a little Miss Witter. I am thankful it is not another bouncing Dr. Have not heard any particulars, presume all are doing well. Rather think you will find the Dr a converted man when you get home, as little Willy who is spending the winter with her folks says "He shall buy his papa a big chair and a great big Bible just as soon as he gets home."

I said, I think, in my last that Walter was going to unite with the church, but I believe it was considered not advisible[sic]. Mrs N. Hubbard, Mr and Mrs A. Bliss, Minnie and Walter are all in Boston.[1] They are a good deal worried about Mr Bliss. They say he will never be fit for business again.

Do you know anything about when your time is out. There are as many different times set as there are families who have friends gone, and I want to know from head quarters the exact time.

We expect Anna B.[2] tomorrow but I am afraid she will find it rather dull. I have been thinking she could ride some as it was getting good going, but it has been snowing all day and we shall have slosh again. We have a great many storms Sundays, at least it seems so.

Rebecca thinks she can't write tonight and has gone to bed. She has had a busy week, as they are getting ready for an exhibition of the Band of Hope and they are disposed to put a good share on her. Mr Allen was in Friday evening, and I was speaking of not wanting them out evenings, for I was afraid it would make them sick. "Well, do take care of them, for if they are sick we can't have the exhibition, that's all".

Monday afternoon Ellen Shaw and her baby were here.[3] In the evening the committee met, also two dialogues, and with the noise and interest in their pieces I was as tired as I care to be. Tuesday Laura came and sat with me nearly all the afternoon. Directly after tea Mr Barrows came begging and sat a long time. Before he left, Eunice came in, in a few minutes Mrs Morse, and she had hardly got her things off and Mr Hyde came and they all spent the evening. Had as pleasant time as we could without Frank. Mr H. said he should write as soon as all the schools closed telling you of the joys and sorrows of a school committee.

[1] Aaron Bliss, born 1814, and his wife Almeda Vincent. They had a daughter Marion M., who married C. Walter Brown in April 1863.
[2] The identity of this guest is uncertain, but since she came from the eastern part of the state, she may have been related to Francis Bird of Walpole.
[3] Ellen Paige married John Shaw Apr. 30, 1861, when she was 18. They had a daughter Caroline, born Mar. 26, 1862.

Wednesday Eunice and I visited in the afternoon the High School. They have reading, rehearsing, Gymnastics and compositions each Wednesday. Mr Palmer is liked very much.[1] After school we called on Mary W. Tarbell[2], went home and in a few minutes Miss Drinkwater came and staid to tea. Had been through tea but a few minutes and Mrs Calvin Upham came to spend the night. Thursday Dea Paige and Mary came to have a talk with me about their affairs. Mary came before meeting and I told her I knew of nothing then but I should be alone and she said they would both come after meeting, but during the time Mrs Tom came and took off her things so they only sat a few minutes. I promised to go up as soon as I could, but I have one of my hard colds and I do not know when that will be. And beside those I have mentioned, Mrs Charley, Mrs Sam Brown, and the old lady Tarbell. Now ain't that enough for one week with all my work to do. Mrs Charley and the old lady have gone to Fiskdale for a few days.

The bell rang long ago and I guess here is as much as you will have time to read. Now be a good boy and stay at home Sundays and I shall enjoy myself very much more than to think of you as roving all over that awful country of Squars[squaws] and Turpentine, but we were very much amused with your visit and excursion in general.

Poor fellow, I wish I could run down and bring you a shirt or two. I would start a box if it were not so uncertain about your being there long enough to get it, but she must have exchanged your shirt. It would not shrink like that would it. But I must go to bed, for sitting up late makes folks look old you know and I shall have my hands full to get back where I was when you went away without late hours, though a good share of the winter I have sat up till eleven and after, for I could not go to sleep. But I am getting to do up my thinking in the day time.

Good night. Now don't forget about the Sundays and if I thought you could find any one to give it to you I would send you all a kiss.

Your own Rebecca

Competent northern housewives like Rebecca suffered pangs at not being able to supply the needs of their distant soldiers as they would have at home. "In countless letters, soldiers' wives and mothers and sisters insisted that their menfolk tell them what they needed" (Silber, Daughters of the Union, *178).*

[1] Charles Palmer was the principal of Hitchcock Free Academy.
[2] Probably Mary W. Tarbell, born 1815, daughter of Elijah Tarbell, Jr.

Monson   Mch. 16, '63

Capt. Lincoln.

Dear Sir—

A box of canned fruit was sent to you from this place last Friday by Adams Express.

It was contributed by Mrs. Kittredge, wife of Rev. Mr. K. & forwarded at the expense of the "Ladies P.A. Socy." designed for hospital use, or for you to appropriate at your discretion, where it is needed most.

I write as Sec. of the soc'y. as the ladies thought it advisable to inform you by letter of its being sent.

My little girl of 5 yrs. <u>insists</u> on <u>her love</u> accompanying this note. I told her you did not know her & I could not write it but with tears she says "Why Mamma, he is a soldier, isn't he? & <u>I love all the soldiers</u>," so I tried no more to dissuade her from her kind thoughts & wishes & promised to do as she desired me.

Hoping the box will be rec'd. & that it will do its mite towards giving "aid & comfort" to <u>loyal</u> ones in your midst, I remain.

Very truly Yours.

A.M. Field—-

[*Detached, undated page*]

You say nothing of what Mr. Paige's folks are going to do. Did he sell his place? Should the note be paid you will inform me immediately. If H.F.B. knows of any good place to loan the money he can do so. C M[?] Wood will probably pay the interest on his note on the first of Apr., F.W.B. on the 5th, and the interest is due on the Paige note the 4th of May. Should the interest on these notes all be paid you must keep a good acct[sic] of the whole. Has S.W. Brown paid his note for the Heifer? Did Bemis of Warren pay the money for the difference in oxen? Look to all these things.

I now intend to go to Ohio with you in the fall if everything comes 'round safely. There is yet some doubt when our time is out. My own opinion is that it will be the 30th of July, though there are those here who feel confident that it will be in June. It seems a long time to you, what do you think it is with me? I am not only deprived of your society, of which Heaven knows I ought to think as much of as you can of mine, but the children are far away too. And we have for the most part a dull routine of duty to occupy ourselves with. A few friends, the letters from home, with the consciousness of trying to do my duty sustain me in my efforts.

Mrs. Prouty says when I talk with her of the relative hardship of the soldier and his wife at home that she believes after all that the dear women suffer most. I spent the eve with her again last night and she seemed almost to wish she had the power to change the order of the seasons so she might strike out summer in New Berne and thereby abate the necessity of her returning north. And I tell the Lt. that if he waits for her to say when it is too warm to stay here august will certainly find her here. Who can blame the woman. She returns, if at all, to spend the summer with his folks. And although good people, you will readily understand that some other house might be so pleasant.

I had a letter from Jim by the last mail. His tone is entirely changed in regard to the war since he was out to see you. And he now feels that the Rebs must be put down by force of arms, says the tone in N.Y. is altogether different from what it was a month ago, or has ever before been. And it now seems as though they mean to have a united North. God grant they may. The rebs have fed their hopes on the division the <u>Copperheads</u>[1] at the north were going to make. And when that hope fails, if our folks act with determination and promptly, I believe the monster may be crushed in a short time.

I have a letter to write the good ladies of Monson so must say good by to you.

Frank

[1] Copperheads were northerners who opposed the war and wanted to make peace with the South.

Although the Lincoln marriage had many features of a partnership, Frank's absence transferred unaccustomed burdens of financial management to Rebecca, in what Silber calls an "ambivalent assumption of economic authority" (Daughters of the Union, 55). These new responsibilities were made more difficult by inflation and other economic distortions brought on by the war. At that time, especially in rural areas, people did not customarily turn to banks for personal loans. Instead, an elaborate network of personal financial obligations existed, in which men loaned money at interest and took mortgages from one another. While based ultimately on trust, these transactions were carefully recorded and were treated as assets or liabilities for estate or property tax purposes.

Dear Frank

It has come to be the middle of the month and it seems but a little while to look back since the first of Jan. But it seems an age to look to the first of July. We have fine sleighing now and thursday night was five degrees colder than any night this winter and what should our hog do but have a party. She had nine pigs but only four are alive, and two of those Lewis brought into the house and did not think they would live to get in, but we warmed some milk and he rubed[sic] them, and soon got them so they breathed nicely. I sat up with him till after eleven, and he said after a while he laid down on the lounge, leaving the pigs in a basket, hardly expecting they would be alive in the morning (one had been injured, had a deep gash in the side, so he put on a plaster of Adams salve). In just three quarters of an hour he was waked by a capering over the floor and a loud grunting and there was his wounded pig! And he took it out to the pen, but the other we kept in the house till last night; but I assure you Lewis worked and watched faithfully as he did not go to bed for two nights.

Henry Brown has been in this evening. He says you owe him a letter, but that he should write if there was anything to write. I suppose Sam has written all about town meeting. I have scolded every man I have seen since town meeting. We started the box thursday morning and suppose it went to you in the saturday steamer. Anna is with us yet, she took Rebecca and Etta up to Mr Paiges Monday and they were to call at Mrs Cooks on their way home, and you [know] the gravel walk up to the door has some rather large stones. Well, they were covered with snow and so the girls thought my caution quite unnecessary, and just as they were at the door hit a stone and broke the whiffletree, so they took out the horse and led her home. So they have to bear a laugh from everyone that comes in, but Lewis took an old one and went directly down for the sleigh.

Tuesday I had to go to Palmer to get some cloth to match your shirt but could not, so Eunice says you must put on the thick one first and wear it as long as you can. I took over my <u>children</u>, and Mrs Tom took Eunice H., and we went to the Alms house, then through the village home. When we started for home my horse was for getting <u>home</u>, so I let her come and although we had four, and only two of them we were home long enough to spread the table and cook oysters before they came. They stayed the afternoon, and Eunice til evening, and we nearly made your shirt.

The next day people came to bring the things, and <u>Boss</u> came at four to pack it. He and Mrs Charley were here to tea, got one all packed and Mrs Morgan came in the edge of the evening with more than we had allowed room for, and then he took them all out and put them in a larger one, but I left him in his happiness and went to the society. Had not been this winter and probably shall not go again. It was at Mrs Morses, and I wanted Anna to go out once, so we went and had quite a pleasant time. [*Paragraph of news about unidentified people, probably in Walpole, deleted.*]

There, Anna has just gone to bed. Now I shall sit and look at Frank a good long while. If you want any thing send for it, for I did not know what more to send. The box came (the express bill I mean) to $5.50. There was a sleigh ride yesterday of Herrings getting up and he invited the war widdows[sic] to go with him but no one went but Mrs Sherman.

Your Rebecca

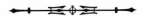

Newbern   March 16, 1863

Mrs. F.D. Lincoln

Your husband requested me to write & inform you where & what he is &c. At 5 ¼ o'clock the 13 inst Our Brigade was ordered off on a march immediately—they were off in a very few minutes. They went out some ten miles & returned the next day at 12 M. At 5 PM were ordered off again over the same rout[sic] & have been gone almost two days. The reason for this march is to find out if the Rebs were coming in force on this road, as it was reported they intended to attack the place from all sides. If they found a force they were to fall back & draw them on to make an attack on the place so that we could bring them within range of the forts. We heard from the Reg this morning. They had seen no enemy & I presume the Regiment will be ordered back before long. The Rebs did attempt something on the other side of the Neuse River, but one little fortification & the gun boats made them skeedaddle pretty soon. Our side did not lose a man. I do not believe we shall see any force to amount to any thing—it would take a very large force to take Newbern & no one here now expects an attack.

Your husband was usually well when he left here, but I presume they have had a pretty hard time. The roads are muddy. He had some letters yesterday & I think some of them from you & I have sent them to him. We have had no new cases of sickness since he wrote you & all the boys in the hospital are getting better. Lyman Parker is gaining very fast. I think Charles Alexander does not gain as fast but is still gaining. I write this letter as your husband sent to me to do before another mail goes. I was told mail closes in ten minutes at the camp. This is singular if it so, for all mails have been advertised here some hours before they leave. If the mail has closed here I will carry it to the city office.

Truly yours in great haste
G C Homer

<u>Regimental Order No. 42</u>   New Berne   March 5, 1863

In pursuance to orders from Head Quarters this Regiment will be ready for marching with 3 days cooked rations at one hour's notice.

<u>Regimental Order No. 43</u>   New Berne   March 6, 1863

The ordinary camp duties, drills etc. will continue as usual but commanders of companies will see that their men are supplied constantly with three days' cooked rations and are in perfect readiness to march at an hour's notice.

New Berne   March 17th 1863

My Dear Rebecca

There is something very singular about the letters you send to me & receive from me. You say that the other folks get theirs two or three days before you get those I send, and I am always among the last to get mine from you. It has happened several times that we have had one mail follow another in two or three days, and at such times most of the Brimfield boys would get theirs in the first. Mine come <u>from</u> <u>you</u> invariably in the last. The last two mails we had, I received letters from my friends, from Mr. Hyde among the number in the first, but those from you came in the last three days after, and in your letter of the 1st you speak of Mr. Hyde's being in and of his intention of writing—rather late news as I had had the letter in my pocket for three days.

On the other hand, tis full as strange that you should not receive my letters as early as the rest, for there has been no mail from here till now that I have not sent one or more letters to you; and if others have sent more they certainly have not sent in advance of mine. <u>Now</u> for the first time two mails have left here, which will be of no use to you, and however much I may regret it 'twas impossible to avoid your sad disappointment. For more than a week we have looked for a mail, a part of which time I have been away, charging George if the mail came and returned before I came home to write you, but none came.

Friday at Dress Parade we all had an invitation from the Col. of the 25th to join them in celebrating the anniversary of the battle of New Berne[1] the next day, and we had hardly time to signify our joy with the invitation when a courier rode in with the news that "the Rebs were coming down on us like the Devil" (as he expressed it). We were ordered to be ready in light marching order to go immediately to meet them on the Trent road (<u>light</u> marching order means all we can carry on our backs). In a half hour we were ready and started about six to go as we supposed about 7 miles. I charged George again about writing you should there be a chance to send a mail before we returned. We pressed on till about 8 when we came to the place where the Rebs had attacked our outpost, composed of four companies of the 25th.

The enemy had fallen back a little to rest for the night. After a consultation among the Cols[sic], four companies of our Regt., Co's B, C, E & K were ordered forward a half mile to take a cross road which led to a point where a company of our cavalry were stationed to protect them if need be and prevent if we could the Rebs from outflanking us.

So we tramped on through the mud & water, some times knee deep till midnight, when we came to the point where we were to rest for the night. Luckily there were buildings & tents with good fires for our use. Resting a few moments two companies were set as pickets and myself & Capt Kingsbury[2] were ordered to relieve them alternately in two hours. So our boys had a chance at the fire for two hours, which you will believe we enjoyed as we rarely enjoy sitting by a fire.

At 2 I took out the company, all in good spirits, and I think they never have stood guard two hours since we came more contentedly than they did that night. Twas a beautiful night as you ever beheld. And as I stood looking at the waning moon, I took at least a melancholy pleasure in meditating on my situation here, for the happy thought would come that the dear ones were resting securely at home with no thought of the danger that threatened us, and although my reason told me that our situation was perilous, still I was strangely impressed with the conviction that we should come out safely.

At sunrise in the morning there commenced a heavy cannonading which we knew must be at New Berne. And we soon were convinced that we had been drawn one way to fight while the rats tried the game of taking or trying the force we left. We listened & speculated while the roar of cannon grew louder and more constant till 8, when the courier came with the news that the Rebs had appeared in large force before New Berne and demanded its surrender, that the 46th were ordered back to the city, and adding as a bit of pleasant news to us that we could not with safety go back to join our regt by the rout[sic] we came, as the rebs had cut off our retreat in that direction, so we must make our way back as best we could.

Well after marching two hours or more through the swamps we came out on to the main road with the enemy in our rear, glad enough to know that if we were to fight we were going to have a fair chance. Arrived here about 1, tired enough I assure you, having traveled 24 miles in nineteen hours and stood as pickets 9 during that time. Found four letters one from ____, one David Parker from Mr Hyde and a big good one from my old friend Sylvester[?] Crawford. Ate my dinner and took the letter from A to Prouty's, staid there till 4 and came back just in season to hear the order to fall in for another march in light marching order, rations for a day.

---

[1] The battle of New Bern took place March 14, 1862.
[2] Capt. Daniel E. Kingsbury of Holyoke, commander of Co. B.

My God, I was about ready to give out, for besides the fatigue of the previous march, I had slept none for two nights, but go we must, and we tramped till eight and stretched ourselves in the open field to rest our weary limbs by the side of good fires on a gentle slope. A few rods in front were the regt we came out with.

I got but little sleep as there was an alarm about mid night and we were all roused. The Col. was so anxious that we might be caught napping that I did not lie down again till after breakfast. Then for the first time for three days I got a good sleep. We stayed there all day on Sunday, one of the most delightful days you ever see. I declare it seemed sackrilegious[sic] almost to be arrayed in the trappings of war on such a day, when it seemed as though the infinite Father was trying to show us how pleasant were the paths of peace.

About 12 the mail came, two letters from home, one the last one giving the acct[sic] of the Exhibition and of the arrival of our dear friend Anna. I have often said it, but it will bear repeating, you know but little how much the mail does to lighten our burdens, how much joy there is in getting a letter from home. A letter with nothing in it in the way of news, nothing that would interest us for a moment were we there, would be quite a treasure; but when they come bearing the accounts of the happy times all are having at home, they really seem to give me as much happiness almost as I could enjoy were I there. Hope there will be pleasant weather so that Anna can enjoy riding over the hills and through the pleasant valleys of Brimfield. Oh if I could be there for a few days and feel that I was not neglecting my duty! But this is depressing.

We staid on the ground where we encamped Saturday night till near five Sunday eve when we started on and marched till dark when we encampted[sic] in one [of] the most beautiful groves I have seen in the South, a grove of pines standing a few feet apart about thirty feet high, the earth carpeted with the leaves thereof, no brush, where the rebs had built bough houses enough for us to sleep under (they had occupied the same the eve before).

We had a good sleep and started the next morning at sunrise, the 46th in avance[sic]. About nine were met by some of the cavalry, who said that the reb cavalry were in camp about two miles ahead, in large force. We were drawn up in a battle line, while a few of our cavalry were sent ahead to try to entice their force back for us to shoot, but the cowardly devils ran as soon as they saw our boys coming. So after waiting two hours we started for home, knowing well that it was of no use to chase such long legs, and arrived here about 4, having marched better than 20 miles since morning.

And now we are notified that we are to pull up stakes and move to Plymouth to protect the negro's[sic] while they build some forts at that place. We shall probably go Thursday of this week and remain six or eight weeks. On one acct. I had rather remain here, viz. the mail does not come directly from the North to Plymouth but comes to New Berne & then back there, so that letters will be a week or more on the way generally, and of course you will suffer the same inconvenience in getting our letters to you. Tis hard but we must submit. I cannot tell if the danger be greater or not, but we probably shall have no marching to do there. The danger, if any will be from an attack. I have heard that P. is a pleasant place & healthy. Of that I will write when I get there. Tell Etta I shall not enlist again till I see her and have a fair understanding about it.

Now a word about business. Lewis had better get as much as two and a half tons of plaster[1] and sow one ton on the west side of the house pasture, one on the farther pasture, and use the rest for planting. Tell him to sow over the flat on the west end of the further lot and use the rest above the barway. If you have no money and he has or can get it, tell him I will pay him for the use if he will get it, as I have recd[sic] no pay yet, nor do I know when I shall. He must sell stock so as to keep no more than the value of nine cows in home lot & five in the other. If there be no other chance, let him sell at auction. He will use his own judgment as to <u>what</u> he will sell & how, also how & what to plant. Assure him that I shall trust entirely to him and will find no fault if he does as best he can.

I have just learned that our time is not out till the thirtyeth of July, so there is but little prospect of his being relieved till some time next fall. Should he be drafted he may make the plea that he has a widowed mother with her two children dependant on him for support, and I think that will clear him. Should he need any advice on any particular thing about the farming[?] he _____ with, so far as I can judge he is doing as I expected he would. You will engage Mr. Morris[?] to look at the trees a little this spring and have him set some pear trees, some standards in the old garden and dwarfs in the front yard. He may be the judge of the kind to set. Have him look at the trees in the lot by C.L. [Lumbard] to see if anything is needed there. Lewis will scrub the trees with the whale oil soap suds as you have seen me do it with a scrub broom.[2] Tell him that a lowering day is best to do it in. Have him make the engagements for doing the haying in season. I do not expect that he will do just as I should, but I know that he will be faithful and trust will never regret coming to my assistance.

I am to take tea with Mrs. Prouty today. They seem to regret my going away. She some expects to come north in the course of a month.

[Written along margins of previous pages.]
If she should, you will go to Spencer to visit her. The boys are all getting along well. Tell Dr. W. that I think the name is a good one for the baby but I think that the name alone will be <u>hardly</u> sufficient to accomplish his object.

I can tell him if he needs instruction. You will continue to direct as you have till you hear from me again.

---

[1] Plaster of Paris (gypsum), a form of calcium sulfate used to improve soil fertility by reducing acidity.
[2] To protect fruit trees by removing overwintering insects. As late as 1900, soap made from sediment produced in refining whale oil was used as an insecticide.

[*Continues on front first page.*]
I have had a letter from Jim Hartshon written in good spirits and flattering to me. In it he sent his picture. Tis a good one, and he looks therein as though he was enjoying life. Says the Whiskey Club have had no regular meeting since I left but are waiting anxiously for my return.[1] After we remove I shall try to answer some of the letters and my friend Mr Hyde among the rest. Excuse the bungling[?] style of this letter for my head is full of kettle drums.

Yours Frank

The stunning Confederate victory at Fredericksburg altered the strategic situation in the East, relieving pressure on Richmond and allowing the South to take the initiative. These effects spilled over onto the eastern North Carolina theater, which was always subsidiary to the main action in Virginia. The Confederates strengthened their forces in the region and placed them under command of General D.H. Hill. As a native North Carolinian with a reputation for competence and aggressiveness, Hill would seem to have had an incentive to free the state of its northern occupiers. His manpower was now approximately equal to Foster's and he had greater freedom of movement, but a fatal paralysis seemed to afflict southern efforts in the region.

*Hill planned an effective attack from several directions on New Bern, but, as Trotter describes, he "was never sure, from one hour to the next, exactly how far he wanted to push things" (*Ironclads and Columbiads*, 193). Frank's description of the movements of the 46ᵗʰ Mass. is accurate, as is his account of the major attack on the town, with a small fort (Fort Anderson, after its commander) and gunboats holding back a hesitant rebel assault. However, he treats the engagement lightly and minimizes the danger to the Union position, either because he did not fully understand the situation, or to avoid alarming Rebecca.*

Frank introduces a rather startling aside, in admitting that he was considering extending his military service. It is doubtful that he would joke about something so serious. Although he had freely criticized many aspects of military life, it must have held some attraction, despite the fact that it was harming his financial position and the management of his farm, as well as separating him from his family.

[1] A James G. Hartshorn was born in Walpole in 1815 and married there in 1841 (Walpole Vital Records), which suggests that the Whiskey Club was a group of Walpole acquaintances. Recall that in his Feb. 11 letter Frank says "I sacrificed the society of friends such as few ever have to come to Brimfield."

New Berne   March 20th 1863

Dear Rebecca

I should have told in my last letter perhaps more fully the the[sic] force that made the attack on New Berne and the result of their efforts, though as to the first there is little but conjecture, and when we come to guessing why, we guess very differently. There are however some points known which give some clue to help us in forming a judgment. In the first place it is known that they had 18 guns in position in front of us the night we first went out, for on the field they occupied the position of the pieces was plainly marked. Again our cavalry saw their cavalry encampment the last morning we were out and they judged it to contain 700 at least. Now the infantry to support such a force of cavalry & artillery would not be less than 10,000 under ordinary circumstances, and Lt. Lyon had a talk with an old man who lived on the road and he thought there were as many as 13,000.

It seems strange that they should not have advanced on us when we were in front of them if they had any thing like the force, for we had not more than 1300 in all, and no reason can be assigned for it but on the supposition that they were ignorant of our force and supposed it to be much larger than it was. The General in command forbad the firing of the artillery lest they should discover our position and strength, so we probably gained a reputation with them for power, as some people do for wisdom by holding their tongues. So you see that had I been as noisy as is my wont I perhaps would have been in Richmond tonight. Are you not glad that even military power is able to keep me still in the presence of an enemy!

Well, in the move[?] in the direction we went the result was simply this, they used a deal of ammunition uselessly, for they did not hurt a man of ours. We made some long and weary marches, killed a man or two and wounded some few others, and they ran away. In the attack on the city we know what the few prisoners tell us of their force and that is all, except that the field they occupied in its appearance after the battle would lead one to believe that they told the truth.

New Berne is on the left bank of the Neuse, coming up. The right bank is occupied by more or less Rebs all the way. Just opposite of the city is a point from which Gen. Foster feared they might attempt to shell us, and about two months since he placed a regiment on that point and commenced a fort under the protection of the gun boats. We (the 46th) were on the bank just opposite the site of the fort and were removed to be out of reach of the enemy guns, should they attempt to drive the force from the work. The fort was just ready for the guns when the Rebs made their attack, expecting to take the fort, plant their pieces in it, and then blast away at the city while the force we went out to meet poured into us on the other side. To do this they had as near as we can learn some 8 or 10 thousand troops and eighteen pieces.

When they opened the gun boats poured the shot and shell into them with an accuracy and zeal that must have astonished them as it surprised us. And in less than 4 hours they gave it up as a bad job. How much they suffered it is not easy to tell, only this: we know that the ground occupied by their artillery was litterally[sic] covered with the missiles they sent, and we destroyed one of their guns. Not a man of ours was seriously injured. We have all sort of rumors as to who had command of their forces. The best opinion is that Gen. Hill was in front of us and Pettigrew on the other side of the River. Tom thinks that Longstreet was there, as it is supposed he came this way some ten days since. Whoever may have had command I think is well satisfied that New Berne is not to be taken without a fight that will cost dearly, and I hardly think an attempt will be made again at present.

We have our things packed and are waiting the transports to take us to Plymouth, where we are to protect the contrabands while they build some forts to protect the place. Shall probably be there some ten weeks unless driven away. Shall not probably have to make any more long marches, but may be obliged to fight to maintain our position. I am told that the Rebs have quite a force seven miles above Plymouth and a fort there. We shall have the 25th with us and shall be protected by Gun Boats in the river above Plymouth.

Could I have my choice I should stay here, for we shall have to wait our mail at least a week longer. You of course will suffer the same inconvenience. Our sick boys will be left in the Hospitals here and will miss us sadly. All the sick however but Lyman Parker are much better, and I shall leave G.H. to look after him should he live till we go, of which there is a strong doubt. Poor fellow he got along well, never one improved as he did till Sunday while we were off, when he was taken worse and sank quickly so low as to know nothing and has remained in this slipping state since. I have been each morning at sun rise to enquire after him and get the same answer each time. It grieves me sadly to think of the distress the mail must carry to his dear parents. Lyman is the only boy that I urged to come, and I can but feel that his parents will look upon my meddling in the matter as the cause of their sad loss.

Tom sends a box to his wife by express today. In it is a paper of poor shells to Etta, some that I gathered on Bogue shore. They are of little value except in the fact that I picked them with my own hands.

[Written across first page]
Also there is a pipe in the box, the root to make which I got at Roanoke Island and blocked out. Henry Lumbard finished it. You will keep it for Dea Parker to smoke in when he comes to visit you. Have Lewis set maples in the places where those died last summer if he gets time & can find them.

My respect to all. Tell the children I am promising myself a treat in music when I get home.

Yours

Frank

I send a few leaves of Holly which I picked in Roanoke. I know not if the Holly grows in N.E. but if it does they are worth keeping as come from the Island where the famous battle was fought.

Regimental Order No. 49   Plymouth   Mar. 31, 1863

Commanders of Companies are hereby ordered to ascertain and report to these Headquarters as soon as possible the names of the men who were absent on the occasion of the march of the Regiment on the Trent road on the 13th, 14th and 15th inst.—the reasons for such absence if any . . . .

*With the passage of several days, Frank has obtained fuller information about the Confederate attack at New Bern. The figure of 13,000, supported by 39 pieces of artillery, corresponds to what Gen. Foster reported to Halleck, based on information from deserters (*OR*, Ser. I, vol. XVIII, 183). Writing on March 15, Foster summarizes the affair by observing that "The enemy are retiring from an attack on this town, which was intended to have been strong, but was feeble, very feeble, in all places except on a work on the north side of Neuse River." With good reason, Barrett refers to it as "the New Bern fiasco" (*Civil War in North Carolina*, 156). Frank is correct that Hill was in overall command, with Brigadier General James J. Pettigrew in charge of the force that opposed Fort Anderson. Longstreet commanded the department of Virginia and North Carolina but was not present in North Carolina at the time. It is also true that one of the Confederate guns was lost by explosion.*

Dear Frank

I expected a letter last night, as I know you returned to Newbern several days since, but was disappointed, and Mrs Monroe[1] told Sissy almost every family who have friends there except us had one, but presume when it comes it will be a history for all to read for all look for a letter from you almost as anxiously as I do.

We are enjoying Anna's visit as well as we possibly can. Some of us go to ride nearly every day. Monday we called up to Mrs Morgan's. She was going to a party in Warren that evening given to Dr Hastings, who was home on a furlough.[2] She was brim full of happiness, as her sister was at home also, and she is a very lovely looking lady and the Dr thinks so too. When I got home I found A. Smith. He took tea and spent the night with us. Poor fellow, his health is very poor, a general weakness of the system and a hard cough, though he says it is nothing but a cold. He does not speak as encouragingly of Hospitals as you do.

In the evening Mr Wyles came in, but I do not remember a word he said, for it was regular <u>Wyles talk</u>, and Anna said after he was gone "What a silly old fool he is," and it is so I think. He grows very childish, or else it is because I see more of him than I used to, but he says the same things over and over, so I know when he begins just what is coming.

Tuesday there was an Installation at Warren, so as it was very fine sleighing Eunice Knight, Anna, and I went over. Mr Perkins gave the minister his charge and it was <u>grand,</u> and in it he said that they might have all the advantages of books, seminaries, and every accomplishment, but if there was not a <u>man</u> behind the pulpit it would do no good. By that he meant, he said, a person who knew what he believed and <u>dared</u> utter it. The sermon was by Mr Jagers' brother in law but it was not much, and Perkins shone all the more.

Coming home we were just behind Mr Hyde, and we fairly flew, it was such nice smooth traveling. In the evening he came down to see us, told me to remember him to you, says he begins to count the days himself to your return. We had a very pleasant time. During the evening Lewis came in with a whip, and so I asked his opinion, and he says it is a much more genteel one than the other. We lost the old one when we went to Palmer, though Lewis says we used it up.

Thursday went to meeting, called in with Eunice a few minutes, and then she went with me to call on Mrs Brown. She is a singular looking sight, perfectly red and white, but they think her old trouble is gone and I suppose the Dr had no hopes, for Mrs Witter told me what he thought ailed her three weeks before she was taken with the smallpox. If it was as he expected, there was no chance, but they say the smallpox destroys all humors, and I suppose they may term it a disguised blessing.

---

[1] Amos Munroe kept the Brimfield hotel.

[2] Dr. Joseph W. Hastings. At that time Hastings was a 1st Lt., assistant surgeon in the 21st Mass. He was promoted to major and made surgeon of the 33rd Mass. May 15, 1863, and served to the end of the war (Higginson, vol. 2, 382).

[*Continued on top margin of first page.*]
Etta says be sure and give love to Father, but she is so busy she can't write.
[*Letter ends with no signature, or an additional sheet may be detached.*]

New Berne   March 25

Dear Rebecca
   Your letter of the 15ᵗʰ came this morning. I felt I must write a few words to you though we are under orders to be ready to leave for Plymouth on a half hours notice and expect that notice at any moment. When we get there you must not expect to get word from me very regularly for a time, though I hope and have some reason to believe that some arrangements will be made whereby we shall be able to send home & receive letters from you full as directly as we do now.

   I suppose the box you sent came on the same steamer that the letter did, but if so we shall not get it for a day or two. I am not particularly anxious for anything but a shirt and suppose I can wear the one I have on (one of Ira's) till mine comes. He happens to have an extra one which is too large for him, and he has let it out to me to <u>shrink</u>. There will be no mistake about its being small enough after I have had it washed once.

   I wonder that Lewis has not his hog trained to a better sense of propriety, not to say decency, than to have such a party on such a night, but I suppose the saying is as true in regard to hogs as of human beings (there is no accounting for tastes). Lewis ought to have insisted that she should call in <u>one</u> of the <u>Dr.'s</u>. I don't know as I think as either of them would have done any better than you & Lewis did, for I think it pretty good luck to save both patients, especially as one was so badly wounded.

   And so Anna has really had a chance to ride over the Brimfield hills in a sleigh! It must have been rare sport for her, especially the ride through Cooks door yard. She will have something to laugh about for years. Luckily she did not wear false teeth.

   So you sit and watch my picture. Oh how bootless it is for you to imagine how and where I am while you gaze. That night did you dream that I was stretched out on the ground in the pine woods getting a little rest to prepare my weary legs for a march of twenty miles the next day? Could you have known that we were to chase the enemy in hope of a chance to tempt him to turn and face us, would you have gone quietly to your bed? And when a dread starts over you that perhaps the next mail may bring some terrible news to you don't you feel when a letter finally comes full of hope & confidence that you never will worry again?

I am not aware that I owe H.F.B. a letter, unless he thinks that one of his is worth two of mine. Very certain am I that I wrote him last. I am not surprised, though provoked, at his defeat. He perhaps has yet to learn that he has as good friends here as anywhere, and he certainly ought to have known that they are as persistent in their support as those at home.

Lyman Parker died last night at 12 o'clock. His body is to be sent by the first opportunity. Sad indeed must be the news to his father & mother. May all these at home must feel that the loss of one of the brave boys that came out with us is a sore loss.

[*Written across top margin, previous page.*]

Lt. Howe even expects to come north in the course of three weeks. So you may see one of my boys.

[*Written across salutation.*]

Have not much in the way of news to write. I have been a good deal of late at Lt. Prouty's. Am sorry to leave them, and I think they regret my leaving. Mrs Prouty expects to home in a short time. Should she, you must go to Spencer to see her.

Yours
Frank

Regimental Order No. 47   New Berne   Mar. 26, 1863

Pursuant to order from Brigade Head Quarters, Companies C, E, F, G, H, and K will be prepared to embark on the steamer "Escort" for Plymouth N.C. with their camp equipage at 2 o'clock P.M. this day.

Companies I and A will await in camp the return of the "Escort." The detachment left in camp will be under command of Capt. Leonard of Company I and commanders of companies will at once report him the names of their sick and convalescent to be left in Newbern.

Pvt. Lyman Parker died March 25, 1863, the first Brimfield man in Company G to die in the service. Although Frank does not openly blame himself, as in his previous letter, the young man's death weighed on his spirits and may be responsible for the morbid tone of this letter. This expresses the essential contradiction of forming militia-type units composed of men from a local area. All of them would have known many of their comrades, and as neighbors and friends would have been devoted to one another's welfare. Frank Lincoln, the elected captain, was more of a father figure than a stern commanding officer and had no hesitation in placing himself in that role. But when a man in this kind of home-town unit died, the loss was more painful, and if the regiment had ever been engaged in a heavy battle, the casualties could have been devastating. Partly for that reason, higher officers seemed to show some reluctance to commit the nine-month regiments to battle; but, as the letters reveal, the troops expected to see combat, and there were several occasions when they were at risk. As much as anything, it was the enemy's hesitancy to bring about a pitched battle that spared them.

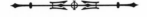

Plymouth   Apr 1st

Dear Rebecca

    I wrote you last from New Berne informing you that we expected to leave for this place soon & just after putting the letter into the office we had orders to be ready to move at 2 that day & I took the letter from the office and scratched the fact in pencil on the envelope, in accordance with that order, or as near in accordance with it as such moves are usually made in the army. We started with bag and baggage about 5 that day to move from our old camp to the boat, where we waited till after sun down before embarking. I took the time to go back to the city and bid Mrs. Prouty good by. I was very sorry to leave her, for I felt that for the next two months at least there was little probability of seeing a woman whose society I should enjoy, and I have presumed to be so familiar at Prouty's as to call in at any time and stay as long as propriety would allow. And I think they regretted to have me leave; at any rate, she so expressed herself, and it was too silly a matter for a decent woman to lie about.

    She said that if she left before I returned, Merrick [Lt. Prouty] should write me that I might inform you. I feel under obligations to them, not alone for the pleasant hours I have spent at their house, for Merrick has been with me, or I with him, to Roanoke and to the battle ground of New Berne, and beside passing away what would otherwise have been tiresome days, I was able to get through him information, which if it be worth nothing more, may be made to interest my friends at home when I come.

– 90 –

You have ever been anxious to hear me talk at home. Well I am laying up loads of talking matter, which I think if you "look me right in the eye" while I relate, you will be quite a military character, fit at least to be my orderly if I should come again. And should I be cheated out of the chance of coming by the greediness of those we deprived of the privilege of coming before, you shall be my 1st Lieut. the rest of my days.

Lt. Prouty was at the wharf, and just at dark we steamed off in a boat so crowded that the men nearly all had to stay on the upper deck night and day. Officers of course have the privilege of the cabin, and I tried to have my sergeants go below to sleep, but they thought it would be such [a] romantic thing to sleep on the deck, my efforts were in vain. It was a delightful eve, and I stood on deck till near eleven watching the fires on the shore. I know not the cause of it, but each time I have been up the sound these fires have been lit & Lt. Prouty told me that it had ever been so when he had been. Take the map and you can trace our course down the river, up through the sound, leaving Roanoke on the right.

I doubt if a more pleasant trip can be taken in a steamer on the coast. Nowhere on the route do we pass outside of the land, and I think even you would feel quite safe, provided I assured you every half mile on the route that the water was hardly over my head. I do not speak of its being pleasant on acct[sic] of the scenery, for that is not so beautiful, the shore being for the most part covered with lofty pines & cypress. But the sound is generally so quiet, and you glide along so smoothly that it is truly fascinating. There are a few points when the sand hills rise high above the tallest pines, one of these is what is called Naggs[sic] Head, curious to look at. You will perhaps recollect that old Gen. Wise was at this point sick as papers said at the time the battle was fought at Roanoke, and his son who was wounded in the battle attempted to cross over in a boat but was prevented by the fire of some of our soldiers.[1]

I was pretty well paid for my visit to the Island in the pleasure I took in pointing out to our boys the different military points on the shore of interest, which though plainly to be seen, one would not notice perhaps if they were not pointed out, or noticing would hardly understand what they were. We passed up to the mouth of Roanoke river and stopped for the second night. There was no trouble in finding enough of the boys to sleep or stay in the cabin this night, for one night in the open air in this climate at spring time of year generally is sufficient to satisfy the most curious. I said stay in the cabin, for as for sleeping even Ira, who is a

---

[1] General Henry A. Wise of Virginia commanded the defense of Roanoke Island. Though a political appointee, he had a reasonably competent grasp of the military situation. He was ill in bed at Nags Head and not present at the battle on February 8, 1862, where his son received wounds from which he died.

regular Van Winkle, could not sleep. A hundred horses directly over your head will generally contain ways & means to keep one awake if they are never so patient, and there was one nervous devil, directly over my head, who I thought did his best all night to keep up a <u>row</u>; otherwise he must have been practicing dancing for my amusement.

In the morning we started up the river a little before sun rise. Roanoke courses into the sound at its head, and yet its mouth is so secreted that one who did not know just where to look for it did not discover it till within a half mile. Tis a deep but narrow stream, so narrow at its mouth that a smart boy would be able to throw a stone across. The land on either side till you get up to this place seems lower than the river bank; indeed most of the way it looks lower than the surface of the river. Plymouth, which is eight miles from its mouth, is on the right bank (left as you come up) and is built on the bank, which here rises gradually from the wharf some 50 feet; and back of this is a level tract reaching back perhaps a half mile to the woods, beyond which I know nothing as yet and probably shall not, unless we go on an expedition, as the bush whackers[1] so invest[sic] the woods as to render it unsafe for one to travel in that direction.

Six months ago this must have been a beautiful place, for besides being laid out in regular streets at right angles accented on each side with noble elms, there are parks here of the same trees set at just the distance from each other as to make a complete shade when in full leaf. And before the raid made on it by the Rebs (which happened about the time we went to Goldsboro) the main streets were lined with pretty buildings, so it is said, and from those left and the foundations of those burned I should judge it was so. It had been from the first mainly loyal, and when the Rebs found that the 25th had been withdrawn to go on the expedition, they vented their spite on the inhabitants by burning the better part of the place.

There is however enough left for our purposes. During Saturday and Sunday we were able to get fairly established in quarters more comfortable than any we have ever had, the boys all having good bunks to sleep on, (Tom, (say to his wife) took advantage of being here alone to build him one on his own hook, stuffed with hay & husks so as to be almost as good as a sofa), which they built of good dry boards, such as no house in B. can boast of. Our company street lies in one of the parks I spoke of and will be shaded entirely. It is covered with nice turf, which is as green as your yard will be by the middle of May. Don't you wish you was here? Don't? Well, I do. We have <u>good Water</u>. Think of <u>that</u>! <u>Good</u> water! Hurrah for our side.

Well we are here how long to stay I don't know, but probably six or eight weeks. We have no drill, but the men work on the forts eight hours each other day, or fell the timber so as to give a longer range to the guns when mounted. I can but think the Company will have better health than they would have had at N.B. even if

---

[1] Irregulars and bandits who made it unsafe for Union soldiers to travel around except in large groups. They reinforced the ominous dread northerners felt in the South, with its gloomy pine forests, dismal spaces, and poverty combining to produce a sense of brooding menace.

they had had the same labor to perform, except the officers, who have here <u>nothing</u> to do, and I don't know as I should be able to do any real labor if I had it to do. Yesterday I went out three different times to try my hand at shoveling, and each time after a few minutes trial gave it up tired enough to go to bed. I mean to persevere till I am satisfied that I am completely used up.

I left G.H. at N.B. to look after our sick for a few days and gave instructions to Kinbury[1] who is in the Hospital as Nurse how to proceed after Homer came away. Orville P.[Parker]* & [Albert J.] Bixby* were also left "being a little down at the heel." Shall expect these three here in the next boat. Lt. Howe was also left, waiting for his papers to come North. He will come to B. If he gets there & will probably bring the body of L. Parker. You can send any little notion you may wish by him. But I have written enough, so Good by—Frank

[Written in pencil upside down across top of second sheet.]
I send in this two flowers taken from a vine that looks like the ivies, it covering a tomb in the burying ground as completely as a mat would and looking prettier.

[Written in pencil upside down on inside and front of first sheet.]
There is one very peculiar circumstance in relation to the trees here. More than a month ago the buds began to show signs of leaves putting out and the peach trees were in bloom, and they do not seem any farther than they did at that time and vegetation generally is about as it was a month ago. The weather is not as cold as in N. E. probably, but a good part of the time since we came tis hardly comfortable without an overcoat. I will write again by the next boat.

Yours. Frank

[Written in pencil upside down across top of last page.]
Apr 2nd. A boat is just in from N.B. bringing nothing for us except the news that Little Washington had been attacked by the same force that attacked New Berne.

---

[1] Possibly Pvt. George L. Kenney, who had been detailed as a nurse under Special Order No. 71, March 9.

<u>Regimental Order No. 50</u>   Plymouth   Mar. 31, 1863

The camp of the Regiment in honor of its highly esteemed Brigade commander Col. Horace C. Lee hereby designated and will hereafter be styled as "Camp Lee."

Frank's outline of the military situation is generally accurate. Confederates drove out the federal garrison and captured Plymouth on December 10, 1862, just as Foster was preparing his march on Goldsboro. The Confederates burned much of Plymouth because they considered the town to have Union sympathies. Frank's description shows that he sees a resemblance to New England towns.

After retreating from their inept move against New Bern in March 1863, Hill's Confederates moved against Washington, North Carolina, with what should have been overpowering force. Once again, a strange indecisiveness afflicted them. Foster displayed much more vigor and imagination, making a daring escape by boat, gathering reinforcements, and relieving the siege. It was another in a long list of bungled operations by the South in eastern North Carolina.

Dear Frank

Do you remember one year ago today? Two fasts have now passed that will never be forgotten.

Yesterday Mrs. Charles and I called down to Mr. Parkers and from the bottom of my heart, I feel for them. The fathers grief is quiet, the tears roll one after another down his cheeks, while Mrs Parker has no command at all over her feelings. You spoke of your influencing, of being afraid Mr. P. might think you influenced Lyman. He did not speak of it, but says he can not express his gratitude to you, but he does hope he shall see the day when he can thank you, for your kindness to his boy, not alone after he was taken sick, but from the first of going to Camp Banks. He used to say, "You don't know father what a kind Capt. we have got and how much he loved him," and his letters have all been the same.

The children have just come in from singing school. Olivia said her Uncle D. had been down there and talking of you, said he wanted to see you, and he should like to see you when you first met your family. He guessed you would hug that Etta for a while. But will that time ever come, it seems so long. We are having awful weather. Our <u>winter</u> has been since March came in.

Mrs. Morgan has been in this evening, went up to her fathers yesterday, came home this morning. Calvin Ward[1] paid his interest money yesterday.

Mr. Hyde comes out squair[sic] footed when he has any thing to say. Last Sunday he was speaking of different kinds of amusements although sinful carried to an excess yet there were those like the bowling alley and billard[sic] table that was a kind of worsted[sic] work for men who had not an intilect[sic] nor ambition for any thing higher, and it has not set very lightly on some shoulders. Today he said "he thought the disunionists at the north should be punished equally with those of the South, that the great political ship of State had been drifting this way and that. They had thrown over first one part of her ladening[sic] and then another to lighten her, and there were <u>some</u> who would have thrown over <u>Abraham</u> <u>Lincoln</u> himself if they could have had their way. <u>Shame</u> on them and the cry should be <u>down</u> <u>with</u> the <u>traitors</u>." He got so excited that we think he burst a suspender button, as there was a space between his vest and pants during the last of his sermon where his linen was perfectly visible, to the no small anoyance[sic] of all the <u>young</u> ladies.

Sunday eve. I think I spoke to you of having Bridget back, but she is not coming. They have prevailed on her to stay at Mr. Browns. I think they give her pretty high wages, but I expect now to have Mary White, the little girl who lived at Paiges two years ago and has been nurse at Mrs. Wyleses since. I am disappointed, for I thought B. would know all about the work, and I could do some sewing. We

---

[1] Calvin M. Ward, son of Julius, was born 1820 and married Sarah Ann Brown 1844.

have not either of us had a dress of any kind made since you left Camp Banks.

I saw an account of three com. of the 46th going to Plymouth but Co. G was not mentioned. Are you not going? My right eye aches so tonight I could not write if I had anything to write, which I have not. Charles Allen was in Friday evening

[*Written across margin of first page.*]
and told Etta that Albert drank worse than ever. They do not say any thing about it to me. What is Howe coming home for? Why don't you send Charley Alexan[der] with some one? I hear Thompson is at home.[1] Our baby pig died last night, so we have not but three now. How about that great battle that was coming off at Charleston? that was to end the war. Don't you run after any rebels of your own accord.

Your Rebecca

[1] Pvt. Eli Thompson was discharged from the hospital at New Bern March 27.

According to family tradition, this cradle was built by the father of George Cox around 1790. George Cox was Rebecca's father. Later the cradle passed down to Rebecca's great-grandson Ronald W.L. Peirce.

Courtesy Judy Reid Mathieu and Jill Reid Lukesh.

Plymouth   Apr 9th

Dear Rebecca

     Homer came up to day and brought the mail but failed to bring the box, though it had been in N.B. nearly ten days. I have just written Prouty that the box was there and contained a shirt which I was so badly in need of that I had been under the necessity of wearing the one I now have over three weeks without taking it from my back for [a] few minutes to examine it critically to see what it might contain, which was not strictly true as I did give myself a thorough washing. But I have worn it so long that I became a little suspicious as to what it might contain, especially after hearing that one of the most tidy captains of our own and a capt. of the 25th had found a "grayback"[1] apiece on their coat collars the day before. However I found mine all right in that respect and not very dirty, so I concluded to try one week more.

     We have been very busy since coming here, the whole force working every day, not even excepting Sunday, as it has been supposed that if the Rebs found out our exposed position they would pass over from Washington, where they have been at work for ten days and attack us. But we are now in a comparatively good shape to defend ourselves should they come, and of course the probability of their coming is lessened thereby. Besides the shoveling and "slashing" which the officers have to superintend, the captains have to act as General Officers of the day here, and as such have to visit the pickets twice each day, which you will understand is no small job when I tell you that these pickets are out on four different roads and the least travel we can make takes us at least seven miles to go our round. This would not be very bad could I have my horse & buggy to use, but I not only have not that but any other, so am obliged to foot it. But it does not come my turn but once in 12 days to do this job, so I must bear it with good grace. Tomorrow I have to go, or I would not be sitting here at twelve o'clock scribbling to you while Ira snores so as to jar the tent.

     As yet I have not visited the country around here and can tell you but little about [it], but from what I have seen I should judge that outside of the village there was but little to interest one. Tom & I went out this morning about three miles when we heard that a lovely secesh[2] woman had a gun, to get it. We did not find the old lady at home, but a housekeeper, and we took the gun & came back. On the road we met the proprietor and she screamed out at Tom "Aint that my gun you have got there?" "I think quite likely it is a gun you call yours," I answered. "What did you take it for; all my things is protected." "Yes Mam but you have no business with a gun," and we left her chewing her cud and muttering something about its "being pretty business for us to take a gun from a poor woman who had protection papers." Now that old slut has two sons in the reb service, and she would be glad to pitch our whole union force into the river. And yet is dependent on us for everything she has but corn & horse and thinks she is terribly abused if she cant keep a gun which belongs to one of these rebel sons.

---

[1] A louse.
[2] Rebel (secessionist).

And the government does protect as well as they can, not only the lives of persons that there is every reason to believe are secesh at heart, but their property. I am getting to believe that [it] is best to deal out a little justice on our own hook, if it can be done no other way, & Lt. Lyon is much stronger in the faith than I am even.

For some time the boys have had no meat but salt horse, as they call it, and today we fell from that to pork. I have been on the fortifications to work. At noon Lyon started off with a party of "non commissioned officers" with pistol & knives, and when I returned there was a very nice piece of beef hanging in our kitchen in the shape of a three year old heifer nicely dressed, so I guess they will have one or two pretty good meals, wont they think? And Lyon & the rest tell the adventure with as much boast as one should have in a tale where as many as three rebs were caught. Well boys will be boyish, and the good sober people at home must not look upon it as a very serious matter if they do take a few things which they do not pay ready cash for.

[This sheet numbered 2; next sheet 4; page missing?]

George brought the sad news of the death of C. Alexander.[1] I was very much surprised as well as sad on hearing it, for I had hoped that he would be spared to his friends. After my visit to Hospital, when first I saw him, it struck me that he had not improved any, if he had not failed in my absence. I talked with George H. about it and told him, as he had written to _____ [2] and received word from her, he would both see the Dr. and find out what he thought and write them so that they might not be disappointed in their hopes of his recovery.

He did so and said that the Dr. & nurses considered him better and they had tried to have him sit up more and thereby try to get a little exercise, stating that they saw no reason why he should not be gaining strength. George talked with Charles encouragingly and told him what the Dr. & nurses said. He wrote his folks of his situation. I saw C. the day we left and told him we were going but I should have someone to look after them for a while. Besides Kinbury, who was in the other Hospital as nurse and would visit him daily, he begged me to have G.H. if I could, & I did. He still seemed no better to me and I told G. that he had not better write too encouragingly to his folks, though I had little fear of his dying and no thought of our losing him so soon. I would write to his mother but what could I say? I am sick at heart trying to write to bereaved friends.

[Last page; no close.]

[1] Pvt. Charles E. Alexander of Brimfield died at Stanley Hospital, New Bern, April 6, 1863, of "malarial fever."
[2] Possibly Jane; he had a sister with that name.

Now I hope Rebecca you will conclude hereafter, should I fail to scribble as much as usual, or be a little more muddy, that we are in a dangerous position, or that we <u>apprehend</u> danger. I had much rather you would attribute it to the rations. Nor must you blame me for withholding our real situation, for had you known it as we did, it would, could, have done no possible good and caused much unnecessary trouble.

Be, rather, encouraged that I have gone through two thirds my time safely, having as good health as one could possibly and are now so fat that I have not a garment big enough for me, except my overcoat. And our community, I think, have cause to rejoice that, thus far, we have been in the service with so little loss. Bitter indeed will <u>some</u> regret our coming, and long hence will the memory of our departure cause them to heave a sad sigh. But they should reflect that they had no guarantee that their friends should be spared to them had they remained at home.

Since coming here all the Holland boys <u>here</u> have had the measles and some three or four others, among whom was C.[Charles] Brown*, but most of them had the disease in a mild form and are mostly well, so as to take their rations, and are anxious to be out more than I will allow, especially mornings & evenings, which are delightful; but I am a little fearful of their effect on the convalescent and so keep them in their tents from about sun set till after sunrise. We have no sick ones <u>here</u> now among the <u>men</u>, though H. Lumbard does not get entirely over his Rheumatism. Lt. Howe has been rather poorly since he came up and I fear will have the fever & ague though he insist[sic] on the contrary. He has been in the hospital for two days and has not been able to do any duty but once since he came. I left him at N Berne with his papers waiting only a signature to go home on a furlough, but when the trouble commenced at Washington he could have nothing done and so came here. Whether he goes at all will probably depend on the probabilities of his having the ague.

In my last I wrote that I sent some eye stones, but after the mail had gone found that I had them in my pocket. Guess I will not send them this time, as the letter will be heavy enough without them.

Yesterday I spent two hours or more conversing with one of the N.C. ladies of the upper tier class, but having not the inclination to give much of an acct of it. She treated me very civilly, as it was her duty to do, I being officer of the day & I promised myself the pleasure of another interview should we stay here many days. Should I have it will write the whole unless—. I did not tell you that she had a pretty daughter of about eighteen, did I? Well sometime perhaps I will tell the whole story. My best respects to neighbor Hitchcock, and tell him that perhaps I should have written him had I not known that he "plowed with my heifer."

[Written in reverse direction on top of first side.]
A little sweaty here today, the thermometer indicating <u>93 in the shade</u>. Think of that you frost bitten New Englanders.

Yours, Frank

Regimental Order No. 51   Camp Lee, Plymouth   Apr. 12, 1863

      All cleaning of fish must be done on the banks of the river. All swill or other refuse from the cook house, must be first deposited in covered barrels and then emptied into the river.

      The same regulations as to use of any part of Camp ground for <u>sink</u> <u>purposes</u> as was ordered in camp at Newbern must be observed in the camp . . .

Special Order No. 88   Head Quarters 46th Regt. M.V.M.
                              Plymouth N.C. April 14, 1863

      In accordance with special order No. 37 from Post Head Quarters Capt. F.D. Lincoln will immediately report with his command armed and equipped for duty at Post Head Quarters.

                        By order
                        Col. W. S. Shurtleff, Comdg.

Under General Order No. 54, 18th Army Corps, the 46th Mass. was part of the 2nd Brigade, commanded by Col. H.C. Lee, of the 1st Division.

Special Order
N 88
In accordance with Special order N37 from Post Head Quarters Capt F. D. Lincoln will immediately report, with his command. Armed & Equipped for duty at Post Head Quarters.
By order
James G. Smith
Adjt
Col. W. S. Shurtleff
Comdg

Dear Frank

It is two weeks since I have heard from you, and looking at you from this distance, you seem to be in the most perilous position you have yet been in; but I do not sit down with folded hands disconsolately, but am as busy as ever, and if anything more. Anna came from Springfield Wednesday. She saw the bear skin Jason Lewis sent home. They have it stuffed and it looks finely, she says. You have never spoken of any such game. I should not think even military commands would keep Cook from going a-hunting.

Mr Hyde has taken his meals with me for nearly two weeks, but is not coming anymore, as Mrs Morse is well enough to be around. We shall miss him, it seemed so good to have some one who can talk at mealtime. Oh, Frank, how can I wait three months more. I shan't know any thing by the time you come. There is no such thing as conversing with Lewis. He is so set. If it isn't yes or no, it is so and so, and that is the end unless it is about the work or cattle. He lost a calf last week, and as Sissy says, we had sick calf for every meal for three days. I kept telling him not to worry, but it did no good, just as soon as we sat down to eat he would begin, and Mr H. was here. I finally told him I should not worry as much if all the cattle were sick. It grew weak, lost the use of its legs; first he gave it gin but it wouldn't live.

Lewis has got the wood cut, tomorrow he looks over the potatoes, and next day takes them to Palmer at fifty cents a bushel. Then he commences farming.[1] Our spring untill the last week has been remarkably cold, but the weather is delightful now, and every thing is springing up with a rush, so I shall soon commence my farming. The children occupy the east room, as Lewis has their bed down in the little room and I have their room for a clothes room, so you see we have to make a few changes.

Lyman Parker's funeral was last Monday and Charlie's is to be tomorrow. Mrs A. was very bad for a few days but is quite calm now. I do hope he is the last one to be sent home in this way, and do you not think these two were the least able to go constitutionally of our boys? The Bliss that lives next to Proutie's [Prouty] has a son brought home dead.[2]

Walter and Minnie are finally married and gone west.[3] I had a call from them the day before they left. We have some nice laughs out of Etta's impulsiveness, yet she is just as when you left. One day Mr H told a story he heard the night before of a man in town who built a barn and carried back to the store all the pieces and heads of nails and had them deducted, but did not know who it was; but Lewis knew we found it out by his looks, but make him tell we couldn't any of us (he delights in that sort of thing).

---

[1] Lewis would be looking over last year's potatoes to see how many were in condition to sell or to use as seed before starting another cycle of plowing and planting. During this busy season, he was living at the Lincoln's, if he had not before.

[2] No soldier named Bliss from Brimfield is recorded as dying in the war.

[3] C. Walter Brown and Marion M. Bliss were married April 9.

So Sissy called to Sam, who went along soon after and asked him; but he had forgotten but said he would find out and tell her. So at tea time he came into the yard and wanted to have her come out, so both went, and in rushed Etta saying "I know who it was, Mr Hyde, it was Capt. Longtail."

[*Written across top front margin*] It would have done you good to see him laugh. He was as childish as either the children about finding it out because L wouldn't tell.

I have not seen Lieu. Howe yet, am afraid I shall not.

Rebecca

After months of separation, Rebecca's need for companionship and intellectual stimulation, which her children and neighbors are not fully providing, has become increasingly urgent. She is representative in this respect of the higher type of New England woman, who played a vital part in civilizing a continent.

Brimfield   Apr 20 /63

Capt. D F[sic] Lincoln—
Dear Sir
You wrote to me at the time of Lyman's Death saying his wages was due from the 31 of Dec. and you thought that I had better send on a power of Attorney to someone and have it collected there when the paymaster comes around. Brown has made out one and I will send it to you and if you can collect it I wish you would do so. And if it cant be collected in this way please inform us and I will try some other way. Orville informs me that Lyman was owing some small debts and I should like to have his wages collected so that Orville can settle up all his affairs, for he knows all about them better than anyone else.

Charles Alexander is buried tomorrow. All well at home.
Yours Truly
David Parker

P.S.   Please write soon and let us hear from you and all the rest of the boys.

This letter from the father of the dead soldier Lyman Parker is made all the more pathetic by its simple New England stoicism. The sorrow of this one death, noted in previous letters, brings home the tragedy of the war's losses almost more poignantly than the casualty lists of the famous battles in which thousands perished.

Dear Rebecca

I was to give you an acct[sic] of my visit with the southern family of the upper tier class, and at the risk of being a little tedious I will be somewhat minute. Indeed, I want you to feel that you are somewhat acquainted with them. The family is composed of a man & his wife, a son & daughter, Norcum by name. Until the Rebellion the old father was a trader in this city and the old lady, I should judge, had charge of the plantation containing about 13,000 acres, having about 20 slaves. Of the two she is a little the most of a man; at any rate has given the man directions in regard to the management of affairs.

They were, or considered themselves, the aristocracy of the village, living part of the year in town & part on the plantation about a mile out. After the yankees came and the troops occupied the city, they took up their residence permanently with the few slaves who saw fit to stay on the plantation, for you know they could not bear the thought of living here among the "mud sills."[1] Their city residence is occupied by the major of the 27th [Mass.]. The house is not what you with your northern vulgar ideas would consider grand, being about such an one as George Hitchcock occupies, but here they have a more sensible idea of what is proper for an aristocratic family. Tis not necessary for a man of wealth to live in a mansion or ride in an elegant coach. Not at all, but he must own negroes and the household to maintain their position, must never be known to do a single thing for themselves. It would be thought very vulgar for a lady to dress herself or comb her own hair. Mrs. Norcum has not probably been guilty of doing either of the above acts for years.

Well, I had a curiosity to converse with this family, knowing something of their history, and so one day while acting as officer of the Day I broke over the rule I had meant to govern myself by, and called at the house. The old lady was by the door, and having a picket post in the back yard which I was obliged to visit, I opened the conversation by inquiring if the Picket was troublesome to them. "Oh no capt., they behave very well indeed." "We felt that it was necessary to place a guard in your yard as there is a bypath leading from it into the woods, as we must guard against any surprise at such a time as this," (it was while we were expecting an attack at any hour), "but we do not mean the guard shall molest peaceable citizens." "Well they have not disturbed us in the least. Mr. Norcum & I are very glad to have the guard here, for we feel safer for it. Wont you walk up and have a seat Capt."

Straps make a sight of difference with the treatment one receives from even the nobility of the south, especially if accompanied with the sash. Well, I accepted the invitation and sat down under the piazza of the little cottage which

---

[1] A term borrowed from architecture to apply to social structure: as a building rested on its mudsill, the lowest members of the social order were called "mudsills".

they call a summer residence and had a talk with the Lady and her husband. She is by nature as coarse as cousin Jim and goes in the class of "Strong minded" women; he an effeminate man, who had been educated a Lawyer (and the old lady said he was a good Lawyer) and practiced[sic] selling [tapr(?)=turpentine?] but a man of considerable refinement; indeed, had he been the woman & she the man, to my mind, each would have played their part in life better.

But to go on with my story, we had a long talk about the war and the slaves. She thought it a very wicked war but didn't know as she could say who was most to blame, the north or south. I thought the war full as wicked as she and might have told which I thought was entirely to blame in bringing it on, but did not think it best to state my views (did I not tell you I was getting very prudent). As for the slaves, if she thought the poor creatures could take care of themselves or could be placed any where by themselves, she for one would be very glad to have slavery abolished. But capt[sic], you have no idea how shiftless and lazy they be. I asked her if she did really think there were any considerable number of them that would not get a living of themselves were they free. "Why yes, Capt." and then she would go through a long _____ about this and that slave of hers and how shiftless they were with a master to look after them, taking it for granted that were they free they would be as lazy as herself.

I of course did not contradict or try to argue the question but played the part of an anxious enquirer for the truth of the case, only once suggesting that the negroes I had seen about New Berne seemed full as industrious as the poor whites. I struck the right vein for the old lady, "the poor whites were a lazy shiftless set and she had some times thought they would be better off if they had some body to look after them, though she did not suppose they would have a right to make slaves of them." I wanted to get at the old ladies idea of the right to make slaves of the one more than the other but knew if I attempted it my cake would be dough, so lost what might have been very interesting.

[Next page numbered 3; page 2 apparently missing.]
. . . home: for the past ten days it has been delightful, with the exception of two days which were a little warm for the season.

I have just got your letter of the 19th. Tell Lewis not to fret his soul about a sick calf or dead pig. I did not suppose six months would pass without some things happening even in Brimfield. About the only evidence we ever have of any life there is the fact that men and animals do now and then die.

I learn by the same steamer that Lieut. Prouty and wife have lost their child and have gone home to bury it.[1] Sad indeed to them must be their passage

[1] Frank M. Prouty died Apr. 23 at the age of 16 months. The Proutys had earlier lost a daughter at seven months. Their last child, and the only one who grew to adulthood, was born 1864. (Charles Henry Pope, *The Prouty Genealogy*; Boston, 1910, 116.)

home, and how lonely must [be] the days after his return. The boy was an interesting child even to strangers, and the mother must feel as though all was lost. I want you to visit her in Spencer at a proper time with the children. She is an excellent woman and I feel extremely sorrowful at her loss.

I sent by the Lieut's Brother my great coat. Should you go to Spencer you will take it home with you. Should you feel that it would be pleasant, ask Mrs. P. to make you a visit. When I left her she said that she certainly should go to see you if she returned before I did, but perhaps in her sorrow she will not feel like doing so. Oh what a sad parting must there be when he returns to N.B.

We have had some dozen boys sick of the measles and have got through them well. Boys are all hale.

The Rebs have all left this region, and I have not the least idea we shall see any thing more of them unless we go after them. Their boast that they would drive the Yankees from the state in thirty days did not even amount to frightening the children in any place they attacked. Had they come here at one time we probably should have had the pleasure of taking a visit at Richmond, I mean the officers, for unless they had proved the greatest cowards the world ever knew, we should have been obliged to surrender to them; but as good luck would have it they did not see fit to come, and now if they come they will rue the day. But I must close . . .

Yours Frank.

I am actually so poor that I have to mark my letters soldiers letter!

Frank is correct in stating that the Rebels had withdrawn after their bungled attacks on New Bern and Washington. His mention of visiting Richmond is a sardonic reference to the notorious Libby Prison, where captured officers were held. As Regimental Order No. 53 suggests, conditions grew more relaxed in the federal garrison. By mid-April Foster had regained the initiative and launched a series of probes and raids into the interior. Confederate hopes of accumulating strength in this region were dashed by Lee's decision, after his victory at Chancellorsville in early May, to gather his forces for an invasion across the Potomac.

Frank's strong powers of observation and vivid descriptions must have delighted his followers in Brimfield, who probably chuckled at his comment on the placidity of life there. His long accounts are in the tradition of 19th Century travel narratives, with which he was undoubtedly familiar. Like other observant northerners who traveled in the South before and during the war, Frank treats the experience essentially as foreign travel, so deep was the cultural gulf between the regions.

Regimental Order No. 53   Camp Lee, Plymouth   Apr. 25, 1863

     Hereafter Guards will be instructed to suffer the orderlies of companies, non-commissioned Officers, Clerks and servants, members of Band Field music, citizens and all soldiers except members of the 46th and 25th Mass. Regts. to pass the camp lines until 9 o'clock P.M. without written passes.

     Any member of this Regiment who shall pass or seek to pass camp lines by representing himself to be a member of any other Regiment will be punished with the most severe punishment allowed by military law or practice for such offenses.

Regimental Order No. 54   Camp Lee, Plymouth   Apr. 29, 1863

Commanders of Companies will exercise their commands two hours each day in Company movements and the manual of arms. They will give their personal attention to this duty unless on other duty or reported sick. They may select such part of the day between Reveille and Retreat as may be most convenient, taking care not to interfere with other camp or post duties—and will excuse no member of their companies from the drill . . . .

Brimfield   Apr. 26th

Dear Frank,

                I received a short epistle from you last night, but felt rather vexed that the <u>long</u> <u>letter</u> should not come also. But I am so glad to get the fact that you are well and comparatively safe, though as the time shortens I tremble the harder, for I know you will have to work yet, and the hot weather, how think you, you will bear that?

We are having a regular March day today, quite a contrast to some of the days we have had during the past week. Anna left wednesday. I took her to Warren & came home by the way of Tylers, the nursery man[1] , as it had been arranged with Mr Woods. We got three dwarf & four standard pear trees, four mountain ash, three evergreen trees, and three horse chestnuts. These ornamentals are for the west side of the yard. The east side I shall leave for you.

It was a beautiful day, and Etta and I enjoyed piloting our selves through the bye roads as she and those like her only can. Mr Woods was on his way to Brookfield. I do not know how much the trees come to, as I am to settle with Mr W. when he gets through. He is to bring them tomorrow and set them out.

I think Lewis will have to hire a good deal beside in haying. He is so moderate. He is to have Mr Upham (or expects to) tomorrow to lay the barn yard walk, then he is going into the planting. I offered him some money before loaning any to the town (this spring I mean), but he would not take any; had rather have it all in a bunch.

I have now the sixty from Bird, twenty-five from Bemis, and some for potatoes, and there is no more to come, and what I had received before, I have told you about. Don't know as I can make this last till you come, but shall try and not have to get any I have loaned. If I do get out, hadn't I better call on Jim.

Mr Paige is to be married tuesday morning.[2] We are invited, but do not see how I can go, as my dress is so rusty and there is no time to get one, as he only asked us last night, and I had rather stay at home than to go alone.

[*Section of news about people in Walpole deleted.*]

Our crooked necked nannie died this week.[3] Now I believe I have told every word of news. There has not been any one in this week. I have not made those calls yet that I have been going to make for so long a time.

Anna and I spent Tuesday after noon at Mrs Toms with several others, Eunice, her mother, and Mary, Aron Bliss, his wife and daughter, Mrs Hubbard and Homer. Had a very pleasant time. Write so as to have your letters ready every chance.

                Rebecca

---

[1] David Tyler was a nurseryman in Warren. As noted earlier, although there was a railroad station within the Brimfield limits, it was more convenient for residents of the center village to travel to Warren; and more trains stopped there.

[2] Paul W. Paige (1807-1876) married his second wife, Catharine P. Brown, April 28.

[3] Presumably a goat, and probably a family pet. Goats were not common farm animals in New England.

In planting ornamentals the Lincolns were participating in a widespread movement to beautify private and public spaces by means of landscaping and planting. Many famous city parks and cemeteries in the North were developed in this period, and the dignified town commons that seem so characteristic of New England were given their present form. Many books and magazines offered advice on creating attractive "pleasure grounds" and making homes more tasteful through landscaping. The impulse has deep social and intellectual roots, reinforcing the fashionable domestic ideal of the age, trying to recapture a lost and glorified rusticity, and providing a refuge from the increasing pressures of modern life.

Women were generally responsible for taking care of the dooryard garden, but this letter shows how the war increased the scope of Rebecca's burdens. These added responsibilities were challenging even to competent, intelligent women. Writing of a farm woman in Michigan, Silber describes how she "had to negotiate an economic battlefront that brought her into a new set of commercial relationships, some of which were enriching and empowering, but she also learned frustrating lessons about her economic dependency and vulnerability, and how difficult life could be without a man around the house" (<u>Daughters of the Union</u>, *42).*

Plymouth   May 5th

Dear Rebecca

We are still here waiting for the transport to take us to New Berne. Nothing has transpired since I wrote worthy of noting & I would not write a line had not some of the boys written & you seem to think you must have a letter as often as any of the girls, though the contract was that once a week should suffice, and even that is twice as often as you used to expect one while we were doing our courting & it cant be that you think more of getting one <u>now</u>? for you know they were worth "<u>every</u> thing" then.

Our boys who have had the measles (18 in all) have all recovered but two, from Holland. One of those, Henry Moore*, is as deaf as a haddock & the Dr. thinks will never be otherwise.[1] The other one, Bennett, looks badly to me and I sometimes fear for him. He got pretty much over the measles and one night ate so heartily as to give him a Diarrhoea from which he has not recovered. I honestly believe that overloading the stomach causes more sickness than all the other things in the army. And still tis almost impossible to check the practice; for <u>me</u> tis absolutely, for I have talked till I am sick of the effort and have made up my mind that if they will not take warning from what I have said and <u>they</u> seem, they may suffer on for all my saying anything more.

I have had a difficulties[sic] with my bowels such as I never had before, which kept me in the Hospital for two days but have got bravely over it and now have my usual health. We have had fine weather especially mornings and evenings and live in the most pleasantly shaded street in the world. But good by, for the boat is ready.

[*No formal closing.*]

---

[1] Henry Moore was discharged before his term expired, on May 28.

Brimfield, May 5th

Dear Frank,

        Now don't be frightened because you have an extra letter, for it is only to say a barrel of dried apple will start tomorrow for Co G from the ladies of Brimfield. I told them of your disappointment in not getting any in your box, and if they wished to send some so all could have it, I would receive and attend to the packing, and I think if word had been given throughout the town there would have been enough for two or three barrels. Warren Tarbell wanted [to] send some spirit, and brought the largest quantity of apple of any one, but it was all headed before he got here, and he felt very bad I tell you. I will put down the names of those who sent.

Mrs. Aron Bliss

"	Henry Wyles	Mrs N. Hubbard
"	Alfred Hitchcock	also the cheese
"	_____ Morse	Mr Lyman Upham
"	Tom Morgan	and his brothers family
"	W.[William H.] Sherman	Mr Bixby
"	C.[Cheney] Newton	
"	W.[William] Upham	

Eunice Knight sent part of the nutmegs & the grater, Rebecca the tobacco & Etta the lozenges. And a small box is in for Henry Stebbins.[1] The extras are on top and the top is the end which has most writing on, I mean the manufacturers marks, as it is to be marked to you in the street. If you use the nutmegs you grate it in after it is cooked. Most of it is very nice, though some will want to be washed pretty hard.

    Mr Robinsons people had news of Wilsons death last night; it seems very sad.[2] We are having a cold rain storm. Lewis got all ready last night to go for plaster today, but the storm prevented—hopes to go tomorrow.

    I hope you will get the barrel soon, and will get it cooked nicely. If you have oranges there, cut up some peel and stew with it. I think it is the pleasantest flavor of anything.

            Good night, love to all,
            Rebecca

[1] Probably Abner H. Stebbins of Brimfield.
[2] Pvt. H. Wilson Robinson of Brimfield, serving in the 27th Mass., died at New Bern April 25, 1863.

Perhaps wistfully, Rebecca is trying to strengthen the reminder of home provided by the dried apples by suggesting a favorite recipe for their preparation. Oranges, brought from Spain, were available at that time of year in New England, and she probably thought that they might be obtainable in New Bern as well. To William Tarbell's disappointment, the Brimfield barrel had been headed (closed) before he arrived. However, shipping ardent spirits was forbidden by regulations, and his thoughtful gift might not have reached the soldiers.

Dear Frank,

I was going to write but there comes neighbor Hitchcock.

Well, it is nine o clock. Mr H. Stayed and talked a long time. He says he is all behind hand with his work. George has been sick for three weeks, and he is very lame this spring, says he has had the worst time that he ever had.[1] Mr H. had not gone when Mr Wyles came and he is but just gone. He and Sissy have had a great time. She was appointed with Ellen Warren to collect money in this district for buying new books for the library, so she asked him to give her something, though she knew he belonged to Ellen's round. Still, she thought he ought to give her something too, as there were no Wyles'es[sic] or Hitchcocks in our part of the district. And so he kept her talking for a long time.

You do not know How much I would like to hear from you tonight, to know if you are enjoying yourself or are suffering with the heat, as I suppose you have very warm weather now. It is two weeks since I had a letter ———. I cannot write, my face aches so. I have had the head and face ache for several days. I don't know whether it be cold, or nervousness. It came on the night news of the defeat of Hooker came.[2] Isn't it dreadful. I pray you will have no such battles in N.C.

Lewis has sowed the plaster as you requested. It cost $20.

Mr. Spaulding is going to close up in the meat line[3]; the slaughter house has been complained of, and he brought in his bill of $13. It is for meat and a barrel of flour. In the winter Fitz H. Knight[4] wrote home that there was no reason why it would not be 25 dollars a barrel before fall, so I got an extra barrel, as he advised his folks to get enough to last; but I have heard nothing of it since, though it is pretty high. By the way Fitz has a baby. It weighed four pounds—a bouncer. Want [wasn't?] it.

They are going to repair the Church, and have been to see how much I would give.[5] I told them I would ask you, but they might put down fifteen dollars. Should you have given more?

It has stormed nearly all the week but was pleasant yesterday, and I had for callers Mrs Hubbard, Mary W Tarbell, Ellen Paige, Eunice & Mary, and Mrs Hendrick Webster today.

---

[1] The Lincolns' neighbor, Alfred Hitchcock (1801-1871), had a son George Morris Hitchcock, born 1837.

[2] The battle of Chancellorsville, VA, May 1-4.

[3] This may not be entirely true, or Spaulding may have changed his mind, as Hyde records that P.F. Spaulding kept a market at the time of his writing. It is possible that he no longer engaged in slaughtering.

[4] Fitz Henry Knight, son of Dr. Ebenezer Knight, was born 1835 and died in Troy, N.Y., 1867.

[5] Hyde (125-26) describes the alterations, which were completed in 1864 and cost about $3400. This was the third church structure on the site and replaced one that had burned in 1847.

The Prouty girls came home with me to dinner, Mary Paige & Dell just at night, and the men this evening. I have done the house cleaning as far as the dining room, and I don't know what I am to do. Shall try what I can do in the line of patching, as carpets that used to be 75 cents are two dollars.

The children are both pleased with their schools. Etta had a perfect mark for each day last week. Mary Knight[1] has a room at Mrs Morses and has her children, the Wyles children and Jim Warrens, big business for a girl of her age don't you think so.

Mr Hitchcock says he has tried every one he knows of to help him in haying, but has found no one yet.

Your Rebecca

[1] Mary T. Knight, a daughter of Dr. Ebenezer, was apparently running a private school for young children.

New Berne   May 14th 1863

Dear Rebecca

In the absence of any thing better to write about, I am going to give you a description of our quarters. I think I wrote you that on our return here we came into Barrack[sic]. Possibly you have but a faint idea of what they are. I am certain I had[sic] before I came. These we are in are about a fair sample of those made for the Union soldiers, so far as I have seen. And those made by the rebs differ but little from them, except in the material they are constructed of and the size of the buildings, theirs being made of logs generally hewn on two sides so as to have them form something like a joint, as carpenters say, having the cracks filled in with mud, and a building for each company, whereas ours are framed sheds long enough to hold a regiment covered with rough boards running from the eaves to the sills with the cracks covered with a thin slat nailed over it. In a word, they are covered just as C.R. Brown's[1] barn used to be, with the exception of having rough boards in stead of smooth.

The Barrack is about 27 feet wide and partitioned off on the length so as to give a room for each company, besides a small one for the sergeants and a kitchen about 12 feet square. In the center of each companies[sic] quarters is a door and each side in front two windows nearly opposite of the door is an old fashioned

[1] Dea. Cyrel R. Brown (1798-1869).

fireplace, and just to the right of it the back door; passing out of this you turn into the kitchen, which is framed on to the main building after the fashion of the salt boxes which the grandees in Walpole place on almost all their houses. There is no passage from the quarters into the kitchen without going "out doors," for you know that the Army regulations prohibit the soldiers from going into the kitchen, and although the rule is violated a hundred, perhaps a thousand, times each day by a single company, still the regulations are so far complied with as to put them to some trouble to do it. The only direct communication between the kitchen and the barracks is by a slide window just big enough for one to put his plate and cup through to get his rations.

On the outside of the room all around from the doors are berths for the men to sleep in, most of them calculated for two to occupy and so arranged that two will sleep near the floor, and above just far enough for those in the lower bunk to sit up is another and above still another, which comes so near the roof that the occupants must move to the front side to sit up straight. Between them & the next is a passage just wide enough to walk through conveniently, and so it is arranged around the whole room.

In the middle of the room is a space 12 feet wide or more running the whole length. On the left as you go in is the sergt. Room, being of the width _____ [*illegible (overwritten)*] barracks (6 feet & ½) and perhaps ten feet long, having on each end single bunks, leaving space enough in the center for a small table for them to eat from. The room is well ventilated from the roof, and being white washed all over, presents the appearance which I think you Brimfield ladies would call comfortable.

The quarters of the officers of the companies are made so as to look very much like those of the men on the outside. Indeed they are made in the same style of the others, except as the rooms are smaller. We of course have to have more doors. The officers of the right wing of the regt occupy a building on the right of the company barracks, those of the left on the other. The three officers have one room 12 feet by 20, with two doors and two windows on the front and the same in the rear. The doors in the rear lead into a small room, which was calculated for a kitchen. Evidently the rooms were made with the intention of being divided in the center, giving the captain one and the Lieuts one of the same pattern.

I occupy one end of our room, having a bunk with a bed tick and a little coarse grass in it to sleep on. The Lieuts have the other, and we meet in the center. Howe has a platform to write on, and George has built one to do the company writing on, while Lyon & I use a table. Lyon, George, Charles Kittridge*, who is feeble and not able to do military duty, mess together.[1] Kittridge makes the tea, sets the table, sweeps the room and does any chores he feels able to do & George does most of the company writing, gets the clothes for the men, and sort of looks after the odds and ends, smokes, chews, drinks now & then a glass of _____ [sic],

---

[1] Kittredge was discharged at the end of April.

lies on my bed all he wants to if it be not covered with others, and on the whole gets along first rate and is a very useful member of the company. Really I have been more surprised in him than in any one of my acquaintance and should be almost lost without him.

He is known through the regt. as Co. G's old gentleman, and although he sometimes gets a little sensation over having the Darkies inquire for the "ole gemen, Mr. Homer, bleves you calls him," generally takes things in good part and gives as good jokes as he gets, to say the least. No member of the company has relieved me of as much as he & although I do not have the same feeling towards him that I do towards Tom, yet I do feel under obligations to him and many others of the company, are whether they feel so or not.

You sometimes ask what we talk about. Writing of jokes in connection with George reminds me of one which caused considerable merriment. He started up all of a sudden the other afternoon, put on his dress coat and stood in the middle of the room bent about double looking for all the world like one of seventy. And I asked, "Where now George." "I'm going down to the undertakers." The first thought that came into everyone's mind was that he was going for his own coffin. And to finish the matter Cook said "Don't let him cheat you George, you wont need embalming." It may seem to you like making light of serious matters, especially for us, but could you have been here & seen him & heard the declaration & the response I don't believe but you would have laughed till your sides ached.

Enclosed I send a couple of verses, cut from some paper which I read to some half dozen of our boys the other day. When one of them exclaimed God, if it want[sic] for the curly hair I should think this was my wife, which caused a good deal of merriment. Now read the verses to our war widows & have them guess who the fellow could have been.

[Written across salutation, first page.]

Shall send in the course of a few days some money home, but can't tell just yet how. Lieut. Knapp[1] expects to go in the next boat and has offered to take it for me & says he shall visit you with his wife if he has time. He is a lawyer from Chicopee. Should he come, you will bear in mind he has been quite friendly to me. I must write of Sarah in my next.

Yours

Frank

[1] 1st Lt. George H. Knapp, Co. D, of Chicopee.

Frank provides a valuable description of the company's living arrangements, noting a characteristic difference between northern and southern building methods. George Homer, who Frank describes vividly, presents a puzzle: at 38, he was younger than Frank, but relatively old for an enlisted man, even in a militia company. He died in 1867, indicating that he really was in poor health. The poem Frank mentions has not survived; from the context, it may have been in the vein of humor at the expense of blacks.

General Order No. 63   Newbern   May 11, 1863

All persons are forbidden washing themselves or any plate dish or any other thing within twenty feet of any well on the camp ground . . . .

Regimental Order No. 68   Newbern   May 29, 1863

All firing by members of this Regiment is strictly prohibited except by permission from Head Quarters.

Dear Frank

Etta is full of Cain and Sissy is making a great scratching with her pen, so between the two I am afraid I can't think very fast. Rebecca heard this week you were not well. How is it? I had rather know from you if you are not than to hear of it from others.

Everything is looking beautifully, the grass is growing finely. For two weeks we have had a great deal of rain, and when the sun has shone it has been very warm. I have just got my yard spaded for my flower seeds. I find every man is not a Frank. I told Lewis as early as the middle of April he could spade it anytime and put on some manure, but it didn't get done so I hoed as much as I could and Friday had Johny[sic] Collins come and help me, and now if my things do well. I think the yard will be looking very prettily when you come home.

People here are talking very much about the greater part of Foster's army reenlisting, and for fear you may in a state of excitement promise to, I will tell you that I think it would not be a greater sin for you to shoot Etta than to leave her again as you have now. I have never told you how she has mourned because I thought it was not best, but this week I was given to understand that there was no doubt but you would go back but I can't write about that.

I heard some news yesterday but doubt if it will be so to you, as the Holland boys may have had it in their last week's letters. One of the Newel[sic] girls at East Corner[1] is going to have a child and lays it to a Holland man. He is brother to Mrs Elijah Allen[2], and as he has left that place suddenly for parts unknown, it looks rather suspicious. Dear me, won't Mrs Newell have something to do now beside tending to her neighbors' affairs, poor woman.

If you was here I should like to go to walk. I have not been out of the house on Sunday except to Church since you left.

I visited at Mrs Knight's tuesday with Mrs Paige, Mrs James Warren, Mrs Muzzy, Mrs Witter, and Mrs Wyles. Mrs Sam Brown was asked but did not go. She and Sam start for New York tuesday.

All have gone to bed and I am alone once more, and so it will be for a dozen sunday nights at least. I am afraid you will think I do not try to write but the only places I have been this week was to call one evening down to Mrs Charlie's and to the party at Mrs Knight's, and Mrs A. Converse[3] is the only one who has been in. Oh, yes, Lucy came one afternoon, but she does not grow any more inter-

[1] East Brimfield, a mill village on the Quinebaug River.
[2] Elijah Allen's (second) wife was Ursula McFarland. The Albigence Newell family lived on the Sturbridge Road in East Brimfield; he was a clothing maker.
[3] Probably Almira Sedgwick Converse, wife of Alfred L. Converse, the son of Marquis Converse, a prominent resident.

esting, though her story is not measles now, it is smallpox. Every time I have seen her since mid winter she has had it all to go through with.

Mr Woods came to look at the trees this last week. He says they are all doing well. I settled with him, it was eleven dollars and forty-odd cents.

Sissy is writing you of her composition. I hope you will think it worth a little praise, and if you do, do not fail to give it, as she needs a great deal of encouragement. She has so little confidence in herself, and it is true what she says at the commencement, it is all her own except two or three ideas, but she expressed it all herself.

Your Rebecca

[*Overwritten on top of first page.*]
They have the measles at Tom's, are all getting along nicely except their colored girl; she has them hard. I have not been up, for I have not mustered courage to drive our horse till yesterday since my Tower Hill ride. Shall go tomorrow if pleasant. Love to the Boys.

R.

In the most powerful statement in all of her letters, Rebecca forcibly squelches any temptation Frank might have had to re-enlist.

Brimfield.

Dear Father.

I have not written
since I commenced going to school.
I study, the First steps in numbers,
Eaton's arithmetic, Grammer, read every
other day, and spell wensdays. beside
writing in journals, Monday, and wensday.
and writing a composition or speaking
once a fortnight, I have spoken once
and written once, the ~~title~~ to the piece
was, "God save the ~~union~~, and
the composition I send now.
a week ago saturday ~~evening~~ we had
company all the ~~evening~~ afternoon, but
perhaps Mother has told you. but
monday evening, brother and I.
went down to call on Miss Lounsbury
and Ruth Nessil, Mr Winslow and I
went out to take a boat ride

Rebecca Lincoln in later years.
Hitchcock Academy.

Dear Father
Mather Rebecca and myself
went down to Mrs Lyons. ~~this day~~ after
had a very pleasent time then
went to deacan Paiges. then went
Hame. ~~we shall~~ dactor Witter
sent a man up to the school
the ~~other~~ day, to vaccinate the
scholars. becars the small pox
is round Mrs J Brown has
it. dactor Witter gave it to
her. He peels very Badly about
it. Nearly all the scholars have

Brimfield

Dear Father

I have not written since I commenced going to school. I study the First steps in numbers, Eatons arithmetic, Grammer[sic], read every other day, and spell Wensdays[sic], beside writing in journals, monday and wensday[sic] and writing a composition or speaking once a fornight[sic]. I have spoken once and writen[sic] once, the title of the piece was, "God save the union," and the composition I send you.

A week ago saturday we had company all the afternoon, but monday evening mother and I went down to call on Mrs Lumbard and Ruth Merril. Mr Winslow and I went out to take a boat ride, had a splendid time and am going again. Friday night I went onto slut[1] Hill begging. The Sabbath School is going to get some new books, and I am one of the collectors. Great bisness, ain't it. I managed to get twenty-five cents at Mr. J. Browns and the same at B. Shermans. In all I have five dollars and ninety-four cents. I had this street and past Astin[sic] Hitchcocks[2].

Saturday we went down to Southbridge, and mother carried her straw bonnet, and they are going to fix it <u>for me</u>. I am going to have a bonnet, then it will be "<u>big</u> Becka with her new bonnet on." Miss E. Knight wanted me to have it, and mother finerly[sic] concluded that I was a little too large to wear a hat.

We called at Mrs Charles, coming home. She has been out to ride twice, once that morning. The baby was asleep, but Luvan woke it up, and Mother told her she didn't know how to hold it.[3] Took it and held it for a long time, then they put it into the cradle and Etta rocked it. They don't like Byron's picture. Mrs C— says she can't bear to look at it, for it looks so sad, and I declare, I should think you would be ashamed to look so like _____ ——[*commas under dashes, possibly to represent beards*] as C—Lumbard, __ T—Morgan and Byron, and I presume all the rest do.

---

[1] Although it is startling to the modern reader to find a well-bred 13 year-old girl using this word in correspondence with her father in 1863, this seems to be the most accurate rendering of the handwriting. Our discomfort arises largely because the definition has shifted; she is using the common meaning of untidy or slovenly. This is supported by the fact that Frank's reply on June 12 uses the same word without criticism, though he corrects other features of his daughter's composition. "Slut hill" is probably a family usage. The *Oxford English Dictionary* gives similar constructions such as "slut's corner" (a corner left uncleaned by a sluttish person) and "slut's hole" (a receptacle for rubbish). There were Browns and Shermans on Prospect Hill, the nearest hill to the Lincolns and which Rebecca would have thought of as "going onto" from her location on the plain.

[2] Probably Samuel Austin Hitchcock, founder of the academy, who lived at what is now 15 Wales Road.

[3] The Charles family owned a large and prosperous farm in East Brimfield on the main road to Fiskdale and Southbridge. Luvan, born 1842, was the daughter of Abraham Charles. Abraham, born 1807, had an infant son, Frederic Abraham, born March 10, 1863. A child of Abraham's second wife, the baby was 25 years younger than his half-sister, Ellen Adelia.

Today Mr Hall preached. He has had the rheumatism, and walks with a cane. Mr Hyde is going to take his meals at the Hotel and sleep at Mrs Morses.

I forgot some money I had not collected, which will make some over six dollars.

My First Composition.

Girls and boys, or rather ladies and gentlemen, this is my first composition. I presume you would have found that out, if I had not told you. I have indeed handed in three compositions, but that is nearly all I had to do about it, but when I asked mother to write this, she said No, and be it known to you friends, that when my Mother says no, she means it, so now you see, I have set sail in my own craft.

I first thought of a subject for a composition. A friend invited me to write him a letter. I commenced, honored friend, erased that, as well as respected sir and dear friend. Another advised me to write about flowers. Now you know there is no limit to what could [be] written upon flowers, neither to the news that could be communicated to a friend from such a place as Brimfield. Now would you like to know how much I wrote on flowers?
[*Remainder missing.*]

[*Letter from Etta.*]

Dear Father

Mother Rebecca and myself went down to Mrs Lyons Saturday, had a very pleasant time, then went to Deacon Paiges, then went home. Doctor Witter sent a man up to the school the other day to examine the scholars because the smallpox is around. Mrs J Brown has it. Dr Witter gave it to her. He feels very badly about it. Most all the scholars have left school. Mr Bacon has taken A. and Mary away. Emma Dale is sick and so is Ellen Brown. I am getting along in Arithmetic very well. I have nobody to disturb me on Mr Woods and he don't only when I say something wrong. Mother and Mrs Morse came in the other day and she told me she would't stay in there a minute for anything. Mother had a letter from Mrs Plimpton and she said if nothing prevents she will come in 7 weeks. Ain't that good. Now goodbye from

Etta

Letters from the children of Civil War soldiers are rare, and these are especially valuable because they describe the course of instruction the girls were receiving.

My dear child Rebecca

       Some time since I received a letter from an old pupil of mine in which she wrote that "she could hardly realise[sic] that I had a daughter as old as she was when she attended my school." And really I have some little trouble in bringing myself to think of you as being almost 14, for it seems but yesterday that I held you in my lap, a little child.

    Sometimes I wonder if I seem to you as my father did to me when I was young, for he seemed quite an old man as long ago as I can remember and never looked any older than he did then, till the last year of his life. And I wonder again if he felt no older than I do. Excepting when I have been on some march, I feel almost as young as I did when but little older than you are.

    Now look at the picture and then wonder if you shall feel but little older than you now do when the deep wrinkles on the brow shall indicate the age of your father. May Heaven so guide you, my child, that forty years shall not make your face show so much of trial, trouble (shall I say fretfulness) as mine. And I have faith that it will, for you have started in life with a much fairer prospect than I did.

    On the next few years will your future usefulness and happiness depend, I mean, on the manner you spend the next few years. Your destiny is, in a far greater measure than you think, in your own hands. You have this spring commenced on a new era in your life. You will be subjected to many trials & temptations that as yet you know but little of, for you will now mingle with those older than yourself, whose characters are well-nigh formed, and you must not expect to find them all worthy of being followed. Better heed the counsel of those what have seen more of the world, and have had to regret in bitterness, the folly of slighting the advice given them long ago.

    You have commenced your studies in the high school. Don't, I beg you, get that silly idea into your head that some other than the studies you should pursue are to be taken if you would be thought a <u>lady</u>. Remember this, that nothing short of a mind well-stored with that knowledge which prepares one for usefulness can make you worthy of the respect of any but simpletons. In no other way can you so well develop your reasoning powers as by a thorough study of arithmetic and English grammar. Remember that these two principles, ever acted on, are the foundation of all moral worth, viz always do what you believe to be right, & do whatever you undertake <u>thoroughly</u>. Govern yourself by the first in all your intercourse with your mates, and the other in all your studies, or whatever you are required or each action leads you to do.

    I did not think to write just such a letter as this, and I fear you will think tis too much like the talk of a school committee; if so, bear in mind that <u>I</u> have had no school to lecture for a long time and perhaps the committee, the school committee at home, leave some things undone which they ought to do.

[*Written across salutation, first page.*]
I have seen the Walpole boys a number of times within a few days. Their regt. is now doing guard duty in the City. I met Ed Ridge going around with the guard (he is corporal), and afterwards saw Charles Gray on duty. Rob & Jim & H. Fuller I saw at their quarters. Their company occupy one of the best houses in the city. [*Additional Walpole news deleted.*]

Farewell my daughter.

Your father

Keenly feeling his absence, Frank is determined to fulfill his educational responsibilities at a distance, and perhaps, as he implies, offer the valedictory that the school committee for some reason was unable to provide. Frank is remarkable, in an era when there was enormous pressure on the middle class to maintain separate and distinct spheres for each gender, in not wishing to compromise or water down his daughter's education. One detects a deep bond of sympathy between father and daughter, and perhaps a resulting touch of jealousy on the mother's part.

Dear Frank

I received a long letter from you last night, also an express package with the $500 directed to Mrs Capt. Lincoln, so you may make up your mind I am not going to be anything short of that when you get home. I don't have anyone to Cap'n it over now, but look out!

I was up to Mrs. Tom's one night this last week, and she was relating some of her troubles and says "you don't have anything to fret about." Whether I do or not, she nor no one else will know it. Lewis is just as faithful as you expected he would be but Oh! so tiresome. He would not move out of his course I believe to make a fortune. He says he shall charge $40 for next months work and some extra for this.

Willard Rice[1] was here Wednesday to bring your overcoat. What a heavy thing, have you ever worn it?

W. is as hard on the administration as ever and says the war is but just commenced. He acted just as lazy and odd as ever. He came to tell the Knights & Mr Homer of the death of a cousin. Do you remember a lad by the name of Adams, who was here two years ago, I think, dressed in soldier's rig? It was he. I remember of your calling him a little boy.

The trees are in bloom today. Ours are not all blossomed out; perhaps the baldwins are not intending to do very much this year.[2] They have kept well this winter. Lewis looked over a barrel two weeks since, that was headed when picked, and found one bad and about a dozen speckt just a little.

I have had for callers this week the same old story, Mr Wyles, Hyde, Dea Paige (oh yes Mrs Dea is a little out of the line), George Hitchcock his wife and Laura, Mary Paige and Mary Brown and Mrs Charley.

I called down to D. Parkers tuesday night. They seemed pleased to see me. Friday their daughter buried one of her children.[3] Mr P says it is a great loss to him in a pecuniary way, having Lyman go a way last fall; he has had to plough up a great part of his strawberries.

I cannot think of a word of news, except we have eight chickens and another hen setting, but I guess I won't count the chicks.

Laura told me that Albert Allen went to Boston again of his own accord, and they were in hopes he would stay, but he came back in two days. He is so ugly they don't know what to do. He was taken up this winter, and one of his Catholic friends bailed him out. His trial comes on soon. Hard as it is, I should rather you would be at New Berne than in his place.

[1] Unidentified.

[2] Baldwin was a popular variety of apple, favored, among other reasons, for its good keeping qualities. One of its characteristics was that it usually bore heavily only in alternate years.

[3] David Parker, Jr., born 1810. The Parkers had a daughter Charlotte B., who married William H. Holdridge in 1859.

I hope you do not keep George Homer company on any thing except smoking, and I hope you keep yourself looking as neat as possible. There is a great deal in the papers about the officers drinking &c. Do you think it is so in your Regiment.

I hope I shall see the man from Chickopee. It is stormy tonight, so no one has been in.

Little Ett has been writing a composition tonight. The title is "The life of a doll". It is a pretty little thing. She is very much pleased with her school, and I think is a good girl. She is marked ten most of the time. I shall go into the street tomorrow to see if I can lend the money.

Rebecca

[Partial letter (essay by daughter Rebecca).]
But this morning Saturday, we went to ride and called at the distillery, and I will try and tell something about it. It is about twenty eight feet long and fifteen wide, it has three windows each of a different size. The building is two stories high. In one corner of the lower room is a large brick fireplace, with a boiler above, and above that is a copper cap as large as a small tub, and when they want to put in the cider they take off the cap and put in a large wooden tunnel through a hole in the floor of the upper room, and pour the cider through this tunnel.

The cap is then put on and a fire made underneath. When the cider gets to boiling the steam goes into the cap, from thence into a pipe called the worm, this goes into a large hogshead and quirls round it six times. The water keeps coming into the hogshead and when it cools the steam it converts it into a licquid[sic] called <u>low wine</u>, Mr Brown called it the worm that never dies but the thought occurred to me that there were many <u>mortal</u> worms that it did kill and not only their bodys but their souls. The water comes from a field some distance by means of a trough, of six long rails, and if the barrel gets more than full is let off by a pipe which goes into a tub and then away, the low wine goes through the same process as the cider and makes high wine or Brandy. Our party were treated to some low wine, and as weariness compelled me to partake, I thought I should not be expelled from the Band of Hope if I did so, though I must say I prefer cold water.

Sissy's essay shows advanced literary skill for her age, as well as a clear understanding of the distilling process, in this case the production of cider brandy, or applejack.

New Berne   May 30th

Dear Rebecca

With just a moments time I scratched a few words to you yesterday to let you know that I had sent some money to you by Lieut Knapp in hopes you might get it in season so as not to think that someone was going to ruin you & the family by making a present of such a sum. I received pay from the 15th of Oct. to the first of March, and after paying my debts here had $545.00 left and thought that 45 would be all I should probably need till I got my next pay, even should I not be paid again till the end of my term of service.

There is now a strong probability that we shall be mustered out of service in Mass. on or about the 22nd of July, at least the officers of the nine months men whose term of service expires next month say that they expect to return to be mustered, and some of them even say that they have received official information to that import. I am told too that the 2 years men of other states who have just been discharged were mustered in this manner, and that their time counted from the date of the muster of the last co.[?] From these statements I am led to conclude that we shall have the pleasure of troding[sic] the soil of New England some two weeks earlier than I have ever before expressed to you; but you must not set your heart too much on seeing us on any particular day, as something may happen to make it necessary for us to stay for a few days after the expiration of the nine months, and surely the intense desire that you all have for our return would not prevent your saying yes to our staying a few days were it deemed necessary if your will was to decide the question.

I am told by one of our Captains who has just returned from Westfield that many of the people at home hope we will, and think we ought to, reenlist, as we have been here long enough to get that knowledge of military matters necessary to be efficient soldiers, besides being acclimated. Very clever that, is it not. Most of the boys, I imagine, will answer "they cant see the point." For my part I would just remind such disinterested Patriots that with the love of country and disinterested patriotism they have ever manifested, it will take but a short time for them to acquire a sufficient knowledge of tackticks[sic] to make them quite efficient soldiers. And besides they should remember that we "were getting great pay" for our services with the $150.00 bounty, so great that some of them seemed almost to envy us the chance.

Now if they are drafted they can save 300 by coming, and the adage is 'a penny saved is a penny earned' and will besides receive 100 as bounty, making 400 in all. To my poor brain that should be an inducement sufficient to make such as grudged our boys 150 anxious to come (but I forgot that some of them disdained the idea of taking any bounty if they should come). Well, to them I would say that it seems to me there is a grand opportunity now for them to display their patriotism, such an one as has never been offered before. Let them embrace it by all means.

As for me, after they have spent 9 months in the service I will consider if my duty requires me come again and let them know the conclusion.

The bbl[sic] you sent has not yet got along, and it may not come for some time yet, as the means of transportation are not what they used to be. But if there be nothing perishable in it, tis just as well so far as I am concerned, for George got a box a few days since containing apples, and we have in our mess a supply for the present and plenty for the Sergts.

I read the letter to the B. boys in regard to the things and F. Cook came near fainting when he heard that part where you tell of Tarbell's returning with the liquor, exclaiming "how could the woman refuse such a donation when there was such a grand chance to have sent it?" "How, Frank," I asked. "Damn it, empty out the apple to make room of course." Well we had a good laugh.

Tom has got a fiddle, and they keep sawing away on it most the time when off duty. Last night they had a dance, and there is another going on now, and I don't know but he will forget he has a wife to write to yet. I did not attend the hop last eve as Dr. Potter called over to see me and remained till after taps. We have a good room to dance in now and the evenings are cool, so I think I shall lead in some of the figures.

Give my thanks to Mother Bliss for her present and tell her that the boys voted unanimously that she was the sweetest girl they could bring to mind.

[*Written across first page salutation.*]
I am sorry for neighbor H. Tell him to keep up good courage, for I think he is a little apt to be despondent. You seem to think we must suffer with the heat, but as yet there have been but few days very bad and the nights are quite cool. Tis very dry & dusty. Last night was the first of my sleeping without drawers, and really I think that Davie Crockett's girl with her bear skin petticoat would have been comfortable compared to sleeping between two such blankets with bare legs. Had I been brushed off with a scrub broom I hardly [sic] it would have irritated more but I shall get used to it I suppose.

Good night

Frank

Frank displays odd prescience in suspecting that his regiment will not return home at the scheduled time. He also lands a few more jabs at those men back home who found reasons not to join him. By this time in 1863, few illusions about the war remained, and volunteers could be attracted only by offering substantial bounties. Soon the North would have to resort to drafting men, as the South had already begun doing. The inability to find men willing to fight could have been taken as a signal to make peace, but neither government saw it that way.

Frank's letters make no mention of an important engagement in which the 46th participated, the expedition against Gum Spring, about eight miles from Kinston, May 20-23. Hoping to capture a Confederate outpost, Foster dispatched Col. Lee's brigade, consisting of the 5th, 25th, 27th and 46th Mass. regiments, accompanied by three pieces of Riggs' artillery and a cavalry unit. An attack on May 22 captured 165 Confederates, and on the following day the expedition fought off a counterattack. During the initial attack the 46th supported the artillery; later it supported the 25th, advancing farther to the front. After the battle, Col. George H. Peirson of the 5th Mass., who had commanded this part of the force, reported that "The 5th and 46th Mass. manifested great enthusiasm to distinguish themselves and add to their character as regiments; had serious work been required of them, I have no doubt they would have done it with spirit and determination." The expedition suffered casualties of two killed, five wounded (one in the 46th), and one missing; Sgt. Andrew S. Bryant of Co. A in the 46th was awarded the Medal of Honor for gallantry. (OR, Series I, vol. XVIII, 362-369; Barrett, Civil War in North Carolina, 162-163.)

After this engagement a period of inactivity set in that lasted beyond the 46th's term of service. One obvious reason was Foster's diminishing manpower. On May 5 he wrote to General-in-chief Halleck "I must . . . recall to your mind that by the first day of July the effectives in this department will not be more than 5,000 men, as 500 artillery are now being mustered out . . . and in June twelve of my fullest regiments are to be mustered out, their term of service then expiring (nine months)." (OR, Series I, vol XVIII, 700.) This letter is interesting in implying that the nine-months regiments had become nearly as valuable as longer-term units, and also that, while Frank in the following letter considers his company "quite small in numbers" the regiment was still "one of the fullest" from Foster's perspective.

New Berne   June 2d

Dear Rebecca

I send this letter as far as N.Y. by G. Homer, whom you will probably see in a few days after getting the letter. He has a furlough of twenty one days on acct. of sickness of his wife. Homer will tell you all the news or, if he should fail, Lt. Howe goes with him and will come to Brimfield before returning, but probably not till next week, as he is to go from N.Y. to Philadelphia before coming home.

We have discharged seven[1] men from our Co. to go into the service for three years or the war, and Lt. Lyon expects to receive a commission for the same duty. Shall I? Don't go into hysterics now, for I have no thought of the kind as yet. We have also discharged three sick men within a week, so we are getting to be quite small in numbers, though still the largest co. in the regt.

It seems foolish for me to sit here & write when you will so soon see George or Howe, who can tell you more in five minutes than I can write in an hour, so good by. I am very glad Etta is getting along so well in her school. Hope she will go through with as little trouble as she seems now to have. Rebecca I suppose you thought there was no necessity of writing about. But again I say good by.

Yours.   Frank

---

[1] Two others were later discharged for this purpose, for a total of nine. See Roster for names of those discharged. The May 27 entry in Watson's diary reports that General Foster mustered the regiment and solicited men to enlist in a heavy artillery regiment being formed. This is confirmed in William C. Harris, ed., *"In the Country of the Enemy,"* 179, which adds that the 27th was Gen. Foster's birthday.

[Regimental Order No. 70, June 2, was the last entry in the company orderly book.]

New Berne, June 5th 1863

Dear Rebecca,

Have I ever written you a letter since coming here that really suited your fancy? One I mean on reading which you did not feel that you would have liked it better if I had been a little more minute in giving the very things I did in the every day course of life, or perhaps in the social intercourse I have, if there can be said to be any such thing as social intercourse in the life we live. And from the very meagerness of my letters in this particular have you not been a little suspicious that I did really have some society that for some reason or other I chose to keep a little dark about? How is this now, Rebecca? Be as honest and frank as you can and let me know.

That question of yours asked by a prefix that the "papers give bad accts of the temperance of the officers in the army." "Do you think these stories are true of your regts." Was there the most remote suspicion in your mind at the time you wrote it that Frank might perhaps be one of the guilty parties, or did you ask the question out of womanish curiosity? Say, will you tell me plainly? You must do it plainly, for you know when at home you suffer me to guess at half you would say, or what you think by looking in your eyes. And although I can see them plain enough <u>now</u>, I did not at the time you asked your question.

Well, Rebecca, I will answer your question first and then will try to give you a good idea of how I get along with time when not on active duty. Our Regt. is not open to the charge you speak of, so far as I know. On the contrary, my impression is that most of the officers are full as temperate as they were when at home. With two or three exceptions I think that even the sedate matrons of Brimfield would not think it necessary to hold temperance meetings for their benefit.

Nor is there any point in which their behavior indicates great moral depravity. Of two of the Lieuts. I have heard things which certainly would not be very much to their credit as married men, & what I have seen has rather confirmed me in the belief that the stories were true. But with these exceptions (of course I shall not mean to include myself in the exceptions), I know nothing against morals of our officers. There may be much more than I know of these things however, for I do not mingle with the officers much, just enough to be on good terms with them all and that is all. My associates have ever since coming here been my men. And while in tents I have and now though in barracks giving us room enough, there is but little of the time when there are not men enough of the company to make it social.

Outside of the camp I know no one but friend Prouty's family, excepting a few negros and officers of other regts., just well enough to "pass the time of day". With the Lieutenant's family I visit a good deal, that is to say I go there as often as each other day or eve & he calls when it suits his convenience. Sunday they asked me to call them on my way to church and return with them to dinner. I went to church on my own hook however, but returned then to dinner and had an excellent dinner.

But I forgot, I must tell you everything we had and all about it. Well, the table is just like yours with the exception of having different legs, and was set with as much neatness as any one can set one. A good nice white cloth (and a white cloth looks wonderful to a soldier), a very good set of white ware with good knives and "silver forks," a very pretty caster and three glasses (she declared she had but three). We had some nicely boiled ham, good mashed potatoes, green peas, good bread & butter (woman's bread, not baker's), and an apple pie made of some apples I gave her from the bbl. sent here. I could not help offering her some, as she said to Merrick in my presence she did so wish she could have some from home. Now there isn't that particular enough? And was it not a good dinner?

I forgot to tell you that the eve I took tea with them we had fresh black berries. "How forgetful you are and how provoking that you can have blackberries while we shall wait them two months." Well, my dear, this living down south is not all bitter, though Heaven knows there is bitter enough in it for the south. Well, I staid till five o'clock, and the lady & Merrick were talking about coming home with me to see our dress parade when she asked me rather hesitatingly if she better, and I told her I thought it hardly proper on Sunday eve, which she readily fell in with & claimed it was not right for Merrick to go & leave her alone, & I commanded him to stay, which I had a perfect right to do, he being a Lieut. only & of course must obey. So I came alone, after making arrangements to go with them someday during the week on a sail over the river to visit the fort the rebs tried to take from us on the famous fourteenth of March on Tuesday, there being a fine breeze no matter what happened between for I am on social relations now and am deter_____

[Apparent missing page(s); concludes with overwriting salutation.]
Saturday, June 6th.
Your letter last Sunday is here. I don't now feel just like finding fault with you about the silk dress. Do in those things as you think best, knowing as you do the means we have. Should Howe come after you get this, send by him a couple of my shirts if I have any fit to wear. These are not full enough over the chest, and of course are inclined to gap. Should you not see Howe, send them by Homer, if he comes. I mean to try to go to Morehead to day with Lt Prouty, but don't know as I may be able to get away. Am very happy over the thought that the children are getting along so well with the schools. Send by I will with by the next mail[sic].
Yours
　　Frank

Frank is responding to Rebecca's letter of May 24 by gently chiding her, or displaying annoyance, perhaps both. Possibly there was another letter from her which has not been preserved, since it might have been remembered as a source of friction. Frank seems to have little sympathy for Rebecca's attempts to find topics that will promote dialog or to find something newsworthy in the placid existence of Brimfield. He seems not to understand that she may not have had the time or inclination to write the colorful descriptions he was able to produce fairly regularly (another of which follows).

Rebecca's is the age-old worry of women left behind that their men in military service, removed from the civilizing influence of female company, have reverted to their customary savage state. While he may be distressed by the result, he contributed to her fears with his sometimes heavy-handed teasing. In many of the longer-term units in both armies, there was ample justification for womanly worry, but militia-type units like the 46th Mass. posed less of a threat. Since so many of the men were acquainted, any misdeeds would eventually be reported at home and men could expect to be reminded of lapses by their neighbors for the rest of their lives.

As Frank depicts, the caste system that was prevalent in the army, with its wall of separation between officers and enlisted men, was much less pronounced in the 46th Mass. Frank, at least, felt closer to his hometown friends, regardless of rank, and associated more easily with them than with fellow officers, even though they came from the same county and had a similar background.

Dear Rebecca

In my last I wrote you that I expected to go to Fort Macon[1] on a visit soon, and I had the good luck to obtain a furlough of three days, and on Monday morning with Lt. Prouty and lady I started. We had intended to go without the lady, but one eve last week, when we were making the arrangements, she asked me what objection there was to her going. I said she asked me, and her question was directed <u>towards</u> me, but the Lt. was present, and I suppose you will readily guess why she went through the form of asking <u>me</u>. At any rate I took it that she would like me to put in a slight argument for her, and so I insisted that it would add much to the pleasure of the trip to have her go. And I guess the Lt. thought full as strongly that way as I did, for the conclusion was soon arrived at that we, three, should start on Monday morning.

And we carried out the program to the letter. Went to Morehead, about forty miles, in the cars, took a steamer to Beaufort just over the bay, where we put up at a Hotel kept expressly for visitors of the shore, a southern watering house one of the grandest in N.C., for you must know that Beaufort is the Newport of N.C. To a N.E. man there is nothing very grand about the House except the bill for board, & say what you will about it, $2.50 per day does look quite grand on a bill. And the satisfaction one takes in being able to pay such an one compensates in a great measure for poor food & poorer lodging.

We took our dinner, which was well enough so far as victuals looked, but somehow when one sits at a table where he happens to notice that there are more flies on the ceiling overhead than can find footing on the plastering, it sort takes off the relish for a bread pudding. But we all ate a pretty hearty meal in spite of these little things, for we were hungry as travellers, though I noticed that Mrs. P. confined her attention to her own plate after taking a hasty survey.

After dinner we took a sail boat for Fort Macon, across the bay about two miles. Had a pleasant sail, found the Col. commanding the Fort at the wharf and walked up to the Fort. I confess my surprise at its strength and cannot see why a few men cannot hold it against a great number with perfect safety, nor do I believe but what 300 men, or even two, would, with a fair share of pluck, hold it against ten times their number while their provisions held out. I can not now give you much of an idea of how the fort is made, and so will not try on paper. When I come, should you be curious about such things, I can give a description of it that I think will enable you to form an idea all sufficient for a woman. Suffice be it now to say that I think it is so made that I could content myself to live there with my friends about me as well as I could any where out of Brimfield.

---

[1] Fort Macon guarded the approaches to Beaufort, NC, across Bogue Sound. A masonry structure typical of the "Third System" of coastal defense, it was captured without a fight by Confederates early in the war. After the fall of New Bern, northern forces under Burnside's overall command besieged Fort Macon, and it surrendered April 25, 1862.

Mrs. P. was so taken up with the fort that I did not know at one time but we should have to leave her. After looking over the fort we went down the Island to see where the batteries were planted to reduce the fort. Lt. P. commanded the foremost one of the three and of course was able to give a full history of the fight. No man can fairly realise that a force which would seem in comparison to the fort as weakness compared with strength should be able to reduce it, but so it was. I got a very favorable idea of the Lts ingenuity from the manner he arranged his battery & conducted the fight.

Well, after a while we went to the beach and amused ourselves by watching the waves. We had such a curiosity to walk in and let the waves roll about us that the Lt & I could not well resist, so off with our shoes & socks, rolled up our pants, and walked out as far as we could and not wet our clothes and travelled about for a while, Mrs. P. sitting on the shore wishing she was a <u>man</u>. After a while the thought struck me that perhaps if there was one <u>less</u> man about, it might answer as well, so I tramped off and had not gone many rods before I saw the shadow of what I took to be shoes & hose flying back on the beach. And the next moment a glance over my left shoulder that the man & his wife were wading in the sea together. By Heaven if I could have clutched you then!

Fifteen minutes after the shoes were on the lady, and I returned to put on mine. Then we strolled about till the boat came to take us back to the Hotel, where we had a good supper, & after tea Lt & I walked about the city, which is like all the other Southern cities I have seen. That night, for the first time since I left Boston, I slept on what one could call a bed, and I guess I had a comfortable night's sleep, for I was not aware that I was at Beaufort from about ten till sunrise.

Mrs. P said after breakfast that she had about as much as she wanted to attend to for a long time after going to bed, from which I concluded they occupied a room with the big bugs,

[*Written across salutation, first page.*]
but I, being minus a lady, was put into a small room where there were three beds & four other men, & there was really but little room left for very big bugs. We had a good sail & gathered a few shells in the forenoon & returned at four. Found your letter of the 5th.[1] I cannot now answer it, as the mail is nearly ready to leave. Nor do I really know what to say, had I time. Do your duty, perhaps is all I could say had I days to write in.

Yours, Frank

[1] Apparently missing.

Whatever ripple of discord marred Frank's last letter has passed on and he is back in his jovial, richly descriptive mode. Watching the lieutenant and his wife cavorting revived his longing for Rebecca. With Prouty's assistance, he has gained a clear understanding of how the siege in the previous year was conducted. It is true that the strength of the fort should have allowed the Confederates to make a more successful resistance, but they were hampered by the lack of suitable guns and sufficient ammunition.

It has long since become apparent that Frank and Rebecca are an intelligent couple, aware of the world around them, but it is probable that neither had traveled outside their native region. The war created an opportunity, directly for Frank and vicariously for Rebecca, to visit other places, and he took full advantage. His descriptions show discerning powers of observation. The narrative does not make it clear whether Frank was in Beaufort proper or Morehead City, and he may not have fully understood the distinction. Morehead City was a fairly recent development, having been started less than ten years earlier by John Motley Morehead, a former governor of North Carolina. It rapidly became a favored resort, and the comparison with Newport, Rhode Island, then in the early stages of development as a vacation place, was reasonably appropriate. (David Stick, The Outer Banks of North Carolina, 104).

New Berne   June 12th 1863

Dear Rebecca

You will be indebted to my getting pretty well provoked (I should say mad, but that is a word that does not look well written), for this letter, coming as it does so close on the heels of my last. "What on earth can I have to get provoked about?" Well now listen to see if it be not enough to provoke a stone. I was in at Capt. "King's" last eve. when the chap. came to the door with a few letters. Seeing me, he said Capt., I left a letter in your quarters for you. Is there a boat in, I asked. No, these are a few letters that may have been kept over by the P.M.[postmaster] at the City because there was some thing due on them.

I came immediately to my quarters and found the long looked for letter which I had felt the loss of more than I probably should of any two others you had written; for I had so depended on that letter from home on returning from my tramp through Dover swamp. I declare, it seemed as though I had lost all my friends when I found that with so full a mail there was none for me, and yet I could not bring myself to believe that you failed to write on the previous Sunday. And now after the weeks time to have the mean Devils send up a letter with word that it had been detained at the office on acct of over weight. Was it not enough to make one of far better temper than mine somewhat disturbed?

Nevertheless, I opened it after some hard words about P.M.s in general and ours in particular and found it still worth being thankful for, as it contained, besides one from you of that nature that the date did not materially affect its interest, a very good one from Rebecca and her composition which is, all things considered, a very well written piece.

She must pardon me for making a few corrections in her letter. Wednesday is not spelled Wensday, though it may sound as though it was; there is no such word onto, and she should not have written, I went onto slut Hill, for the on is sufficient. Look in the dictionary and see if what we call "bisness" is spelled as I have written it. I have had so little of it to do lately I hardly know how to spell the word, but my impression is that there is a u in it some where. Now, Rebecca, don't say father is disposed to find fault, for even with the faults I have mentioned I still think the composition & letter very good for one of your age & advantages.

In the letter from big Bec there is a fear expressed that I might reenlist. I think I have written about that matter since you wrote the letter; if not George or Howe will probably set you all right in regard to the matter. I shall not go into the service again, or agree to do so, till I see you, so you can arrange your arguments for me to hear when I come. In the meantime I beg you will loose[sic] no sleep in relation to the matter. I had almost promised that I would not go again without your consent, but I guess I wont quite say that.

My last letter I was obliged to close in a great hurry, so did not say much of the burden or your last, nor yet look the letter over to correct mistakes. So I think likely you will have to fill in some sentences and perhaps I better let you try to guess wat[sic] I would think of the matter you wrote of.

You know my opinion of such ideas, Rebecca, or you might have known if you do not; and although I would not put the least restraint on your thoughts or actions in relation to religious matters, I must beg the same privilege from you. Years ago I made up my mind on this subject, after more serious deliberation on the matter than you may perhaps think, and on those points which you may deem essential have seen no reason to change my mind. I am willing to admit that I do not always do as I ought, but can not honestly say that I do not feel it as much as my friends. But I do not mean to go into any discussion, for a letter is hardly the proper channel to carry on such in & will only say that if you have had any new light, or lived to that you already had, so as to make you a happier or better woman than you were, I am certainly very glad of it, though I should hardly have found it in my heart to complain, did I receive you just as you were when I left. And I hope to return no worse.

There is a new move[?] about the time of the nine months troops, which will perhaps result in four companies going home before the rest of the regt., but whether our time will remain the same I can not tell. Tis pretty certain it will be made no shorter thereby, but may be extended till the 18th or 20th. I had written you, had I not, that the time had been fixed on the 14th to start? It looks mean[?] to me for these companies to go then because they happened to be first mustered, especially as they are not to be mustered out, but must remain there in the service till we arrive. But it is of no use to talk, for they say they do not care what people think or say they are going. Co. A had the same privilege of the rest of what was the right wing, but they have voted unanimously to stay till the rest can go.

We are now at work on breast works to protect N.B. when we are gone, and there is no duty done but the common guard duty kinds. The companies are reduced to quite a small figure by furloughs & discharges for one cause & another. There is not so much real sickness, but a good number that are not

[*Continued across salutation, first page.*]
able to do duty. My own health is for the most part very good, & although I consume much less food than I used to do, I am heavier than I have ever been for any considerable length of time, weighing 184 ½ lbs. For a few days I have felt a little Rheumatic, but hope to be better of it soon. You need not fear that you will not hear if I should be sick. An injunction from the President would not prevent the news getting to you. I forgot to ask Sissy if "quirls" in her composition is meant for coils, or has her Dictionary got a new word in it? Am glad you are so well pleased with your shrubbery. How is it with that bed of strawberries? Mrs. G. sent him some in the last letter.

Yours

Frank

There is little doubt that Frank was tempted to remain in the service. Despite the alternating boredom and danger, some aspects must have been appealing. Rebecca has to exert increasing pressure on the domestic apron strings to pull him home. It is not certain how Frank would have gone about extending his military service, as the company he commanded would have been dissolved at the end of its nine months' enlistment. He apparently assumed he could obtain a new commission.

In an apparently missing letter, Rebecca must have discussed religious issues. Though he was not entirely an unbeliever, religion seemed unimportant to Frank. The exchange is interesting in light of the religious controversy the couple became involved in 15 years later. Frank believed more in secular improvement than in religious salvation, and, as his critique of young Rebecca's essay shows, the instincts of a schoolmaster are powerful.

Brimfield   June 14th

Dear Frank

Do you know that Tuesday is to be my birthday. I think the Col would have let you come home if you had urged <u>very</u> hard.

We had the Sturbridge candidate to preach today. He resembles your brother Charles very much, though he is younger. The other night Mr Hyde was speaking of having seen him at an association in Spencer, and said "he was very much disappointed in him, for he had heard he was a bachelor, and took it for granted he was tall and lank, lean and black, and come to see him he was short, and rubicond[sic], and jocond[sic]," so he concluded he should not judge of any one again, till he had seen them. He said he found you had a great many friends in S. He stopt at Grouts.

I visited the High School this week, it was on Wednesday, and heard the compositions. Sissy had in two, a composition and a piece for the paper, the latter was signed High Private. There was a piece in the week before saying the girls were to be drafted, and she commenced hers by saying the draft has fairly arrived and nearly all the girls of the Hitchcock grammar school came under it, told who were the officers, and it was full of little witty things, at least I think so, and the visitors fairly shook.

I will tell two or three: she had Fannie Warren for Capt, and said she was a very efficient officer, she was as vigilant at detecting sugar cigars &c as Capt Lincoln was in taking whiskey bottles. Clara Hooker was first Lieu[tenant] and complimented her very highly, and says what wonder, if all officers were brought up on a Staige[sic] coach, there would not perhaps be such a lack of courage. I do not know that these were best, but I can't tell the others, though I do of Ida Baker. Now she does not write more than two or three lines in her journal, and she says of her "and last though not least is Capt. Clerk I. Baker, and if you rember[sic] with what rapidity she always wrote in her journal, you will all know how well she fills her post, and would add that she always had on hand a large stock of pens, paper &c and thought none equal to those that came from Herring's store." She is with Frank H all the time out of school. The other was titled Cemeteries, a description of Forrest[sic] Hill and a Catholic yard. It was quite interesting; I think you would call them good.

I have not had a call from Howe yet. We buy our meat now of the Wales butcher, and he told me yesterday that Moore was confined to his bed.
We have had for callers Mr & Mrs Woods, Mrs Hitchcock, Mrs Allen, C. Ward, Mrs Knight & Eunice, Mrs, Charles, beside our daily and weekly callers Mary, Mr W, and H. Mr W says he don't care, he will have one more kiss before you get home, but I looked pretty stiff and cross. Mary claims to be my oldest daughter, so Mr H says he shall be my oldest son, so you see we are not very much puckered when he makes his calls. I think you will like him better the more you are acquainted with him. He is very free and social.

You spoke of "dressing up" when you went to call. Now you need not be afraid of wearing your clothes, for I never desire to see any of them after your return, and I hope if you have a particle of love left for me you will get a thorough suit of black or dark clothes on your way home, so as to be sure to not have to appear in public in any of your souldier[sic] rig.

Monday morning

We had a nice long call last evening from Mr & Mrs Merrick Warren, and he said it was reported you would be in Boston by the 22d of July. Oh that it were here, or I could jump over the time, but we must wait for one day then another till thirty-eight have passed.

Your Rebecca

New Berne, June 16th, 1863

My dear Rebecca,

Last night for the first time since I left home I dreamed of seeing you, when it seemed as though I had been away & had returned to my family. I thought a little preparation had been made for our reception, and I walked passed by this friend & that till I came to the place where you stood waiting my approach & so natural was our meeting that I could hardly persuade myself on waking that I had not met you.

Today is your birthday, and I have set thinking it over. Thirty-five years old and we have been married nearly fifteen! I declare, it hardly seems possible. Fifteen years! Run it over in your mind and see if it seems so long since that twenty-eighth day of September that we started for our new home? Really, it seems a delusion & yet what changes have been made in the world about us since!

I can not feel that time, which seems to have laid its hand so heavily on others, has left the prints of his fingers on us. And I wonder if so many years more are to pass by so rapidly so happily to us! Even these last nine months, with which more of suspense & anxiety have been crowded than into all the rest of the time since we commenced our journey together, as I look back on it, is but a day. These letters, unimportant as I feel many of mine to have been, have served to cheer me out of the fact that we were separated my many long miles, and I have had through them such a constant conversation with you that I am not able to realise[sic], nor yet even believe, that you look now any older than when I bad[sic] adieu to you on Camp Banks.

And if you expect to meet me looking as one whom the fatigue of terrible marches had brought to look years older than when I left, you will be happily surprised, or the next month will work the change. And although I have had anxiety and doubt about our meeting again, it has been but for a moment at a time. My hope has for the most part of the time amounted to a faith that we should meet at the expiration of my term of service and be all the happier that the sacrifice had been made. Thirty-five today! And I most forty-two! A long way on the journey of life to those who believe that all of life is numbered up in three score years & ten, but to me the whole seventy years hardly reaches to the childhood of life.

And if it be a delusion, it is one I delight in to believing. Those whose feelings are such as to add to each other's happiness here are not to be separated hereafter, though the creeds of all sectarianism declare for the separation. "What God hath joined together, let no man put asunder," says the priest in the ceremony of marriage; and he might with truth say what God hath joined shall so remain forever. The sixteenth day of June! How many times this day have you tried to imagine what I was doing & wondered if I remembered it was your birthday, & perhaps if the sixteenth of the next month would bring the 46th Regt home? And I wonder if the day seems as long to you as to me. But I must try to get out of this train of thought, otherwise the few days that remain will seem longer to me than all the rest of the time here.

We are falling off in numbers quite fast by discharge from disability & the new regt. Already we number but 80, & I have the papers made out for four more, among which are those of Henry Bennett, who has finally come to the conclusion that he had better go if he can get his papers; & I think he will get them without any difficulty, as the time is but short for any of us to stay, & there is no probability of his being able to do any more duty in that time.[1]

We have no very sick ones except Bryant Pendleton*, who will probably go in the next boat, if able. Tom has three of the boys at the Hospital [in] Beaufort.

[1] Bennett, or Bennet, was discharged June 17, 1863, at New Bern.

I had him go partly because he has never fully recovered from his Gum swamp march & partly because he had a desire to visit the place. No doubt he will enjoy himself hugely there, as he will have a chance to ride about the harbor, get all the clams & frogs he wants, besides hunting the shore over for things curious. I expect he will be able to add something to my stock of shells, which is not as yet very large or nice. Ned Bliss is one of the boys with him. Ned went as chaplain & will probably instruct Tom in difficult theological points.

June 18th   Your letter in which you speak of having seen George is here. It seems to me that he has grown old fast, but he insists on it that it only because hair dye is more costly here than there. He certainly <u>looks</u> like one of 50 years, and all his ways are those of an old man; but it does not do to talk about the matter, for he is a little sensitive on the subject.

You speak of Sarah's coming and my extending an invitation to her to visit us.[1] <u>That</u> I certainly shall never do; if my sister has to be invited to visit <u>me</u>, & that too at the homestead, it is a fault of hers, not of mine. All I intended to say to you about her was that if she came in my absence I did hope for your own & the children's happiness you would try to appear as though the past was not so held

[*Continued across salutation, first page.*]

in remembrance as to make it unpleasant for her from anything you might do. I hope she will not come till I do. We are having very warm weather here. During the daytime the heat reaches 105, but the eves are quite cool.[2] I have not slept a single night without as much as two blankets over me. There are but a few hours in the day that it is extremely warm, from about ten till three, say. The rest of the day quite cool. I have not seen an evening yet when it was suitably warm for one to sit at the door through the evening. Goodbye.

Yours,
Frank

[1] Sarah D. Lincoln was Frank's older sister, born Dec. 17, 1819.
[2] Watson's diary entry for this date says "It has been very hot to day the thermometer stayed at 98 degrees above zero in the shade."

New Berne   June 21, 1863

Dear Rebecca

Tis Sunday morning just after services. You will not probably be up for a long time but probably will be ready to read this letter, & so as I have washed & <u>combed</u> <u>my</u> <u>hair</u> (the which regulations require soldiers to do twice each day), I will scribble a little while Charley is getting the coffee ready, for you know I have come to the conclusion that coffee made in a good clean pot and tended while cooking is full as good as it is made in an iron kettle holding three pails of liquor & which the cooks keep stewing to suit their convenience. I don't know but I am getting a little dainty, for I not only find fault with my coffee, but it goes rather against the grain to rattle the worms out of our bread & then eat it. I would not object so much to the worms if they were only decent looking "varmints," say like skippers in cheese, but these fellows are wooly like the catapiller[sic], & it seems as though a hand full of them would be unpleasant in one's stomach.

However, we get along in one way & another, though it comes hard for me to loose[sic] the hard tack, for it was the better part of my living. Lyon is altogether different. He seems to like these greasy fried pies and the trash, if that can be called trash, which is nearly as solid as lead, which they cook up here in the shape of cakes. But for my part I had rather drive the worms from the regular army bread and eat it with cold water than to try to make a meal of anything else we have here, except now and then a few fresh vegetables. But you know bread was ever my staff of life, or of food at any rate, and without it, or with that of a poor quality, it never seems to me as though we have anything. We have flour, and the boys bake what they call griddle cakes, which they eat as little children eat the cake taken on the sly from mother's cupboard. I think a better name for our cakes is slapjacks or slapping jacks.

Well, we have been to, rather than eaten, our breakfast, and I will tell you what we had: a pot full of decent coffee, one of tea for Lt. Lyon, sugar brown & white, a few slices of fresh, cold, boiled meat, hard tack with plenty of worms to season them, a piece of skippery cheese, a pail of apple sauce, and cucumbers. Lyon sat & made mouths at this good substantial meal and finally started for some pies, brought some apple & some meat pies from the sutlers. I attempted to worry down a piece of the apple, but some how sweet apple made into pies don't taste good. I am sorry, for most of the pies we have are made of such.

Your last Sunday's letter came last night. I was a little surprised that you had not seen Howe, for when he left he said he should certainly go to Brimfield & I supposed he would try to make his visits so as [to] be back by the time of his furlough expired, but he is not here and his time expires today. Not only that, but there is no boat coming to bring him for a number of days; and the last boat left N.Y. so as to bring the papers of the 18th, & Howe must have known that if he did not come in that there was no probability of his getting here in season! But it is his mess not mine, and there is not likely to be any trouble in regard to it, as we are doing nothing but digging and can dispense with one Lt. from each company, though a Commissioned officer has to go out with every company.[1]

It seems the North are stirred up again by the approach of Lee's army. Really, I don't know but it is the only means of keeping those devilish Copperheads decent, & I hope he will go far enough this time and do mischief enough to scare the whole batch of them, so that they will stop their treasonable language, if not their designs. You wonder how I can wish an advance of the enemy to disturb the peaceful homes of the North. Peaceful homes! I tell you, there is to be no peace there or here till copperheadism is completely put down.

I have worried over our slow progress in this war & wondered at it, and although I am still sad that we deserve the punishment we are receiving, I can but feel that the chastisement is just, and I am as certain that we are not to be successful until that base of all base prejudice of the northern people, which refuses to sanction the full freedom of the African is humbled in the dust as I am of the justice of heaven. Let the base devils swear and cry Nigger; the day is coming when the nigger is to [be] the instrument in saving this country, and these contemptible skunks shall own that to him they owe their <u>freedom</u>. Don't think my crazyness[sic] grows on me. I have lived to see the reasonableness of my former views and to know that they partook more of hunker than radicalism.

But I did not mean to write of politics. I wonder not at your anxiety for our return & that the time seems long! We have now probably twenty five days to stay here, and it seems a long time to me, though tis but yesterday Howe & George went, and they have been absent most as long. You hope to see me in citizen's dress. That can not be, as we shall probably have to go to Springfield as a regiment, & I hardly think you will content yourself at home knowing we are to be at Palmer depot on our way to Springfield on the __[sic] day of July. Besides, I have been thinking I should wear my brass buttons till after the draft, lest some of these fellows might need a little assistance about coming.

---

[1] George H. Howe returned to action Nov. 2, 1863 as 2nd lieutenant in the 57th Mass. By then a captain, he was killed at the battle of the Crater, July 30, 1864, when the Union Army undermined and blew up a section of Confederate trenches at Petersburg, VA, but then failed to follow up the advantage. Howe's body was recovered and he was buried in Monson. The funeral was supposed to have been held in the Methodist church, "but the assembled multitude was so great that not one-tenth of them could gain admission, hence the ceremony was held in the open air." (Capt. John Anderson, *The Fifty-Seventh Regiment of Massachusetts Volunteers* [Boston, 1896] 189). For more information on the 57th Mass., a regiment that suffered devastating losses, see Warren Wilkinson, *Mother, May You Never See the Sights I Have Seen: The Fifty-Seventh Massachusetts Veteran Volunteers in the Last Year of the Civil War* (Harper & Row, 1990), reviewed by Larry Lowenthal in *Historical Journal of Massachusetts*, Winter 1992.

[*Continued across salutation, first page.*]
Am being glad the children are getting along so well, or so much to your satisfaction, at school. Could not Sissy send her productions to me? Did she take with good grace the criticisms I made on her other? Tom is still at Beaufort with four others of the company. He means to take his trip to the seashore before coming home. We have a number sick there in the Hospital, two from Monson & one from Wales. Tis quite warm during the daytime, but cool nights—has been but one night yet that I did not need two blanket[sic] over me. Charley is quite indignant that George should presume to kiss his wife, & only his in open church, but you must not tell her, for there is considerable jealousy in regard to what is written home, and I do not wish anything I might say in sport to come back. J. H. continues to send papers. Had a letter from Bird in the last mail, all [well?] with the club except Bird.

Yours, Frank

During the course of his military service, Frank's political views had become more radical and adamant. As he says, his earlier opinions were more in line with the "hunkers," a moderate, rural faction of the Democratic Party. Now he has come around to the abolitionist side and expresses support for prosecuting the war with unrelenting vigor. His idea that the North must be punished for its failings resembles the statements of extreme abolitionists such as John Brown, who said that the sins of the guilty land must be purged by blood.

Nothing is more reminiscent of home and tradition than foodways, and Frank has strong opinions on that subject as well. Accustomed to apple pies, a New England staple, made from fresh or dried varieties that were suitable for cooking, he expresses disgust at the local version made from sweet, or dessert, apples. Reading this, Rebecca may finally be convinced that her husband will be coming back to New England.

Dear Rebecca

I have just time to write that we left New Berne on Wednesday and are now on board the steamer we came on at Fortress Monroe. Where we are to go or what we are expected to do, I have no means of knowing. Only one thing is settled, I.E., we are not to return to New Berne. We left 25 men who were not able to take the trip with any hope of being able to do anything, though few of them [were] what we should call <u>sick</u> at home & fewer very sick. They will go home by the first chance.

When we shall come or start of course I can not say, but I do not think the chances are that we shall go any sooner than we should had not this move been made. Of the men left at New Berne, Henry Lumbard, F. Cook, G. Parker & Bixby are all from Brimfield. We had the good luck to meet Howe & George at Hatteras & have them with us.

I have just heard from the Col. that we are to remain here through the most of the day and then start for West Point [Virginia], where Keyes is stationed. You had not better write to me untill you hear, for tis not certain or probable that we shall stop in any[sic] anyplace long enough to have a mail come from home. I have not yet got your last week's letter, & before I left New Berne I made an arrangement with Lt. Prouty to send what mail should come to me at N.B. to Brimfield or destroy it.[1]

I can not write you now of this place, as we are all in a hurry to get ready to leave, & besides I have seen nothing of the place, except as I see it from the harbor. If we are in a situation where I can write again, I will improve it. Gen. Foster came up here with us but has returned. Am not well today, but hope to be able to get a little sleep and come out of it better.

Good by

Yours   Frank

---

[1] Lt. Prouty remained with the 25th Mass. and was mustered out Oct. 20, 1864, having served three years.

Instead of a placid winding down of its military service, the 46th was unexpectedly swept up in larger events. When Lee's victorious army moved north, it created panic, and northern leaders hurriedly scraped together whatever forces they could find to defend their endangered cities. Sister regiments of the 46th Mass., like the 44th, had been mustered into service earlier and had already completed their enlistments and returned to civilian life; but the 46th was still in uniform. Even with its diminished numbers, the regiment represented a trained and cohesive unit, and as such attracted the attention of northern generals.

Having volunteered to serve, the 46th could hardly refuse its country's call in that perilous hour, and so the officers agreed to extend its tour of duty through the emergency. They were too far south to participate in the great battle at Gettysburg, July 1 to 3, 1863, but, as part of the Army of the Potomac, they figured in the subsequent action. As Lee's army receded from its high-water mark, the 46th took position on its flanks, ready to defend Baltimore and Washington, or to participate in a climactic effort to crush the invaders. As had been the case in North Carolina, the 46th Mass. happened not to be drawn into heavy fighting, though it was certainly exposed to that risk, and events could easily have taken a different course. Meanwhile, the dramatic alteration in the regiment's destiny gave Frank new opportunities to record his impressions of striking scenes.

Baltimore   July 1st

Dear Rebecca

I have just time to say that we have just arrived in this city under an order of Gen. Halleck.[1] Where to go from here I know not. If I find out in season will write again. We left at Fortress Monroe three men sick, [George] Barnes, R.[Royal] Nelson* & O.[Osbern] Fenton*.

Uncle Cheney has been poorly since the first day out and will not be able to move with us if we have to march. Bill S.[Stearns] has the jaundice & looks as yellow as a saffron bay. [Israel C.] Earle says he does not feel able to do anything but may be able to move if we have to go from here. Rest of the boys with me well, but have no conveniences for writing, so you will start your train as soon as you get this to let the friends in B know.

Yours   Frank

P.S. Uncle Cheney is suffering under a half fever half sea sickness. Guess he will be better when we land. Shall send him home if it be possible when we land, if he wants to go.

Frank

P.S. I see some of the boys are writing but who will write & get their letters off I don't know, so it will do no harm to see them all.

Frank

I suppose F. Cook & the rest of the boys left at N.B. are at home, as I hear they were to leave there last Saturday. Hope they will get safely <u>home</u>.

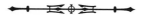

Baltimore   July 2d

Dear Rebecca

Just to tell you that we have gone into camp close by the city of Baltimore. I write these few lines this morning. Can not tell how long we shall remain, but as the mail comes in two days from home, you had better write me here. I think there will be no attempt to keep us longer than the 22nd & should Lee's forces be driven back or defeated we shall probably be sent immediately.

Uncle Cheney is in the Hospital, but is not very sick. Hope his folks will not worry, as he is able to write but thought he would not this morning.

Yours   F.D.L.

---

[1] General Henry W. Halleck, general in chief of the federal forces.

Sunday July 5 63

Dear Rebecca

You will not be provoked if you get a few lines from me each or every other day, and I have need to write but a few lines. To tell the plain truth I feel less able to do any thing than I have for so long a time together since I left you. This jaunting about on a steam boat with nothing to do, impatient all the time to get on shore, which lies within a half mile of one, drinking water that the Horses refuse, is enough to kill any one who is ever alive & I have been "right smart sick" ever since we came in sight of Fortress Monroe. Though I have kept about, I have felt like being in bed.

You have not had from me any detailed account of our trip here, or how it happened that we came. And you will excuse me from attempting to give any acct. of the matter further than to say that we were ordered to go to the support of Gen. Dix, but were delayed in getting to Fortress Monroe till after one of the other regts. had been up the river & found that Dix did not wish our help. But the Gen. in command at Baltimore did want us if we were <u>willing</u> to come, & the officers voted to come to this point, believing that the better sense of the regt. would not allow them to go home at such a crisis as this even if they were <u>permitted</u> to do so.

For one, I am very glad we came as we have had an opportunity to see more of the country that is really worth seeing than in all the rest of the time, besides placing ourselves in a position to do some good. Baltimore is about equally divided between secesh & union in numbers, with a hatred on the part of the former fit only for Devils. The presence of troops here is necessary at a time like this, especially as they are forwarding prisoners here daily. Besides, there was no other point where troops could have been sent forward to the assistance of the Army of the Potomac as well as from this.

Things now look well for our cause, and we shall probably move from here homeward next week, if not the last of this. Uncle Cheney is much better. Charley Upham* is some ailing, but I trust will not be seriously ill. I feel that in one respect we are far better situated than we were at New Berne. We are where we can send to our friends at any time, and they would be able to get to us in two days time. Really, it seems like getting into a new world to be where a letter can come to us from home the next day after tis mailed. Charley got a letter from his wife this morning at 10, which left Brimfield yesterday at nine! Think of that & remember we have waited ten and even fifteen days to get letters from our friends.

[Written across salutation, first page.]
But good by. Hope to see you next week.

Yours. Frank

Harpers Ferry   July 10

Dear Rebecca

You have probably wondered that you did not get letters from me as I intimated you might in my last, but the heading of this, if you had had no other intimation of our moves will explain the cause. At three o'clock Monday morning we were ordered to be ready at day light to leave and came on the Baltimore & Ohio R.R. to this point.

We have & still occupy what are called Maryland Heights, which are just opposite Harpers Ferry & command one of the passes from South Mountain to the Patomac[sic]. The contending armies are to the north & n.west of us at a distance of about 15 or 18 miles, or perhaps varying from 12 to 20. Should we stay here, I think we are as safe as at any point in the vicinity of hostile forces. But whether we are to remain, or how long, I can not and do not know as <u>any</u> <u>one</u> can tell. It will probably depend on Lee's moves. Fighting is going on between the two armies each day in distinct hearing of us, & it is said that Lee has passed through the gap and is making the best of his way to Williamsport! If so, I fear he gets back to Richmond.

I will not go through with an acct[sic] of our moves since we left, but will content myself by saying that although they have been sufficiently fatiguing, no one of us who gets safely away will not feel that all the fatigue has been more than compensated for by the scenery we have passed through and now have.

We encampted[sic] two nights & part of two days on the mountain which overlooks the scenery that Jefferson said (& I think said truly) was worth a voyage across the Atlantic to witness. To stand above Harpers Ferry & see the Patomac, having just received the waters of the Shenandoah, as if to give it strength for the effort, sweep through the mountains where the huge rock is broken off for two hundred feet high on either side for its passage, looking as though nature had at this point made a mighty dam to stay the flood of water, but they in their might had forced the very mountains, rock though they be, to yield, is a sight well worth many privations to witness. But this is only one of the grand sights we have witnessed. Nor can I give you in a letter any definite idea of the grandeur, nor do I think one can hardly form one, without witnessing the scenery. Pen ink & paper are poor at description of such scenery.

Whatever may be the emergency, our Reg. will probably be ordered to move towards home when their time is out and perhaps in season to be at home by this time. The 51st is here & has orders to have three days rations (<u>cooked</u>) in readiness today, with the understanding among them that they are going home. This would take them home by or before their time is up, & I believe that two regts. were sent on Thursday from the field where they expected a battle to commence at any moment because their time had expired. Ours will be served as others have been.

[*Written across salutation, first page.*]

I wrote you that I was sick and you will wonder at my coming and I did start sick enough to be in bed, but I must come if my friends did, so I gave the command to Howe & came & am now much better than when I started.

Yours

Frank

Maryland Heights   July 12th

Dear Rebecca

Very unexpectedly I received your letter of the 8th containing as many as 20 words. Don't think I was not thankful to get even so much, but it did seem as though it was a pity to waste nearly one side of a sheet of note paper. I suppose there is a dearth of news as well as water in Brimfield, though I imagine there will be stirring times there and talk enough if not news as soon as they commence the draft.[1] Perhaps the success of our arms of late will so excite the patriotic sentiment of the people that it will not be necessary to make one, volunteering being sufficient.

I would not have attempted to write to day but that I felt if you had read my last letter you would be anxious to hear as often as you could. You see we remain in the position we occupied when I last wrote, & I have very good evidence that the General in command expects us to stay here as long as we continue in the service. But he can only judge by probabilities, nor can any one tell what the emergency may be, and of course tis impossible to tell with any degree of certainty where we may be tomorrow.

All we know is that the present order is to hold this point. There are rumors to day that Lee has crossed the river. If so, the chase is useless, for he will get quite a start of Meade, and if he follows I believe it will be of little use. If he still remains this side, then there probably will be the hardest fight of this campaign. I am confident that our force will be victorious, and although there must necessarily be great slaughter of our men, I still believe that in the long run it would cost less life than to have the enemy get off without a battle.

As to bagging Lee & all his force, why tis simply ridiculous on any supposition that he looses[sic] all his cunning and they all their ability to run or fight. Doubtless he has been so crippled already that should Meade let him go they are far worse off for the raid & I hope & trust they are to be troubled still more.

The boys at Baltimore were all getting along well when I last heard, but of those at New Berne I know nothing, but suppose they must be about going home. I trust that they will all get back by the time we get there.

New regts. Continue to join us & others are daily expecting to go. The 34th came from Washington day before yesterday, which you know contains the boys from B. that enlisted just before we did. Frank G.[2] & Kenfield[3] were here yesterday morning and took breakfast with us. I cooked some ham & coffee & shared it with Gardner, & the other boys helped the rest of those that came. Ed. Hitchcock[4]

---

[1] A national conscription act had been passed in March, and the first draft was underway. It provoked rioting in several northern cities.

[2] Probably Francis S. Gardner of Brimfield.

[3] Orsamus Kenfield.

[4] Edward Walker Hitchcock, born 1839, the son of Marcus Hitchcock.

was of the number. This is the first time their regt. has been out of sight of the capital, & they think this quite a tramp considerable to bear for these fellows.

Tell Etta to keep a little of her mirth till I come, for it will be quite a rare thing for me to see a mirthful white child. The children we see look like disconsolation itself. Good by.

Yours   Frank

Frank was enjoying the spectacular scenery at Harpers Ferry, a point of great strategic importance on several occasions during the war. General George G. Meade, commander of the Army of the Potomac, won at Gettysburg while almost entirely on the defensive and has often been criticized for allowing Lee to escape to Virginia without a major battle and thus prolong the war for nearly two more years of horrific bloodshed.

Frederic[sic]   July 18th 1863

Dear Rebecca

We are relieved from military duty and are [on] our way home, thank God. For a week have been in the army of the Patomac. I am now on my way to Frederic to get Tom, who was sent yesterday to the Hospital. The Regt. comes on the next train, & I expect to join it at Monocracy[sic; the Monocacy River, a battlefield during another invasion of Maryland a year later]. We shall probably be at home on Wednesday, perhaps sooner. The cars shake so I cannot write, so good by.

Frank

Most of the 46th arrived home Tuesday, July 21 (some of the men who had been discharged from hospital had returned more than a week earlier). The Palmer Journal *(July 25) reported that "They were a good deal browned by a southern sun and exposure to the weather, but they appeared in excellent spirits . . . ." The town of Wales gave the heroes a "reception supper" on July 23; while there is no record of similar festivities in the other towns, the* Journal *was surely correct in observing "There were many open arms to receive the long absent ones; and tears of gratitude flowed from many eyes . . . ." Frank probably came home to Rebecca in uniform and had to don it again on the following Tuesday, when the regiment reassembled in Springfield for the mustering out ceremony that took place July 29. Even then, Frank's military duties were not finished, as he was responsible for distributing the soldiers' final pay, which did not appear for several more weeks.*

After deaths, re-enlistments and early discharges, 72 men of the approximately 100 who had served in Co. G remained to assemble at the final muster. Overall, the 46th had mustered a total strength of 43 officers and 904 enlisted men. Of that number, one had died of wounds and 32 of accidents or disease.[1] Despite the gratefully low losses, the men had every reason to take pride in the service they had rendered their country.

A surprising piece of information provided by the Journal *was that the troops had brought back "a couple of young contrabands" and that Capt. Lincoln took one of them home with him.[2] This tantalizing report was not expanded in subsequent editions, so we know nothing about how these people came to be with the 46th, what became of them later, or even whether they were male or female. If, as seems likely, they came from North Carolina, they may have accompanied the 46th on its tiresome detour to Harpers Ferry.*

---

[1] Thomas Wentworth Higginson, *Massachusetts in the Army and Navy during the War of 1861-65* (State of Massachusetts, 1896, 2 vols.).
[2] July 25, 1863.

SERVING IN OTHER WAYS

With pressure from his family pushing in the same direction, Frank Lincoln resisted any temptation he may have felt to extend his military service. His devotion to the cause remained strong, and he found other ways to aid the war effort. Probably helped by the influence of Francis W. Bird, he was appointed by Governor John Andrew to the Massachusetts Board of Cattle Commissioners on May 24, 1864. Documents in the Lincoln papers show that the captain approached this assignment in his usual dutiful, competent style.

With little dissension Brimfield met repeated calls for manpower. Assembled at town meeting, the citizens taxed themselves to pay bounties, burial expenses, and support of soldiers and their families. In those years of trial and agonizing disappointment, this small New England town and its pure form of democracy shone with glory. As a leading citizen and a veteran, Frank undoubtedly used his prestige and speaking ability to sustain Brimfield's commitment to the struggle, no matter the cost in lives and money.

One of the memorable events of the war in Hampden County was the Soldiers' Fair held in Springfield in December 1864. Intended to raise money to aid the thousands of wounded or discharged soldiers passing through that crossroads city, the event represented a rededication to the Union cause, energized by victories such as Sherman's capture of Atlanta. Coming after years of sacrifice, the fair still succeeded in raising $18,000 (50 to 100 times as much in today's currency). Brimfield was an outlying, largely agricultural, town with little industry and no wealthy benefactors, yet it contributed $149.80 to this total, an impressive figure coming after years of extra taxation and personal donations to the war effort. A note on Springfield Institution for Savings letterhead indicates that Frank Lincoln was in charge of the Brimfield campaign.

At the first regular town meeting after the war, in March 1866, Capt. Lincoln proposed spending $1250 to erect a monument in honor of the Brimfield men who died in the war, and his motion was approved. This monument, one of the earliest Civil War memorials in the state, was completed rapidly and dedicated July 4th, 1866. Frank presented the main address at the dedication, confirming that he was the Brimfield citizen most closely associated with the war effort.[1] He delivered a noble patriotic speech, such as might have been uttered by a Roman senator before the Republic became corrupted—proud but without the pompous rhetorical flourishes typical of the time; rejoicing in what he considered the triumph of righteousness without gloating over the defeated foe. He did not elevate those who died above others who served, on the grounds that all had risked their lives; and, mindful of Rebecca's letters, he recalled with honor the immense sacrifices of the home folks.

---

[1] Published as fourteen pages of a pamphlet.

The Brimfield Civil War Monument was rededicated at a special public ceremony, September 24, 2006.

Probably the surviving record preserves only a small portion of Frank's personal activities related to the war. The collection in the Hitchcock Academy includes the following two unusual and important letters from W.G. Leonard, a chaplain with the U.S. Sanitary Commission in eastern North Carolina. This was William G. Leonard, who had been pastor of the M&E church in South Wilbraham (now Hampden) and left to become captain of Co. I in the 46th Mass. He had returned to, or remained in, the area where he had served after the regiment was mustered out. At 35 when he entered service, he was close to Frank's age, and although it is unfortunate that he is not mentioned in Frank's letters, the two men were surely acquainted.

In carrying on this work in North Carolina, Rev. Leonard was consistent with his principles. Before joining the 46th he had apparently not been a passionate abolitionist, believing more in practical action than in fiery exhortations from the pulpit. Writing to a female church member while he was serving in the 46th, he explained, "While I regard slavery as a great wrong, and pray its destruction, I think the attention of a congregation should not be constantly engaged with the subject. An anti-slavery or anti-rebellion lecture in South Wilbraham will do but little good here. No slaves are there, nor slave-holders. . . . True, we should pray for the nation's prosperity, the dreadful strife to cease; but to pray that the South should be annihilated, the slaves all sent to Liberia, or some other definite object, beyond our knowledge of what is best, is to pray at random."[1]

U.S. General Hospital
Smithville N.C.
June 26" 1865

Capt. Lincoln.

Dear Sir.

When I was Negro Superintendent of Negroes[sic] at Pt. Lookout, Md. I persuaded two Colored families to go north with me to labor in Wilbraham. They went the last days of March 64. Their names were Willis & Cole. Mrs. Eliza Cole had money due her at the U.S. Hospt. but could not get it. I took her papers & when I returned I collected it. I wrote to know her whereabouts. It seems that the families had left Wilbraham & engaged to Mr. Merrit Esqr. of Springfield, & he had sent them to Brimfield to work on his farm. He wrote me to that effect. I wrote him I would send the money to him if he would be responsible for it & that it should reach her. I have never heard a word from either since. I have the money & would like for it to reach the woman, Mrs. Eliza Cole. She has a husband & son. If you will give me any information of their whereabouts, I will be greatly obliged.

If she is there, will you be the medium of payment?

Our war is over and our soldiers can scarcely be made to care for the sick among them. Our best troops now are the negroes. We hope to send the last of the white soldiers home very soon.

Yours Truly,
Wm.G. Leonard
Chaplain, U.S.A.

Please direct as above & add via Wilmington, N.C.

[1] Quoted in the Palmer *Journal*, Feb. 21, 1863.

United States Sanitary Commission [letterhead]
U.S. Genl. Hospital
Smithville, N.C.
July 12, 1865

Capt. F.D. Lincoln
Sir.

I am much pleased to hear of Mrs. Cole & to find a medium through whom to pass the honest dues to an honest woman, or who was such when I sent her North.

I had rec'd an inkling of Esq. Merrick's honor(?) and hence was a little cautious about sending the money.

I think Eliza is a good woman and hope she will do well. I will send the money to you by express. I shall be going to Wilmington this week and will forward it by Adams' Express to you Brimfield Mass. Will you just deliver it to her and notify me of the fact. I care for no receipt.

I think those families had better remain North another year as times are mighty poor here now; & the state of Colored society very uncertain. Tell them to have patience and find good men to deal with. I am sorry they did not remain at Mr. Sessions in Wilbraham. But he is a driver. They would have been paid.

I tell you, Captain, we are in the midst of a haughty people. Though conquered, they boast of a <u>glorious</u> <u>cause</u>. Rebels at heart, but shrewd enough to make a good bargain. Haters of Negroes & Haters of the Yankees. It would be far better for our country now to enfranchise the negro; not that they would make a majority against their masters, but it would ensure their good treatment, and but [put?] the agitation down. These Southern masters would manage to secure the negro vote. The negroes will work for them now sooner than for Yankees & cheaper. But I must not discourse these questions.

Notwithstanding the people hate Yankees, I can have large audiences out in the country a little & frequently ride out ten miles and preach. There is a little mellowing: & a little more readiness to do the best they can. There are openings for farmers & mechanics about here.

I would be glad to see factories built & negro girls employed in them & the white girls "snuff dippers" be driven to do their own work.
Yours truly,
W.G. Leonard
Chaplain U.S.A.

Quite likely there was a letter from Frank, now lost, between these two, which would account for the name Merrit in the first letter being corrected to Merrick. Leonard's letters are marvelously revealing of conditions in that part of the South in the first months after the fighting ended (General Lee had surrendered at Appomattox in early April). In particular, it is remarkable to confirm that the myth of the "glorious [or lost] cause" had taken hold at that early date. Leonard had been in the region long enough to become a shrewd observer, and he seems to anticipate the disappointing outcome of Reconstruction in terms of African American progress. Although he would not presume to make the suggestion directly, Leonard seems to be inviting capable men like Frank and Tom Morgan to seize the opportunity to help develop the southern economy.

Although Esq. Merrick is not fully identified, he is almost certainly the same individual with whom Frank had been involved in a fierce controversy a few months earlier. The Lincoln papers contain a petition dated October 19, 1864, in which Frank's prominent signature is second, stating that "The undersigned Republican voters of the town of Brimfield earnestly protest against the nomination of A.N. Merrick as the Republican candidate for County Commissioner because from a thorough knowledge of his character we believe him to be unworthy of public trust and confidence." The subject of this devastating indictment is Ambrose Newell Merrick, born in Brimfield in 1827, the son of Reuel Merrick and Marcia Fenton. A.N. Merrick was noted as one of the few Brimfield residents to have a college education (Williams, 1850). The family lived along the main highway (present Rt. 20) in the western part of Brimfield, an area that became known as Fentonville. Reuel had died in 1832, and the remaining Merricks were no longer living in Brimfield in 1865, though they retained their farm property[1]

In 1864 A.N. Merrick was a lawyer and political aspirant in Springfield. At a Republican county convention on October 13, he was nominated for county commissioner, although leading Brimfield Republicans such as Frank Lincoln *believed they had assurances he would not be a candidate and were prevented by a heavy storm from attending. Brimfield Republicans met on the 24th and endorsed the petition against Merrick, which 59 of them had signed. Although Brimfield was a small town on the edge of Hampden County, this testimonial from the people who knew Merrick best had an impact. The Springfield* Republican, *normally loyal to the party whose name it bore, accepted Merrick's "untrustworthiness as a business man" and took the rare step of supporting his opponent.*

[1] The Assessors' Valuation List of May 1, 1865, shows that A.N. Merrick was taxed on personal property consisting of a horse ($120), a colt ($50), 4 oxen ($450), 17 cows ($680), 5 two-year olds ($125), 25 sheep ($130) and 5 swine ($85), indicating a commercial farming operation. The family farmhouse may have still been standing, as he was taxed on two houses and three barns, as well as 350 acres of land. As a non-resident, he did not pay a poll tax.

Throughout the controversy, Frank took a prominent part, sending a long letter to the Republican and, with Henry F. Brown (who had served a term as county commissioner 1857-60), arguing against Merrick at a special convention on Saturday, November 5. Here the two Brimfield leaders finally laid out specific charges against Merrick. They involved financial dealings and, as the paper conceded, were in the nature of "petty meannesses, merely—not glaring crimes." By then, with the election coming on the 8th, time was running out, and the convention decided it was preferable to stick with its existing candidates rather than make a last-minute change and risk losing.

In the election, Merrick beat his opponent 4694-3528, but his unpopularity was shown by the fact that he ran far behind the rest of the ticket. Whereas President Lincoln carried Hampden County by 3420 votes, Merrick's margin was 1166. In Springfield, where Merrick lived, he reduced the party majority from 1567 to 890. Brimfield, normally a strongly Republican town, supported Merrick's opponent 199-16, a telling commentary; and neighboring towns rejected Merrick by overwhelming margins. As the Republican concluded, he did best where he was least known. (The story is covered in various reports and editorials in the Republican, Oct. 14 to Nov. 9, 1864. The Brimfield petition was published Oct. 28, and Frank's letter on Nov. 1.) According to the family genealogy (George B. Merrick, Madison, WI, 1902), A.N. Merrick left Springfield in 1867 and went on to a distinguished career in Minneapolis and Washington Territory; the genealogy does not mention his troubles in Brimfield and Springfield.

AT HOME IN BRIMFIELD

A long generation behind Frank and Rebecca, Brimfield was graced by Mary Anna Tarbell, a representative of those high-minded intellectual women whose lives are one of New England's outstanding achievements. Believing unswervingly in the civilizing value of education and high culture, she devoted her life to teaching, library work, and preserving history. As a writer, she was fluent and forthright, and these characteristics are especially evident in the obituaries she wrote, which she developed into a minor art form. As the chronicler of Brimfield life, or at least of the prominent people in the center village with whom she was best acquainted, she made their obituaries much more than a formal summary of their lives. Each obituary was really an essay, describing the individual's personality and defining his place within the flow of Brimfield history. As someone remarked, it was almost worth dying to have Anna Tarbell pen your obituary.

Several years after Frank Lincoln died, she wrote that "Francis was the one to whom it fell to stay in Brimfield and maintain the old home," in contrast to his four brothers, who earned success as lawyers and businessmen in other states.[1] To what extent this was a voluntary choice is hard to say, but there is no doubt that Frank remained closely associated with Brimfield for the remainder of his life. After the war, he held numerous town offices, performing the duties of moderator at meetings and serving on various special committees. Despite his manifest abilities as a writer and an orator (he gave the welcoming address at the town's centennial celebration in 1876), and his other leadership qualities, his sphere of action remained limited to Brimfield and adjacent towns. Whether he sought wider influence remains uncertain; if he did, Brimfield's small size and isolation would have been a handicap. His staunch opposition to A.N. Merrick may have worked against him in Republican circles, as it showed he was unwilling to place party loyalty ahead of principle or to yield an argument where he felt that integrity was at stake.

Frank was not known to shy away from controversy. Tarbell's obituary refers to "his fondness for argument," and the minister's eulogy described him, with rather faint praise, as "A man of decided opinions, . . . correspondingly outspoken, a trait which often made his real character misunderstood." Documents in the Lincoln papers show that, after being appointed at town meeting to serve on a committee to supervise building a bridge on the Monson Road, he engaged in a dispute with a "Captain" Shaw.

The most serious and longest-lasting controversy in which Frank became involved was the split in the Brimfield church that began in 1878. This was at least the third serious division in the church during the 19th Century and for Frank must have revived painful memories of the Perfectionist controversy that split his family

---

[1] Palmer (MA) *Journal*, July 1, 1904.

in the 1830s. Characteristically, these controversies took on doctrinal overtones, pitting liberals against traditionalists, which in New England meant adherents of orthodox Puritanism.

In church disputes, both sides defend their position on theological grounds, but personal issues often lie at the heart of the conflict, and that appears to have been the case at Brimfield. Newspapers around the region followed the controversy avidly, probably struck by the incongruity of such a fierce clash raging in a place that appeared so bucolic. A letter from an individual who used the pseudonym "Gloster" openly expressed a common view about the origins of the dispute. A young minister, Webster K. Peirce, had been installed in 1874. When he arrived he was single; as time passed and his confidence grew, he began to inspire "a subdued fluttering in the hearts of his tender hearers of the softer sex." Rev. Peirce perceived the need to make a choice and, "being a gentleman of discrimination and discernment, he was looking for a person of refined taste and mental culture. . . ." This person proved to be Etta Lincoln.

It was common for small-town congregations to contain liberal and traditional factions, which maintained an uneasy balance where the body was too small to divide. According to the popular explanation, the minister's choice of a mate "was the head and front of his offence; the deadly sin that culminated into the Christian hate; not so much by the fair daughters of Eve themselves, but by their disappointed mammas and papas. . . ."[1] Furthermore, Etta possessed a fine singing voice, and her prominence in the choir created another source of animosity.

Peirce's contract allowed his dismissal on six months' notice by either party. His opponents moved to do so, but were defeated by a 57-29 vote of the church membership. However, the parish society, which managed the church's organizational affairs, was narrowly controlled by traditionalists and voted 11-9 to terminate the appointment.[2] One critic said she "don't want to hear any more love preached," and another was heard to complain that Peirce was "too comfortin' at funerals."[3] Rev. Peirce was undoubtedly liberal, not inclined to hurl hellfire and damnation at his congregation; and his opponents, as was typical, accused him of being Unitarian. However, it is striking to note that even after the church split, his new church professed conventional Trinitarian belief.[4]

When 20 supporters of the embattled minister tried to join the church society and were refused, Frank Lincoln and Tom Morgan "were so much disgusted that they at once withdrew from the society." Two weeks later, 250 people

---

[1] Spencer (MA) *Leader*, May 24, 1878.

[2] Springfield *Republican*, Feb. 18, 1878.

[3] Ibid.; Holyoke (MA) *Transcript*, Feb. 20, 1878.

[4] "Articles of Faith and Covenant and Regulations of the Second Congregational Church, Brimfield," 1881. Article 1 of the Confession of Faith affirmed "We believe in God the Father, the Son, and the Holy Spirit, the one only living and true God."

attended a reception at the Lincoln home and presented Peirce with a gold watch.[1] He began giving Sunday evening sermons at the hotel, and these proved to be far more popular than services at the church, where ministers from neighboring towns occupied the pulpit. Peirce, meanwhile, preached in surrounding towns, where he was perfectly acceptable. In October he requested a formal council meeting to dismiss him, and 50 of his followers sought to be dismissed in order to form a new church, referred to as the Church of the Messiah. When the parish refused to let them use part of the church, they rented the hotel hall and in 1879 organized a Second Congregational Church. Rebecca was among the group that was dismissed. With stronger religious in-

Rev. Webster K. Peirce, probably late 1870s.
Hitchcock Academy.

clinations than Frank, she had joined the original church by profession of faith in 1869.[2] Frank, who had never been a member of the older church and had been described as "holding Unitarian views" in one newspaper account[3], joined the Second Church by baptism in May 1880. Daughter Rebecca seems not to have been a member of either church.[4]

In another letter, "Gloster" observed "There is in almost all suburban towns a few persons who seem to take delight in stirring up discord and broils . . . and who had rather reign in Hell than serve in Heaven."[5] Anyone so inclined would have been pleased by the results in Brimfield, where the church quarrel spilled over so that lifelong acquaintances no longer greeted each other in the street. Henry F. "Boss" Brown sided with the traditionalists, placing him in opposition to Frank Lincoln.

At the same time, the town was divided over whether to construct a town hall, and the two issues soon merged. Those who sought to dismiss Peirce tended to oppose the new building, arguing that supporters were looking for a place to hold their breakaway meetings after they left the church. Frank was chosen moderator at town meeting in April 1878, and when the discussion of the town hall

[1] Palmer *Journal*, May 4, May 18, May 25, 1878.
[2] Manual of First Congregational Church, Brimfield, Mass., 1899.
[3] Springfield *Republican*, Feb. 18, 1878.
[4] "Articles of Faith and Covenant and Regulations of the Second Congregational Church, Brimfield," 1881.
[5] Spencer *Sun*, May 3, 1878.

seemed to be stalled, he left the moderator's chair "and with the dignity of former senators and statesmen, delivered one of those most plain, powerful and convincing arguments" that scattered the opposition. The report, obviously prepared by a partisan, concluded that when he "resumed his seat the whole sacred edifice rocked with exciting plaudits that struck terror to the souls of the opposition, and a vociferous call of 'Question' was made from all parts of the hall." Even with this intervention, the new building was approved by only a 95-91 vote. Tom Morgan was appointed to a committee to select a site for the structure.[1]

The church controversy probably colored the remainder of Frank Lincoln's life, though in other respects it stayed on its regular course. Even while the dispute was raging, he led a band of veterans at the funeral of Brimfield's Civil War General Fitz Henry Warren.[2] Rev. Peirce died in 1897, at the age of only 55, and the Second Church eventually disbanded, though hardly any of its members rejoined the original church. Peirce had spent his entire pastoral career in Brimfield; if it had not been for the controversy, he might have followed a more conventional pattern of moving up to a larger church after a few years.

Frank had the instincts and inclinations of a farmer, and had resumed that occupation when he returned from the war. As the years passed, there became, as Anna Tarbell phrased it, "less opportunity for successful farming," and Frank spent the rest of his working career as a traveling salesman for his brother-in-law's paper company.[3] The inability of this intelligent, energetic farmer to adequately support his family on level, fertile land located on a main road provides grim testimony to the increasing difficulties of agriculture, which has now declined almost to the point of extinction in the region.[4]

---

[1] Palmer *Journal*, April 13, 1878. Lacking a separate building, town meetings were held in the church, as had been the practice before the Congregational Church was disestablished in Massachusetts.

[2] Palmer *Journal*, June 29, 1878.

[3] Obituary, Palmer *Journal*, May 17, 1901.

[4] The Assessors' Valuation List of May 1, 1865, showed that Frank was taxed on a horse valued at $100, 2 oxen ($140), 5 cows ($175), 2 yearlings ($40), 4 sheep ($35) and a swine ($25). This assortment of animals was more suited to a family's use than a commercial operation and indicates that the Lincolns depended on other sources of income, or that their farming emphasized crops and orchards, rather than livestock. (Compare to the figures for A.N. Merrick, given earlier.) Frank also paid personal property taxes on $2500 of money and a carriage worth $75. His real estate consisted of the "home place" of 150 acres, assessed at $2000, and two lots, the 6-acre "Lumbard lot" ($100) and the 10-acre "Haynes lot" ($150). Altogether, his annual tax came to $70.09, which placed him approximately tenth highest in the town. The highest tax was levied on the Herrings, who owned the hotel ($992), and Samuel A. Hitchcock, founder of the academy and who had considerable stock holdings ($902). John Wyles was next at $401.

In addition to his participation in town government, Frank remained dedicated to education, serving on the board of trustees of the Hitchcock high school for 25 years. He maintained contact with wartime comrades, being active in the Grand Army of the Republic (GAR). In September 1872 he invited members of his company to a "roll call" at his home, and there were probably many similar occasions that were not recorded.[1] His last appearance in public was at the annual town meeting in April 1901, but by then he was extremely feeble and he died May 8.

In Anna Tarbell's obituary, and more conspicuously in the minister's eulogy, Frank Lincoln's life was treated as a geological epoch, when the rocks were craggier and more sharply defined, before the growing urge to conform eroded a younger generation. Summarizing his place in Brimfield history, Tarbell wrote that "He belonged to a group of men possessed of insight and original power, independent in thought and action; men whose school privileges were limited, but who were educated through self-development, and whose strong personalities and useful lives are looked up to by those of a younger generation to-day." At his funeral, the minister, admitting that he did not know Frank (who, of course, was not a member of his church), regarded the captain with awe and eulogized him with praise bordering on distaste: "He belonged to a generation of self-made men; men of earnest and noble purpose, men of clear, though sometimes limited vision; men tender of heart, though brusque in manner; men who in order to be appreciated and understood, need to be viewed, like the unpolished marble, at a distance."[2]

In one respect Frank was fortunate to pass on when he did, for he was not present when his beloved Etta died less than a year later, at the age of only 48. His wartime comrade Tom Morgan died in November 1906 at the age of 83. In another finely crafted obituary, Anna Tarbell seemed to emphasize the affinity between the two men: "His death removes almost the last of a group of men who are associated in the memories of those who are in active life to-day with the social, public and intellectual interests which distinguished Brimfield in the last century. Mr. Morgan was always on the side of progressive movements, and, until the failure of his physical and mental powers, had maintained a lively interest and taken an active part in public matters." He was associated with Frank in the GAR and the Hitchcock board, and was noted as one of the early promoters of the public library.[3]

Mrs. Rebecca Lincoln survived her husband by ten years, dying March 9, 1911. Once again, Anna Tarbell responded with a thoughtful eulogy, observing that "In the passing of Mrs. Lincoln Brimfield loses one of the last of a generation of women who were leaders in the social life and interests of the town. She never grew old in spirit or manner, even with the weight of increasing years, and she kept

[1] F.D. Lincoln vertical file, Brimfield Public Library.
[2] Palmer *Journal*, May 17, 1901.
[3] Palmer *Journal*, Nov. 16, 1906.

her interest in people and events and in the broad questions of the day to the last." By then the two Rebeccas had taken to spending the Winter with grandson Charles L. Peirce in Springfield, opening the Brimfield house for the Summer. Tarbell affirmed that the house "with its treasures and fine associations has always been a center of hospitality in the community . . . ." Rebecca had become known for her "genius for the cultivation of flowers" and her talent for floral arrangement. She was also noted for loaning furniture and making costumes for the dramatic presentations that were a highlight of the Hitchcock high school schedule and a major community event.[1]

Miss Rebecca, who never married, continued to occupy the Lincoln homestead during the Summer and maintained family traditions. She died in Springfield December 13, 1928, at the age of 79. She had been a library trustee for 41 consecutive years and had been an organizer of the Hitchcock Academy alumni association. The obituary, which bears the Anna Tarbell style, noted that Rebecca "was endowed with superior intellectual powers and artistic gifts and was an unusual conversationalist with a fine sense of humor. The combined dignity and charm of her presence impressed all with whom she came in contact."[2] In that description it is easy to discern the influence of her parents and recognize the girl who had written to her soldier father more than 65 years before.

Rebecca's passing removed the last Lincoln presence in Brimfield, after more than 100 years, but the family's influence remained. In 1904 the youngest Lincoln brother, James D., born in 1823, donated to Brimfield the Danielson-Lincoln Memorial Library, named to honor his mother and wife. The library was "a cherished interest" for Frank, who worked closely with his brother to bring it into existence.[3] The library, still a vital feature of the Brimfield community, occupies part of the former apple orchard of the Lincoln farm, and some of the stone used in its construction was taken from the farm. Brimfield undoubtedly would have had a Civil War monument, a town hall, and a library without Frank Lincoln, but he had a lasting influence on their timing and location. He and other members of his family also had a prominent part in the continued success of Hitchcock Academy.

The restored Lincoln homestead, with its stately, accommodating appearance and lofty barn would probably seem familiar to Frank and Rebecca. If many of the physical features of the town center would be recognizable to the Lincolns, few of the old families they associated with remain; and the secluded, self-contained Brimfield they knew, based on agriculture and local industry, has vanished in the rush of modern life. The village retains its separate identity but has lost something of the vigor and distinctiveness it displayed when the upright figure of Captain Frank Lincoln walked its streets.

[1] Palmer *Journal*, March 10, 1911; Springfield *Republican*, March 10, 1911.
[2] Springfield *Republican*, Dec. 14, 1928.
[3] Palmer *Journal*, July 1, 1904.

Gravestones in Brimfield Cemetery.

APPENDIX A

ROSTER OF ENLISTED MEN, COMPANY G, 46TH MASSACHUSETTS REGIMENT

Source: "Company Descriptive Book," Sherman Room, Brimfield Public Library. Names checked against "Company Clothing Book," same location.

Possible Additional Names
Alfred J. Newton, Pvt., age 23, Enlisted Monson, Aug. 19, 1862. Appointed regimental commissary sergeant Oct. 16, 1862 and therefore not a member of Co.G. Mustered out with regiment July 29, 1863 (Higginson).
Royal A. Wilson, 30, Wales. Mustered in Oct. 15, 1862; mustered out July 29, 1863 (Higginson).

Key to Abbreviations
A=Re-enlisted in heavy artillery.
B=Buried in Brimfield Cemetery through 1918.
I=Illiterate (signed with a mark).
M=Mustered out July 29, 1863.

Recapitulation
Occupation given as Farmer: 54 (56%)
Born in Hampden, Hampshire and Worcester Counties: 73 (75%)
Born outside New England: 10 (10%)
Foreign-born: 6

Total for 46th Regiment: 43 officers, 904 enlisted men; total 947.
1 enlisted man died of wounds, 32 died from accidents or disease.
Source: Thomas Wentworth Higginson, *Massachusetts in the Army and Navy during the War of 1861-65* (Boston: State of Massachusetts, 1896).

Name	Rank	Age	Height	Complx.	Eyes	Hair	Birthplace
Ira L. Peck	Sgt.	21	5 ft 7 in	dark	black	brown	Monson
John Q. Hoar	Sgt.	23	5 ft 9 in	light	blue	brown	Monson
William H. Sherman	Sgt.	33	6 ft 1 in	light	blue	brown	Brimfield
Stephen A. Gammons	Sgt.	24	5 ft 10 in	dark	hazel	dark	S.Glastonbury, CT
Thomas J. Morgan	Sgt.	39	5 ft 10 in	sandy	blue	brown	Brimfield
Marcus H. Chaffee	Cpl.	19	5 ft 11 in	dark	blue	dark	Monson
Helon H. Fales	Cpl.	19	5 ft 11 in	sandy	hazel	brown	Rutland MA
Cheney Newton	Cpl.	43	5 ft 9 in	light	gray	brown	Brookfield MA
Oliver H. Perry	Cpl.	42	5 ft 6 1/2 in	light	blue	light	Sturbridge MA
Francis E. Cook	Cpl.	38	5 ft 6 1/2 in	sandy	blue	brown	Princeton MA
Charles E. Lumbard	Cpl.	29	5 ft 8 in	light	gray	brown	Brimfield
Henry W. Webber	Cpl	19	5 ft 10 in	dark	blue	brown	Holland
John L. Flynt (or Flint)	Cpl.	28	5 ft 7 in	dark	black	black	Sturbridge
Charles E. Alexander	Pvt.	20	5 ft 8 in	light	gray	light	Brimfield
George Barnes	Pvt.	44	5 ft 8 in	sandy	gray	auburn	Sturbridge
Baxter C. Bennet (or Bennett)	Pvt.	18	5 ft 6 in	light	blue	light	Holland
Henry H. Bennet (or Bennett)	Pvt.	21	5 ft 5 in	dark	gray	brown	Holland
Thaddeus Benson	Pvt.	21	5 ft 9 in	light	gray	light	Sturbridge
Albert J. Bixby	Pvt.	25	5 ft 11 in	sandy	gray	brown	Rupert VT
Edward Bliss	Pvt.	32	5 ft 5 in	dark	black	dark	Brimfield
Hiram Bradway	Pvt.	34	5 ft 8 in	sandy	blue	light	Monson
Rodney Bradway	Pvt.	27	5 ft 10 1/2in	light	gray	brown	Monson
Truman C. Bradway	Pvt.	20	5 ft 8 in	light	blue	brown	Monson
Charles B. Brown	Pvt.	18	5 ft 7 in	dark	hazel	black	Brimfield
Joseph P. Brown	Pvt.	34	5 ft 10 in	dark	blue	brown	Brimfield
Jacob Burley	Pvt.	28	5 ft 10 in	light	blue	brown	Monson
Byron W. Charles	Pvt.	18	5 ft 11 in	light	blue	light	Brimfield
Leonard B. Charles	Pvt.	29	5 ft 10 in	dark	blue	brown	Wales
William A. Charles	Pvt.	20	5 ft 7 in	dark	hazel	brown	Monson
David Clapp, Jr.	Pvt.	26	5 ft 9 in	light	gray	brown	Hampton CT
George H.Dillaber (or Dillable)	Pvt.	38	5 ft 9 in	dark	gray	brown	Southbridge, MA
Warren W. Eager	Pvt.	21	6 ft 0 in	light	blue	light	Wales
Israel C. Earle	Pvt.	22	5 ft 6 in	dark	dark	dark	N. Brookfield, MA

Occupation	When Enlisted	Where Enlisted	Notes
bookkeeper	Aug 19, 1862	Monson	M
teamster	Aug. 19	Monson	M
farmer	Aug. 20	Brimfield	B,M
mechanic	Aug. 18	Wales	M
farmer	Aug. 20	Brimfield	B,M
farmer	Aug. 18	Wales	Died at Foster Hospital, New Bern, Jan. 30, 1863, of malarial fever.
operative	Aug. 19	Monson	M
farmer	Aug. 20	Brimfield	B,M
shoemaker	Aug. 18	Monson	M
farmer	Aug. 20	Brimfield	B,M
farmer	Aug. 20	Brimfield	M
farmer	Aug. 26	Holland	M
finisher	Aug. 19	Monson	M
farmer	Aug. 20	Brimfield	B Died at Stanley Hospital, New Bern, Apr. 6, 1863, of malarial fever.
farmer	Aug. 26	Holland	M
shoemaker	Oct. 10	Holland	Discharged May 30, 1863, at New Bern.
shoemaker	Aug. 26	Holland	Discharged June 17, 1863, at New Bern: disability.
farmer	Aug. 20	Brimfield	M
farmer	Aug. 20	Brimfield	M
farmer	Aug. 20	Brimfield	B,M
farmer	Aug. 18	Wales	M
farmer	Oct. 22	Monson	Discharged at Foster General Hospital, New Bern, Apr. 7, 1863.
farmer	Aug. 20	Monson	M
farmer	Aug. 20	Brimfield	M
farmer	Aug. 20	Brimfield	B,M
farmer	Aug. 20	Monson	M
farmer	Aug. 20	Brimfield	
farmer	Aug. 19	Monson	M. Appointed corporal Feb. 1, 1863.
dyer	Aug. 19	Monson	M
miller	Aug. 26	Holland	M
farmer	Aug. 18	Wales	M
carder	Aug. 18	Wales	M
clerk	Aug. 20	Brimfield	M

Name	Rank	Age	Height	Complx.	Eyes	Hair	Birthplace
George A. Fales	Pvt.	18	5 ft 6 in	light	hazel	brown	Enfield MA
William B. Fay	Pvt.	22	5 ft 5 in	light	blue	auburn	Wilbraham MA
Osborn Fenton	Pvt.	18	5 ft 9 in	dark	gray	brown	Willington CT
William F. Foskit	Pvt.	18	6 ft 1 in	light	blue	brown	Brimfield
Henry F. Frost	Pvt.	18	5 ft 8 in	dark	black	black	Ware MA
John A. Frost	Pvt.	18	5 ft 6 1/2 in	dark	black	brown	Monson
Joseph Gagne (or Gagin)	Pvt.	42	5 ft 7 in	dark	gray	brown	Canada
John Gale	Pvt.	18	5 ft 8 in	dark	hazel	black	Stafford CT
James M. Harmon	Pvt.	21	5 ft 8 in	light	blue	light	Brownfield ME
Henry H. Hitchcock	Pvt.	22	5 ft 9 in	light	black	brown	Palmer
George C. Homer	Pvt.	38	5 ft 8 in	light	blue	brown	Brimfield
Francis P. Keefe	Pvt.	18	5 ft 10 in	dark	blue	brown	County Cork, Ireland
John Kelley	Pvt.	18	5 ft 9 in	light	gray	light	Boston
George L. Kenney	Pvt.	22	5 ft 9 in	light	black	brown	Paxton MA
Frank H. King	Pvt.	21	5 ft 8 in	light	gray	brown	Monson
Charles B. Kittredge	Pvt.	21	5 ft 7 in	light	blue	brown	Westborough MA
Merrick Lamphear	Pvt.	20	5 ft 6 in	dark	gray	brown	Monson
Francis L. Lemon	Pvt.	36	5 ft 7 in	light	gray	light	Monson
John Letter	Pvt.	25	5 ft 7 in	light	gray	brown	Paterson NJ
Charles O. Lumbard	Pvt.	42	5 ft 7 1/2 in	light	blue	light	Westfield VT
William Henry Lumbard	Pvt.	33	5 ft 10	light	blue	brown	Brimfield
John C. Maguire	Pvt.	25	5 ft 6 in	sandy	gray	brown	Hingham MA
George H. Moody	Pvt.	27	5 ft 5 in	dark	black	black	Monson
Harlan (Harley) B. Moody	Pvt.	18	5 ft 6 in	light	blue	light	Monson
Frank Moore	Pvt.	18	5 ft 5 in	light	hazel	auburn	Wales
Henry M. Moore	Pvt.	22	5 ft 6 in	light	blue	brown	Brimfield
Peter W. Moore	Pvt.	34	6 ft 2 in	light	gray	light	Montgomery VT
John Moran (Moore)	Pvt.	30	5 ft 8 1/2 in	sandy	blue	light	County Wexford, Ireland
Nicholas Moran (Moore)	Pvt.	22	5 ft 7 in	sandy	blue	light	County Wexford, Ireland
John B. Motley	Pvt.	18	5 ft 7 in	dark	black	black	Saco, ME
George A. Munroe	Pvt.	18	5 ft 8 in	light	blue	auburn	Fiskdale
Elijah Munsell	Pvt.	39	5 ft 9 in	dark	gray	brown	Ludlow, MA

Occupation	When Enlisted	Where Enlisted	Notes
dyer	Aug. 19	Monson	M
mechanic	Aug. 19	Monson	M
operative	Aug. 18	Monson	M
farmer	Aug. 20	Monson	B Died at Foster Hospital, New Bern, Mar.2, 1863, of malarial fever.
farmer	Aug. 20	Monson	M
farmer	Oct. 22	Monson	Discharged May 30, 1863: A
currier	Aug. 20	Brimfield	M
currier	Aug. 18	Wales	M
carpenter	Aug. 19	Monson	M
carpenter	Aug. 19	Monson	M
farmer	Aug. 20	Brimfield	B,M
operative	Aug. 19	Monson	Discharged May 30, 1863 at Newbern: A
farmer	Aug. 20	Brimfield	Discharged May 30, 1863, at Newbern: A
student	Aug. 20	Brimfield	M
butcher	Aug. 19	Monson	M
farmer	Aug. 20	Monson	M
farmer	Aug. 19	Monson	Discharged June 3, 1863, at Newbern: A
farmer	Aug. 19	Monson	M
operative	Aug. 20	Monson	M
farmer	Aug. 20	Brimfield	B,M
mason	Oct. 6	Brimfield	Discharged June 24, 1863, at Newbern: disability.
shoemaker	Aug. 19	Monson	M
silversmith	Aug. 19	Monson	M
farmer	Oct. 10	Monson	M
farmer	Aug. 18	Wales	M
farmer	Aug. 26	Holland	Discharged May 28, 1863, at Newbern.
mechanic	Aug. 18	Wales	Discharged May 30, 1863.
operative	Aug. 19	Monson	I,M
operative	Aug. 19	Monson	I. Wounded slightly in shoulder at Goldsboro, NC, Dec. 17, 1862; Discharged May 30, 1863, at Newbern: A
mechanic	Oct. 14	Brimfield	M
student	Aug. 20	Brimfield	B,M
farmer	Aug. 19	Monson	M

Name	Rank	Age	Height	Complx.	Eyes	Hair	Birthplace
Watson W. Needham	Pvt.	21	5 ft 7 1/2 in	light	hazel	brown	Belchertown MA
Royal A. Nelson	Pvt.	30	6 ft	sandy	blue	brown	Wales
Lyman P. Parker	Pvt.	19	5 ft 10 1/2 in	sandy	hazel	brown	Monson
Orville S. Parker	Pvt.	21	5 ft 11 in	light	black	light	Brimfield
John W. (or M.) Patrick	Pvt.	23	5 ft 10 in	light	blue	brown	Amherst MA
Bryant C. Pendleton	Pvt.	23	5 ft 8 in	dark	blue	brown	Wales
Charles H. Robbins	Pvt.	18	5 ft 8 in	dark	blue	brown	Monson
Charles F. Roper	Pvt.	18	5 ft 5 in	light	blue	brown	Brimfield
George Skinner	Pvt.	23	6 ft 1/2 in	dark	gray	brown	Monson
George N. Skinner	Pvt.	18	5 ft 6 in	dark	black	brown	Monson
Harvey G. Skinner	Pvt.	27	6 ft	dark	gray	brown	Monson
William Smith	Pvt.	34	5 ft 7 in	light	blue	brown	Belchertown
George E. Stacy	Pvt.	18	5 ft 7 in	dark	blue	brown	Monson
George W. Stacy	Pvt.	26	5 ft 6 1/2 in	light	blue	black	Monson
James L. Stacy	Pvt.	20	5 ft 8 in	light	blue	light	Monson
William S. Stearns	Pvt.	18	5 ft 6 in	sandy	blue	light	Ware MA
Abner H. Stebbins	Pvt.	23	5 ft 8 in	light	gray	brown	Brimfield
Charles F. Thompson	Pvt.	18	5 ft 6 in	light	gray	brown	Wales
Eli H. Thompson	Pvt.	28	5 ft 10 in	dark	black	brown	Wales
Isaac Toohey	Pvt.	29	5 ft 6 in	dark	blue	brown	County Galway, Ireland
Charles Upham	Pvt.	27	5 ft 10 in	dark	gray	brown	Brimfield
Alburtus H. Walker	Pvt.	18	5 ft 11 in	light	blue	light	Union CT
James H. Walker	Pvt.	20	5 ft 6 in	dark	gray	brown	Woodstock CT
William S. Walker	Pvt.	18	5 ft 5 in	light	blue	light	Hadley, Canada East
Harris C. Wallis	Pvt.	44	5 ft 8 in	light	blue	light	Holland
Emerson O. Webber	Pvt.	34	5 ft 7 in	dark	blue	brown	Holland
Allen L. West	Pvt.	31	5 ft 8 in	light	blue	brown	Rensselaerville NY
Orrin H. Wilson	Pvt.	25	5 ft 9 1/2 in	dark	black	black	Springfield
Emerson Wood	Pvt.	26	5 ft 9 in	dark	black	brown	Darita NY
Francis N. Wood	Pvt.	19	5 ft 7 in	light	blue	light	Monson
George E. Wood	Pvt.	23	5 ft 11 in	dark	blue	brown	Monson
Henry H. Wood	Pvt.	20	5 ft 9 in	dark	gray	black	Bloomfield PA

Occupation	When Enlisted	Where Enlisted	Notes
dyer	Aug. 18	Wales	M
farmer	Aug. 18	Wales	M; Wounded in head at Goldsboro, NC, Dec. 17, 1862.
farmer	Aug. 20	Brimfield	B; Died at Stanley Hosp., Newbern, Mar. 25, 1863, of malarial fever.
farmer	Aug. 20	Brimfield	B,M
farmer	Oct. 13	Brimfield	M
teamster	Aug. 18	Wales	M
operative	Aug. 19	Monson	M
farmer	Aug. 26	Holland	Discharged May 30, 1863 at Newbern: A
farmer	Aug. 20	Monson	M
farmer	Aug. 20	Monson	M
farmer	Oct. 22	Monson	M
stone cutter	Aug. 19	Monson	M
farmer	Aug. 20	Monson	Sent home sick, Nov. 9, 1862; discharged Feb. 25, 1863.
farmer	Aug. 19	Monson	M
operative	Aug. 19	Monson	M
farmer	Aug. 20	Brimfield	M
farmer	Aug. 20	Brimfield	B,M
dyer	Aug. 18	Wales	M. Left home sick, reported for duty Feb. 26, 1863.
farmer	Aug. 18	Wales	Discharged from Foster Hospital, Newbern, Mar 27, 1863.
blacksmith	Aug. 18	Monson	M
farmer	Aug. 20	Brimfield	M
farmer	Aug. 26	Holland	Discharged May 30, 1863, at Newbern: A
farmer	Aug. 26	Holland	Discharged May 30, 1863, at Newbern: A
mechanic	Oct. 2	Brimfield	M
farmer	Aug. 26	Holland	M
farmer	Aug. 18	Wales	M
carder	Aug. 20	Monson	M
shoemaker	Aug. 19	Monson	Discharged June 3, 1863, at Newbern: A
mechanic	Aug. 19	Monson	M
farmer	Aug. 20	Monson	M
farmer	Aug. 20	Monson	M
operative	Aug. 19	Monson	M